Excellence and Ethics in Counseling

RESOURCES FOR
CHRISTIAN COUNSELING

RESOURCES FOR CHRISTIAN COUNSELING

1. Innovative Approaches to Counseling   *Gary R. Collins*
2. Counseling Christian Workers   *Louis McBurney*
3. Self-Talk, Imagery, and Prayer in Counseling
   H. Norman Wright
4. Counseling Those with Eating Disorders   *Raymond E. Vath*
5. Counseling the Depressed   *Archibald D. Hart*
6. Counseling for Family Violence and Abuse   *Grant L. Martin*
7. Counseling in Times of Crisis
   Judson J. Swihart and Gerald C. Richardson
8. Counseling and Guilt   *Earl D. Wilson*
9. Counseling and the Search for Meaning   *Paul R. Welter*
10. Counseling for Unplanned Pregnancy and Infertility
    Everett L. Worthington, Jr.
11. Counseling for Problems of Self-Control   *Richard P. Walters*
12. Counseling for Substance Abuse and Addiction
    Stephen Van Cleave, Walter Byrd, Kathy Revell
13. Counseling and Self-Esteem   *David E. Carlson*
14. Counseling Families   *George A. Rekers*
15. Counseling and Homosexuality   *Earl D. Wilson*
16. Counseling for Anger   *Mark P. Cosgrove*
17. Counseling and the Demonic   *Rodger K. Bufford*
18. Counseling and Divorce   *David A. Thompson*
19. Counseling and Marriage   *DeLoss D. and Ruby M. Friesen*
20. Counseling the Sick and Terminally Ill   *Gregg R. Albers*
21. Counseling Adult Children of Alcoholics   *Sandra D. Wilson*
22. Counseling and Children   *Warren Byrd and Paul Warren*
23. Counseling Before Marriage   *Everett L. Worthington, Jr.*
24. Counseling and AIDS   *Gregg R. Albers*
25. Counseling Families of Children with Disabilities
    Rosemarie S. Cook
26. Counseling for Sexual Disorders   *Joyce and Clifford Penner*
27. Cognitive Therapy Techniques in Christian Counseling
    Mark R. McMinn
28. Case Studies in Christian Counseling   *Gary R. Collins, Editor*
29. Conflict Management and Counseling
    L. Randolph Lowry and Richard W. Meyers
30. Excellence and Ethics in Christian Counseling   *Gary R. Collins*

VOLUME THIRTY

Excellence and Ethics in Counseling

GARY R. COLLINS, Ph.D.

RESOURCES FOR
CHRISTIAN COUNSELING

―――――――― General Editor ――――――――
Gary R. Collins, Ph.D.

EXCELLENCE AND ETHICS IN CHRISTIAN COUNSELING, Volume 30 of the Resources for Christian Counseling series. Copyright © 1991 by Word, Inc. All rights reserved. No portion of this book may be reproduced in any form whatsoever, except for brief quotations in reviews, without written permission from the publisher.

Quotations from the Bible in this volume are from the New International Version, copyright © 1983 International Bible Society. Used by permission of Zondervan Bible Publishers.

Permission to quote from the following sources is gratefully acknowledged:
"Myself," from *The Collected Works of Edgar A. Guest*. Copyright © 1962 by Edgar A. Guest. Reprinted by permission of Contemporary Books, Inc.
"Informed Consent" (Appendix B) from *Integrative Therapy: A Comprehensive Approach to the Methods and Principles of Counseling and Psychotherapy* by Darrell Smith, copyright © 1990, Baker Book House.

Portions of Chapter 7, "Trends in Christian Counseling," formed a part of the author's closing address to the Australian Congress on Christian Counseling in Melbourne, Australia, March 6, 1991. Chapter 8, "The Future of Christian Counseling," is a revision and expansion of the author's opening address to the First International Congress on Christian Counseling in Atlanta, Georgia, November 9, 1988.

Library of Congress Cataloging-in-Publication Data

Collins, Gary R.
    Excellence and ethics in Christian counseling/Gary R. Collins.
      p. cm. — (Resources for Christian counseling : v. 30)
    ISBN 0-8499-0696-2
    1. Pastoral counseling.   2. Pastoral counseling—Moral and ethical aspects.
I. Title. II. Series.
BV4012.2.C564   1991
253.5—dc20   91-26545
                                                                                                            CIP

Printed in the United States of America

49 AGF 9 8 7 6 5 4 3 2

CONTENTS

Preface	ix
1. Excellence in Christian Counseling	1
2. Ethics in Christian Counseling	19
3. Liability in Christian Counseling: Welcome to the Grave New World	41
4. Theory in Christian Counseling	75
5. Effectiveness in Christian Counseling	93
6. Growth and Training in Christian Counseling	113
7. Trends in Christian Counseling	133
8. Future Directions in Christian Counseling: The Best Is Yet to Be	155
Epilogue: A Letter to Christian Counselors	173
Appendix A: A Code of Ethics for Christian Counselors	179
Appendix B: Informed Consent: A Sample of the Information that Could Be Presented to New and Potential Counselees	185
Notes	188
Index	223

IN APPRECIATION

With this volume, the Resources for Christian Counseling series is complete. All of the authors, whose writings and research comprise this thirty-volume library, wrote these books during the years 1985 to 1991. It is the publisher's hope that the resources found in their books will, for many years to come, greatly assist those who engage in the care of souls.

Dr. Gary R. Collins has served as the General Editor for this series. Esteemed teacher, lecturer, author, and genuine "people-helper," Gary Collins has devoted tireless effort to the preparation of each of these volumes. Word, Incorporated, has been extremely fortunate to have engaged Dr. Collins for this enterprise, and to him the deepest and most sincere appreciation is expressed.

THE PUBLISHERS

PREFACE

WE MADE IT! With this volume we come to the completion of Word's Resources for Christian Counseling series of books. It's been a long journey, one that started about seven years ago when I was invited to serve as General Editor of this series. At first I balked a little. I was intrigued by the idea of a series like this and enthusiastic about the challenge of pulling it together, but I knew nothing about being an editor. The world, it seems, is filled with people who want to write books, but I wondered if good writers would be willing to "sign on" to this project. Could we find competent authors who could write clearly and complete their manuscripts on time? We now have the answer: yes.

As you know, if you have read my Editor's Preface to any of the other volumes in this series, we sought authors who have strong Christian commitments, impeccable professional credentials, and extensive counseling experience. From the beginning we have attempted to produce books that would be useful and helpful examples of accurate psychology and the careful application of Scripture. With each we have intended to give a clear evangelical perspective, careful documentation, and a strong practical orientation; we have endeavored to have writing that is free of sweeping statements or unsubstantiated conclusions. Our goal has been to provide books that would be clearly written, up-to-date overviews of the issues faced by contemporary Christian counselors—including pastoral counselors.

Five years ago the first of these books with the familiar blue-and-silver covers rolled off the presses and now we have come to the final volume. None of us could estimate how many hours have been spent by people working on this project—writing manuscripts, negotiating contracts, editing copy, handling production, and guiding in the marketing. As the General Editor of this series, I am grateful to them all. And I am grateful to the Lord who has guided and abundantly blessed this project.

For me, the journey to this last book has been a pleasant but sometimes bumpy ride. The hardest parts came on those half-dozen occasions when I returned completed manuscripts to authors who had signed contracts but whose work was not acceptable for publication in the series. I learned that it is hard to say no, especially to colleagues whom I respect. I am grateful for their understanding, especially when they were disappointed.

For most of the journey I have been accompanied by some of the finest people whom I have ever known. The thirty or so authors of these books are most prominent because their names are printed in silver on the book covers. I have been enriched through working with each of them.

But no book gets published without the efforts of unrecognized people who work behind the scenes. Perhaps there are several hundred in this category if you add the Word executives, editors, marketers, production experts, secretaries, and people who pack the boxes and send out the books. I am grateful for them all—especially for five who stand out as kingpins: Carey Moore, Ernest Owen, David Pigg, Steve Gibson, and Harry Clayton. These men at Word were the ones who did the most to make this work.

Near the beginning it was decided that I would write the first and the final books in this series. You will notice that these "anchor books" differ a little from the others. In the first, I wrote about innovative approaches to Christian counseling. My fellow authors then tackled basic problem areas such as substance abuse, sexual dysfunction, the problems of Christian workers, and homosexuality. In this concluding volume I pick up some professional issues that need to concern all Christian counselors if we are to be effective in our future counseling ministries. In working to reach this goal, I have appreciated the efficient and insightful work of my researcher, Steven Sandage. He and Dr. Timothy Clinton each read and critiqued portions of the manuscript and I am grateful for their helpful suggestions. I hope you will discover that this book attempts to be practical like the twenty-nine that have come before.

In writing the foreword to each of the preceding books I have tried to say something about each author's qualifications. In this last book I want to express my deep appreciation to the author's wife. Julie Collins has been my helpmate, my most ardent supporter, and my best friend for twenty-seven years of marriage. Without her prayers, encouragement, and commitment, this series would not have been completed and neither would most of my other books have been written. Great will be her reward in heaven, but I want to acknowledge my gratitude and love for her, here on earth.

Now that the Resources for Christian Counseling series is complete, the creative people at Word are already at work on a new Contemporary Christian Counseling series. Can you guess who has agreed to be the General Editor?

Gary R. Collins, Ph.D.
Kildeer, Illinois

CHAPTER ONE
EXCELLENCE IN CHRISTIAN COUNSELING

MICHAEL JORDAN IS A HERO IN CHICAGO! Almost all communities, whatever their size, have athletic idols and big cities like Chicago have several. But Michael Jordan, six-foot six-inch star of the Chicago Bulls basketball team, is in a class all by himself. His name is recognized and respected, even among people who have no interest in sports. When he runs onto the floor of Chicago Stadium, the local fans leap to their feet and shake the rafters with the roar of their enthusiasm.

Long before the fans arrive, however, Michael Jordan gets ready for the challenge of the game ahead. Late in the afternoon of any day when the Bulls are scheduled to play, while the arena is still locked and the lights are low, Jordan runs onto the court and begins his practice—usually by himself. Some vendors will be there and so will the ushers and perhaps a few policemen, all getting ready for their night of work. Few pay any attention to the tall man shooting baskets, changing positions, practicing different moves. Wearing a T-shirt and gym shorts, in place of his famous Bulls uniform, Jordan is fine-tuning his skills, far from the television cameras or the cheers of admiring fans. When the turnstiles open and those fans start pouring into the building, the man who has been lauded as the best basketball player in the world slips back to the locker room until it is time to reemerge with his teammates.

Chicago Tribune columnist Bob Greene likes to arrive early to stand in the shadows and watch Jordan's pregame practice. It is "mesmerizing," according to Greene, who has tried to understand why. "Probably it's this," he writes. "In the course of my work I see so much of the world that is low-spirited and mean and shoddy and common. But in those chilly hours in the deserted Stadium, watching Jordan in solitude honing his craft, I see something that is almost beyond excellence. It is like nothing I have ever seen in my life, and to witness it is a privilege."[1]

CHRISTIAN COUNSELING EXCELLENCE

"Some people have greatness thrust upon them," according to John Gardner. "Very few have excellence thrust upon them. They achieve it. They do not achieve it unwittingly, by 'doin'' what comes naturally'; and they don't stumble into it in the course of amusing themselves. All excellence involves discipline and tenacity of purpose."[2]

Michael Jordan's reputation for excellence depends in part on his God-given height, speed, and innate athletic abilities. But the man is known for his dedication and determination. As a teenager he was dropped from the high school basketball team because they said he wasn't good enough. Still, the determined young athlete kept practicing, kept improving. As an adult, Jordan's consistent pregame workouts powerfully demonstrate his discipline and tenacity of purpose.

The efforts of this famous basketball player remind me of a world renowned pianist who said that if he failed to practice for one day, he would know it. It he didn't practice for two days, the critics would know it. If he missed practice for three days the world would know it. Excellence in music, like excellence in athletics, requires effort and demands faithful dedication to a task.

Early in the 1980s, a book about American business unexpectedly "took off," rose quickly on the best-seller lists, and launched what some have called an "excellence revolution." Almost overnight, business managers, educators, professionals, politicians and Christian leaders—along with athletes and musicians—were talking about the search for excellence.[3]

In the books and seminars that followed, few attempted to define excellence but everybody knew that it had something to do with quality, skill, and doing things well. We recognize excellence when we see it, wrote one observer, even if we can't concisely define it. Excellence involves an attitude toward life that values quality in products, workmanship, performances, and relationships, but shuns carelessness, laziness, and shoddiness. To be excellent does not mean that we have to be perfect, the best, or the most acclaimed. Instead, excellence implies an in-depth commitment to being and doing the best that is possible. This is a goal that excellence-minded people strive to reach. It is a goal that motivates, even though nobody ever arrives. If we think we have reached the epitome of excellence, our efforts slacken and quality slips.

Excellence is intangible and difficult to measure. The excellent athlete is likely to get a good score in the game. Excellence in business often is seen in the bottom line. Excellent science is marked by carefully crafted, well-executed research that is clearly described and able to be replicated by other competent scientists. But none of this can apply to the practice of counseling. How, then, can we know if some person is an excellent counselor?

We who counsel are not like surgeons whose degree of excellence can be seen by other surgeons in the operating room. Lawyers can watch one another in the courtroom and teachers can be evaluated by their students in the classroom. But counselors work in private, committed to confidentiality and seldom observed by peers. Counselees may have opinions about whether or not a counselor is good and helpful, but fellow professionals rarely see us and no counselor ever gets an award for excellence in practice.

"Good practice is the reason for all of our training programs," writes Stanford University psychologist John Krumboltz, but "why don't we do a better job of recognizing excellent practice?"[4] The only counselors who get professional awards for excellence are people who write about counseling or do research. And those people might not be the best counseling practitioners.

EXCELLENCE AND ETHICS IN CHRISTIAN COUNSELING

In the chapters that follow, we will look at counseling excellence from several viewpoints: maintaining excellence in our ethics, seeking to be excellent in our responsibilities before the law, maintaining excellence in relating to counselees, developing excellence in our theories and research, stimulating excellence in our students and continuing education programs, and planning ahead so that we can grow in excellence as we move into the next century. As we will see, Christian counselors are making progress in cultivating excellence but we still have a long way to go.

A Noncounselor's Perspective

Some time ago, I received a thought-provoking letter from a friend who works for a parachurch organization and who described himself as a casual observer of Christian counseling. "I have a few observations about the field at present," he wrote. "Rather than keep them to myself, I wanted to share them.[5]

> 1. The Christian community, including the clergy, has increasingly been open to counseling. Much of this, I suspect, is due to feelings of inadequacy on their part as problems continue to build and escalate in the families of their churches.
>
> 2. There are growing numbers of Christian counselors. Their "business" is very difficult. For many it pays the same meager wages as somebody would get for teaching at a Christian college. For others, even less. Breaking into the field, getting clients and keeping clients is not easy.
>
> 3. Polarity seems to exist between two extremes of counseling. This problem exists in other areas of ministry as well: the balance between interpersonal and transactional approaches, between friendship evangelism versus buttonholing.
>
> 4. Often Christian counselors are locked into ministering only to Christians. Breaking that barrier and ministering to the non-Christian community is difficult.
>
> 5. Fees always seem to be a problem. Those who need counseling aren't always the ones who can afford it. I'm wondering if there aren't more helps available in the local church than are being drawn upon.
>
> 6. Are Christian counselors committed to evangelism? That is, do they feel that the greatest service they can offer to a client

is to help him or her come to know the Lord? Are counselors encouraged to pray for each other, or does that seem unprofessional? Is the counselor comfortable with having gone for an entire year without a single client coming to know the Lord? If a group of Christian counselors were meeting together and sharing would any of them feel at ease standing up and saying. "I had a thrilling thing happen last week. I led a couple of clients to the Lord." Or would they be fearful that such an admission would cause them to be ostracized?

My friend's letter then made some suggestions for change. Could we allow concerned Christians to share financially by helping to underwrite the cost of counseling ministries? he asked. While recognizing the importance of confidentiality, could we nevertheless develop a close group of people who could pray for clients and their counselors? Could we brainstorm about ways in which the average Christian counselor could bring more non-Christians into his or her clientele? Could we view the Christian counselor as a missionary, and teach people to view Christian counseling as something other than an underground activity within the Christian community? Could we reorient Christian counseling to view evangelism as acceptable and normal?

The letter concluded with a comment about the integration of psychology and Christianity. This is a popular topic, the letter-writer suggested, but it seems confined to the academic world. "The counselor, like everybody else in the ministry, needs to be sensitive to the Spirit's leading and power every day. Christian counselors must seek to be Christo-centric in their own lives, in their styles of counseling, and in their willingness to present Christ as Savior."

Some of what my friend proposes might be considered professionally unethical. His observations could stimulate enthusiastic debate if they were discussed by a group of Christians who counsel. But the letter also encourages us to ponder what Christian counseling should be like and what excellence in Christian counseling might mean.

Christian Counseling Growth

Counseling is not a static field. Pick up any journal, read any new book, or attend any professional meeting and you will be reminded that counseling is growing and dynamic.[6] It is a field of changing theories, techniques, trends, and training approaches.

Changing Theories. It is well known that modern counseling began with a basis in psychoanalysis, was influenced heavily by behaviorism, and developed around the client-centered philosophy of Carl Rogers. Many counselors have used the methods of reality therapy, rational-emotive therapy, multimodal therapy, transactional analysis, family systems therapy, Gestalt, therapy and perhaps two or three hundred others. Currently, the focus of interest is on the cognitive therapies.[7]

Christian counseling also has its theoretical approaches. Many are associated with the names of their chief proponents, most claim to be biblical, and some sound like Christianized equivalents of contemporary secular theories.

Some critics have pointed to this diversity and proclaimed that counselors don't know what they are doing. But is this different from the competing theologies that we see in the church, the varieties of denominations, and the diverse approaches to Christian education, homiletics, philosophy of religion, or views of ecclesiology and eschatology? Diversity reflects our different perspectives and conclusions, but it does not necessarily indicate a lack of competence.

Changing Techniques. Religious counseling methods tend to fall into one of three categories.[8] Some are strictly secular methods applied to religious problems and used in religious settings. Others are strictly religious methods such as prayer, meditation on Scripture, or reading the Bible in the counseling session. Most often, counseling methods fall into a third group that involves a combination of the secular and religious. Confrontation, behavior modification, visual imagery, systems theory, dream interpretation, or Egan's problem-management approach, for example, may all be combined with prayer, confession, giving, involvement in the church, or encouraging counselees to meditate on verses from the Bible. It is difficult for any one person to keep up with the latest techniques; most counselors probably use a variety of methods, depending somewhat on the counselee's problems and more on the counselor's training, personality, and personal preferences.

Changing Trends. Writing about trends in counseling can be risky because things change so quickly that any list soon is out of date. Currently there is much interest in genetics, the physiological bases of psychopathology, health psychology, and in cross-cultural and multicultural approaches to counseling. We come from different social backgrounds but too much of the counseling literature has focused on people who are middle-class, white, highly educated Americans.[9] The emphasis on wellness that began over a decade ago continues to concern counselors who seek to prevent psychopathology and stimulate psychologically healthy living.[10] To the surprise of many Christians, spirituality has emerged as an issue in secular counseling, although the emphasis appears to be less on traditional Christian values and more on humanistic, New Age, and Eastern perspectives.[11] Media psychology also has become a major concern as counselors get involved in helping people through radio programs, television, newspapers, magazines, films, and videotapes. The application of computer technology to counseling is likely to increase as our march to a computer society continues.

With the "graying of America" and increased numbers of senior citizens worldwide, a new interest has developed in counseling the elderly. The AIDS epidemic has led to books and seminars in counseling people with AIDS and their families.[12] Counselors in the United States have also become interested in the estimated half-million self-help and mutual aid groups that currently exist nationwide and that encourage people of all ages to help each other with their problems.

In addition, there is growing interest in the environmental counseling that takes problem-solving out of the office and into the communities where people live. The field of community psychology seeks to change neighborhoods, improve working conditions, reverse unemployment trends, eliminate poverty, improve schools, provide adult educational opportunities, and relieve the crowding and noise that put so many people under stress.[13] Is this social action a form of counseling? Some Christians would say yes, and argue that community counseling is most consistent with the methods of Jesus when he met with the needy, poor, confused, and struggling people in the communities of his day.

Perhaps S. L. Halleck was right; there is "no way in which a psychiatrist (or other counselor) can deal with behavior that is partly generated by a social system without either strengthening or altering that system." Every encounter with a counselor, Halleck wrote, has political implications.[14] This could take counselors into areas of political action where we feel uncomfortable and far removed from our training and fields of expertise.

Changing Training Models. Even when a counselor is aware of theories, techniques, and trends in this growing field, a period of formal training is required before one is legally qualified to counsel. In most parts of the United States and Canada, it is against the law to open a private practice, call oneself a psychologist, or collect fees and insurance payments, unless the counselor has earned a doctorate, passed a state or provincial examination, and worked for a specified number of hours under the direction of a more experienced counseling supervisor.

Does this training stimulate excellence and make a person competent to counsel? Not according to Jay Adams who believes that Christians "properly trained in the Scriptures are competent to counsel—more competent than psychiatrists or anyone else."[15] Others would agree. "A biblical counselor does not need to be trained in psychological counseling," write Martin and Deidre Bobgan. "Psychological training tends to undermine the training the Lord has already given through years of Bible reading, listening to sermons and Bible teachings, and applying the Scripture in daily life. . . . By knowing and applying God's Word, by abiding in Christ, and by loving fellow Christians, a spiritual counselor is trained by God."[16]

Some Christian criticisms of professional counselor training have been backed up by secular writers. According to one report, for example, "there is no evidence that the usual training program has any positive value in producing therapists who are more helpful than nonprofessionals."[17]

This could be a shocking conclusion but it needs to be set alongside some other facts:

1. It is extremely difficult to evaluate the effectiveness of counselor training with scientific precision. At present, therefore, conclusions must be accepted tentatively.

2. While the effectiveness of traditional graduate training has not been demonstrated scientifically, neither has the effectiveness of the training proposed by Adams, the Bobgans, or others. Christian counselors and their critics frequently agree that the Bible, God's Word, is relevant to the needs of people today and that Christ is sufficient to meet our needs. But from this it does not follow that a Christian approach to counseling proposed by an antipsychology counselor is innately superior (or inferior) to a Christian therapy approach

developed by an equally committed believer who is willing to utilize some of the insights of psychology. Much of the debate between Christian counselors, therefore, involves expressions of opinions with little backing from carefully collected, empirical facts.

3. As we will see in a later chapter, counselor training has been studied carefully. Perhaps few other professions are as careful or as honest in the evaluation of their educational programs.

Most training programs teach the importance of listening and responding with skill. Most expect students to learn about psychopathology, human emotion, motivation, learning, thinking, and the principles of normal human development. Most stress the characteristics of effective counselors and help students to develop warmth, empathy and genuineness. Considerable attention is given to practical experience under the direction of an experienced counselor. In Christian training programs there is emphasis on the importance of knowing Scripture, applying biblical truth to practical counseling situations, and growing in one's relationship as a servant and disciple of Christ.

Despite improvements in training, we need to give serious consideration to the charges that counselor training isn't as effective as we would like. If we are to approach excellence in counseling, there must be significant and probably greater emphasis on the training and continuing education of counselors.

Growth and Health. Rowland Croucher is a perceptive Australian writer whose books and articles have dealt with a number of church-related issues. His observations on church growth have interesting implications for Christian counseling.

Church growth is not a biblical concept, according to Croucher. We assume that God wants the local church to get bigger. We love to make head counts and share statistics, especially when our churches are gaining in size. Although the New Testament mandates evangelism and fulfilling the Great Commission, it places little emphasis on a self-conscious strategy for church growth and there is no implication that bigger is better. Some of the churches we look to as models of success may not be serving God's purposes at all; instead they stand as monuments to human pride and egocentricity.

It would be wrong to condemn all large churches; many of them are genuinely Christ-honoring and biblical in their priorities. But church growth should not be their major goal. "Aim for church health rather than church growth," Croucher writes. "Living organisms grow anyway."[18]

Could this be applied to individuals? If we are genuinely healthy, including *spiritually* healthy, we grow. The same could be said of Christian counseling, counseling centers, Christian inpatient treatment programs, training institutions, and counselor organizations.

If we aim for health, including excellence, we are likely to grow anyway. If we are careless in our counseling, lax in our training programs, and shoddy in the quality of our counseling publications and materials, ultimately our lack of excellence will undermine our impact and effectiveness.

Christian Counseling Values

In 1980, psychologist Allen Bergin published a landmark article on psychotherapy and religious values. As a graduate student, Bergin had trained with several leaders in psychology, but he felt continuing frustration because his values differed from those of his professors. "I felt constrained from full expression of my values," he wrote, because of the "prevailing, sometimes coercive, ideologies" of his teachers. Frustrated by these attitudes, Bergin later wrote about his own ethically explicit approach to counseling.[19]

The response to his article was most unusual and unexpected. Over one thousand counselors wrote to request reprints and to express support for Bergin's views. Only a handful wrote to disagree. Convinced that there must be a "hidden society" of values-oriented psychologists, psychiatrists, social workers, and others, Bergin began a decade-long series of inquiries into the influence of values, including religious values, on psychotherapy and mental health.[20]

Values are personal beliefs and standards about what is true, good, bad, right, wrong, or beautiful. Despite the lingering views of some counselors that there can be an objective, value-free approach to emotional problems, most would agree that values permeate our training programs, our research, and our therapy.[21] Counselors and counselees both bring their values to counseling. Values guide our work and our lifestyles, and these, in turn, have mental-health implications. "Personal values really do matter," according to Hunter Lewis. "Without functioning values, we can hardly live at all, much less lead a purposeful and satisfying life."[22]

When values are clear and strong, we can cope more confidently with the challenges of life. When values are conflicting and ill-defined—as they are for many people in modern Western societies—we live with uncertainty and anxiety. Many need what one writer calls an ethical therapy[23] that helps counselees sort through the confusion and find clear guiding values.

Choosing Values. Most Christian counselors assume that the Bible gives the best basis for building values. Why do some of us make that assumption while our colleagues disagree?

To answer we must consider how we look at the world and "know" anything. You might want to do the following one-minute assignment. Think of two or three values that you hold—things like "democracy is good," "psychotherapy really helps people," "family stability is important," or "Jesus saves." Then ask yourself, "How do I know this? Where did I get this idea?" Your answers are likely to fall into one or more of six categories or ways of "knowing" and looking at the world. These six categories are the lenses through which we see the world and form our values.[24]

First, we see the world and form values based on *authority*. If you believe that Christ died to pay for the sins of individuals, that he rose again, is alive, all powerful, and able to intervene in our lives, your belief is based on the authority of Scripture. Often your understanding of Scripture is helped by the authoritative theological teachings of the church. Frequently people base their values on the beliefs and instruction that come from those who are trusted as leaders and authorities.

Within recent decades, people in the developed countries have tended to distrust and challenge authority. We don't always accept what we hear from government, religious, medical, educational or other authorities. Despite our pride in being able to think for ourselves, however, many people naively accept what they see on television or hear in a classroom because the information comes from an authoritative source. Each person needs to pick his or her authorities with care. We can't build solid values on weak and inaccurate authorities.

Second, values and beliefs can be based on *logic* and clear, deductive reasoning. Teaching students to think is one of the prime purposes of schools and universities—even though they often fail in this important task. If we haven't learned to think clearly, our minds can easily slide into irrational and erroneous conclusions. We can be duped and manipulated by silver-tongued persuaders who lead us to ideas and values that are illogical.[25] The more clearly we can think, therefore, the better we can assess and select values.

Third, we build values on sense *experience*—what we see and hear and know through our own sense organs. If two people have different experiences they may have different values. Some people have very positive experiences with churches; others have negative experiences. The resulting perspectives on religion are likely to differ considerably. If you have strong religious values they likely are based, at least in part, on your experiences with God and with other believers.

Emotion is the fourth way in which we form values. Often we decide what is good or right or acceptable based on what we feel. The relativist values of the 1960s were based on the assumption "if it feels good, we can do it! Surely it can't be wrong if it feels so right!" This perspective is still prevalent, often combined with intuition.

The fifth way of knowing and forming values, *intuition*, might be defined as unconscious thinking. The unconscious-intuitive mind seems to "just know" what is right or to "somehow feel uncomfortable" about a proposed course of action. Studies of creativity have noted that innovative ideas often come to people who struggle with an issue, and then forget about it for a while (at night, while they sleep, for example). At some later time a solution seems to pop into conscious awareness. Researchers speculate that during the time away from the task, our brains are working at an unconscious level, thinking about the issue until a time when we sense what is the best.

Science is the sixth way of knowing. It involves forming hypotheses, collecting data, and reaching conclusions. Based on science, for example, we believe that the body is a living organism that can malfunction but also can be repaired, sometimes through medical intervention. Values based on science tend to draw from a combination of the previous five approaches.

When we consider how values are chosen, we can understand how they are taught and how they can be changed. Christian counselors who commit themselves to excellence may be influenced by several of the six categories. Because we accept the authority of the Bible, we embrace scripturally based values. The authoritative ethical statements of our professions teach the importance of competence and doing things well. We learn through experience that when things are done fairly and carefully, they are less likely to create problems later. There may be scientific evidence to show that competent counseling is better than incompetence, but even without empirical data we sense intuitively that excellence is better. All of this leads to the link between values and professionalism.

CHRISTIAN COUNSELING PROFESSIONALS

"For all our talk about Christian counselors who see their task as a Christian calling, for all our emphasis on counseling as a ministry, the greater share of Christians presently preparing for a counseling ministry have their eye on some form of professional practice."[26] Some may hope to serve on the staff of a church, writes Fuller theologian Ray S. Anderson, and others may plan to teach or to work for a parachurch organization. But the majority of counseling graduates are moving toward state licensing and certification by professional societies. Most graduate training programs, at least in the United States, focus on professional qualifications, seek professional accreditation and are led by professors with strong professional commitments.

This is disturbing for at least three reasons. First, Christians who counsel are tied to a long history of competent, in-depth pastoral care. Few Christian counselors know or seem to care about the psychologically astute insights that were developed centuries before the modern counseling profession was born. Theologian Thomas C. Oden has become a champion of bygone pastoral-care writers, not because of some fascination with "the archaic exercise of excavating ancient figures," but because many of these historical writers have contemporary relevance for modern Christian counseling. People like Tertullian, Augustine, Gregory the Great, or Luther and Calvin, are almost never mentioned in the Christian counseling literature, but Freud, Jung, and Rogers are cited repeatedly.[27] There is much to be learned from our psychologically perceptive theological forefathers (there were few "foremothers"). But most of us have ignored their insights while we have become experts in building our counseling on the writings of secular theorists.

Second, the fascination with gaining credentials and becoming professionals can lead to exclusivism and can prevent people from getting help when they need it. I travel overseas frequently but have never seen the emphasis on licensing and accrediting that we have in North America.

It could be argued, of course, that without licensing and high professional standards there can be no limits on quackery and counseling incompetence. Our counseling colleagues overseas would agree, but most continue to make few distinctions between professional, pastoral and lay Christian counselors. More than in North America these three major groups appear to intermingle in other countries and show mutual respect for one another.[28] An overemphasis on professionalism can be as harmful as the devastating effects of racism and sexism.

Perhaps the differences between North America and some other countries reflect the unusually large numbers of professionals in the United States and Canada. Where there are few professionally educated and qualified people there may be less need to demonstrate credentials. But when we elevate the professional counselor, we imply that nonprofessionals are of less value and are rarely competent to counsel.

Third, it is well known that many people are skeptical or threatened by professional counselors, disillusioned and cynical about their effectiveness, and unwilling or unable to pay for their services. There may have been a "Golden Era" of psychotherapy, when an endless flow of counselees came for professional services, but that era is over.[29] There has been a dramatic decrease in third-party payments for therapy, declining government support for professional mental health services, and an upsurge of interest in mutual-aid and other lay, people-helping approaches that give encouragement and guidance—without any fees.

As the following pages will show, these somewhat negative observations need not be discouraging. Trained Christian counselors can have an impact in the future but we may need to set our sights on innovative, less traditional, more cost-effective methods of helping. And we must learn to work in settings that may be far different and much less lucrative than the private practice for which many of us have been trained.[30]

What Is Professional Christian Counseling?

According to dictionary definitions, a profession is a group of people who are engaged in an occupation or calling that depends on the acquisition of a high level of knowledge. Most professions have trained practitioners whose skills are widely valued and whose prestige and social status usually is high. Frequently, professionals are viewed as people who have lofty standards, dedication, and competence. They protect society from unqualified amateurs and are committed to serving others, even though they often receive high compensation for their services. Professionals frequently band together into societies with other persons of like knowledge and technical skills. These societies exist for fellowship, continuing education, and/or social action by the members, but sometimes the professions become elitist, discriminatory, and self-serving.[31]

Everybody agrees that psychiatrists and psychologists are counseling professionals and most people would include social workers, licensed professional counselors, school guidance counselors, and a few other groups. But would pastoral counselors be included? The ministry usually is regarded as a profession and pastors, as a group, probably do most of the counseling in the United States, Canada, and several other countries But in most states or provinces pastors could not be licensed as professional private practitioners of counseling unless they had received advanced training beyond their initial seminary degrees.

Christian counselors tend to follow the society by reserving the words *professional counselor* for only a few select groups—usually including our own. We define *professional* in terms of academic and licensing qualifications and tend to assume that professionals are the only people who are competent counselors and committed to excellence. Most of us would agree with Ray Anderson that "Christians can and ought to serve society as professionals in all areas, including the therapeutic services."[32] We who have the training and qualifications to be members of professional societies and to offer legally sanctioned professional services usually seek to maintain high levels of quality and seek to be professionally respected.

But professional Christian counselors might be wise to remember two qualifications. First, *professional counselors are not the only counselors who are committed to excellence.* Lawyers (who sometimes are known as counselors-at-law), teachers, pastors, physicians, business consultants, and lay people, are among those who may lack the counseling experience and expertise of a psychiatrist or clinical psychologist, but who nevertheless have taken counseling courses and are committed to counseling quality. Counselors, including Christian counselors, can have differing levels of training and expertise, but at every level there can be a commitment to the best counseling possible. A dedicated layperson who is sensitive to people and determined to give the best possible help can be more effective than the highly trained professional therapist whose work has become routine and whose commitment to quality care is minimal.

Second, *Christian counselors, including professionals, have an accountability to Christ and to the local body of believers that is of greater importance than their commitment to professional colleagues.* Christians are members of two worlds: the world of the society where we live and the world of the kingdom of God. Christians who work in any field have a commitment and obligation to their secular employers or to their professions, but they have a higher commitment to their God. For centuries, dedicated believers have struggled to maintain the uneasy alliance between these two masters.

Christian counselors should have a strong link with a local church. There they should find a community of support, accountability, and perspectives from other Christians who are not professional therapists. And there they find pastoral counselors, lay helpers, support groups, and other caring resources that parallel and supplement the professional's work. Even though some churches criticize counselors and offer them little support or encouragement, ideally the local body of believers influences and empowers the Christian counselor so that he or she can go forth as a healer and as a representative of Christ in the troubled world.

Excellence in Christian counseling, therefore, involves competence, the best training possible, the highest of ethical standards, a commitment to professional quality, and a mind-set that we are in a fellowship of believers and Christ's representatives in our field of service.

Conclusions

Two dangers threaten the survival of Christendom, according to sociologist Anthony Campolo: mediocrity and success. Both tempt Christians and undermine a commitment to excellence.

Mediocrity has come to characterize numerous people today. Many of us have been taught by mediocre teachers, led by mediocre politicians, involved in mediocre churches, willing to do mediocre work and have been guilty of settling for mediocre spiritual lives. Other people constantly push for success. With the recent emphasis on simpler living and "downshifting," the goals of getting ahead—climbing the corporate ladder, making more money, and having more influence—may all be less popular than they were in previous decades. But the pursuit of success still is a major motivating force for millions of us, including pastors and Christian counselors.

Nobody can be perfect or competent in everything. There are areas of our lives where mediocrity may be okay, so long as we do not use this as an excuse for laziness. In contrast, there is nothing wrong with wanting to be successful. The pursuit of success can be motivating and valuable, providing it does not become a driving force that pushes everything else aside while it idolizes affluence and power. Mediocrity and selfish ambition can both lead to disappointment, anxiety, and a sense of futility with life. In contrast, a consistent commitment to excellence is a more realistic alternative to both mediocrity and success motivation.[33]

Whenever I talk to audiences about the basics of Christian counseling, I often describe the well-known research showing that warmth, empathy, and genuineness are basic requirements for any effective counselor. I sometimes talk about my visits with Paul Tournier, the famous Swiss doctor, and describe how his gracious, caring, loving manner enabled him to help thousands of people through his counseling and his books, even though he never had formal training in psychiatry or theology. Often I encourage people to turn to Galatians 5 and 6 where we read about the fruit of the Spirit and the biblical teaching that effective burden bearers are spiritual, gentle, loving, humble, patient, and willing to do good "to all people, especially to those who belong to the family of believers."

Perhaps the apostle Paul had similar thoughts when he was writing his first letter to the Thessalonians. Some of the early believers were critical of Paul's ministry and a few had even implied that he was a failure (1 Thess. 2:1). He responded by writing about his mission, his motives, and his methods.[34]

A Clear Mission. With God's help, Paul was determined to tell people about the gospel in spite of opposition (1 Thess. 2:2). That was his mission.

Do Christian counselors have clear goals? Like all believers we are disciples of Christ who should be motivated to live lives that please him; and even when there is opposition, we seek to serve as his ambassadors. The Christian counselor has a mission to serve Christ as a people-helper and burden bearer who brings psychological and spiritual healing, even when there is criticism from secular counselors or from fellow believers.

Pure Motives. Paul did not trick people, show disrespect, or operate from consciously impure motives. He tried to show the love of

Christ. The apostle gave himself unselfishly and was committed to encouraging, comforting, and urging others to live godly lives. His statement about motives is a practical and helpful guide for any Christian counselor:

> The appeal we make does not spring from error or impure motives, nor are we trying to trick you. . . . We loved you so much that we were delighted to share with you not only the gospel of God but our lives as well, . . . You are witnesses, and so is God, of how holy, righteous and blameless we were among you who believed. For you know that we dealt with each of you as a father deals with his own children, encouraging, comforting and urging you to live lives worthy of God, who calls you into his kingdom and glory. (1 Thess. 2:3, 8, 10–12)

Honest Methods. Paul did not use flattery. He was not motivated by greed and neither was he looking for praise from other human beings. With God as his witness, he wanted instead to be gentle and caring (1 Thess. 2:5–7). Certainly he confronted at times. He gave instructions like a teacher. He courageously said what needed to be said, even though this brought rejection and ultimately led to his death.

Nobody could accuse Paul of being mediocre or driven by a self-centered pursuit of success. But he was committed to quality and excellence, even though he probably never heard those words. He knew that our competence "comes from God" (2 Cor. 3:5) and he remained dedicated to his task of serving Christ.

There is much of value in contemporary Christian counseling, even though we know there are weaknesses. We who counsel should be aware of the weaknesses and, with God as our witness and source of strength, we must be alert to avoid the pitfalls that our critics so often observe. We may be counselors, but first of all we are servants, disciples of Christ, and people who care for others. Our training and experiences can be of great value, but ultimately we counsel effectively only when we rely on the wisdom and strength that comes from the Lord.

That is the basis of excellence in Christian counseling.

CHAPTER TWO
ETHICS IN CHRISTIAN COUNSELING

COUNSELING IS THE ART of helping people get unstuck. Most of those who go for counseling (at least those who go voluntarily) are stuck in depression or anxiety, mired in difficult interpersonal situations, glued to guilt or to crippling remnants from the past, unable to move beyond a choice point, gripped by some psychologically debilitating physical condition, in need of new knowledge and skills, or in other ways seeking help to get unhooked from unwanted attitudes or behaviors.

The counselor works to help people get unstuck and moving. Most of us stay away from criticizing or berating others to change. Like mudslinging, harsh criticism often knocks stuck people further into the muck of their discouragement and feelings of hopelessness.

More often, the person in need responds best to encouragement, instruction, or guidance. At times one or two caring friends can do the job, using support and sometimes a little push, to help individuals get free of their difficulties. At other times there is need for the psychological equivalent of a good tow truck driver who can use professional tools to unsnarl the hapless individual from the grip of persisting problems.

Sometimes the helper's job is easy, especially if the counselee is motivated to get moving. More often counseling is demanding because the problems that mire people down tend to be complex, difficult to understand, and hard to escape. Counselors themselves can get bogged down, spiritually and psychologically, when their days are spent helping others find freedom. Sometimes this work is more complex because we have to make decisions and judgment calls that are difficult. We face ethical decisions that demand careful reflection and often have no clear answers. Consider the following examples.

> A Christian psychologist, working for a state university, counsels with a young undergraduate who is having problems with guilt, identity, and questions about religious beliefs. The psychologist knows that an understanding of the gospel will help but the university has a strong policy against proselytizing.[1] Does the psychologist keep quiet about his faith or does he raise the issue of religion, in violation of his employer's instructions?

> In the course of pastoral counseling, a woman reports that her husband has been sexually molesting their teenage daughter. The husband is chairman of the church board of deacons. What does the pastor do with this information?

> A Christian graduate student, nearing the end of her doctoral program, is told that she will be dropped from the university for "actions inconsistent with professional ethical standards" if she lets counselees know her attitudes about homosexual behavior, premarital sex, or sin. What does the student do?

> A professional counselor who depends for his livelihood on client fees, has several outstanding accounts. The people who owe the money, all of whom are fellow Christians, appear to be able to

pay but they have not done so. Does the counselor bring legal or other pressure to get his fees?

These are ethical issues. Counselors face them repeatedly and so do many of our counselees.

How are they resolved, especially when there are no easy answers? This chapter gives a practical overview for Christian counselors who lack the time, or perhaps the motivation, to read some of the more detailed books on counseling ethics.[2]

Understanding Ethics

Values, as we saw in chapter 1, are personal beliefs, especially beliefs about what is good, right, important, just, or beautiful. Values are learned and often are chosen freely. Although they can change, most values tend to endure and influence much of our thinking, behavior, and ways of viewing the world. Everybody has values and everybody needs them. Without values our lives would be directionless, chaotic, confusing, and self-destructive.[3] When people have differing values there can be misunderstanding, miscommunication and conflict.

At one time counseling was thought to be value free, but almost nobody believes this any more. There is growing evidence that values permeate the therapeutic process and often change during the course of counseling; most often the counselee's values become more like those of the counselor.[4] Because of this influence, counselors should be aware of their own values and how these might affect their counselees. Probably most Christian therapists would agree that "it is neither possible nor desirable for counselors to be scrupulously neutral with respect to values in the counseling relationship." The counselor does not exert pressure on counselees to change their values. But we know that what we believe can influence others, so it is crucial for counselors to be clear about their own values and how these influence both the counseling and the counselee. "Since we believe that counselors' values do inevitably affect the therapeutic process, we also think it's important for counselors to be willing to express their values openly when they are relevant to the questions that come up in their sessions with clients."[5] To hide your values as a counselor is unfair to the counselee and could be considered unethical.

What are Ethics? Philosopher Norman Geisler gives a concise answer to this question. "Ethics deals with what is morally right and wrong. Christian ethics deals with what is morally right and wrong for a Christian."[6]

But how do we know what is morally right and wrong? Science, including the field of psychology, cannot answer that question. Ethical decisions and choices about personal morality are by nature philosophical and theological. No laboratory experiment, scientific data, or personality theory can answer such questions as:

- "Should I encourage my daughter to leave her abusive husband?"
- "Should I tell somebody about my boss who is stealing from the company?"
- "If my counselee threatens to beat up or murder one of his parents, do I break confidence and warn the intended victim?"
- "Is it okay to hug my counselees?"
- "What do I do if a counselee brings me an expensive gift?"

Historically, men and women have found a number of guidelines for answering difficult questions and making ethical decisions.[7] These guidelines include pragmatism (if it works it must be right), hedonism (if it feels good, do it) and relativism (it all depends on the situation). Sometimes ethical decisions have been made on the principle of "might is right"; the person or persons with the most power (or money) are the people who "call the shots" and tell the rest of us what is good or bad. Aristotle believed that morality should be based on moderation; we should always seek to avoid extremes. Later philosophers built their ethics on a belief in finding "the greatest good for the greatest number." More recently, we have seen ethical systems based around opinion surveys. The ethical codes of most professional counseling associations have been formed in this way. Members are surveyed concerning a number of ethical issues and then a committee writes a code of professional ethics, based largely on the opinions of the majority. As the majority opinion changes, so do the accepted standards of right and wrong.

Each of these approaches has weaknesses that can leave individuals perplexed. How does a counselor respond, for example, if his or her values and ethical standards do not agree with the majority? Might there be some times when the majority opinion should be ignored? In one survey of professional counselors who had served on ethics committees or had written articles about ethics, 57 percent acknowledged that on occasion they had violated the law or gone against their own profession's statement of ethics. These were highly ethical people who realized that in some circumstances (for example, whether you should always report child abuse to the authorities) it was better for all concerned if the counselor did not do what the law demanded.[8] Subsequent research has shown that clinicians usually know what the law and professional ethical codes say counselors *should* do in difficult ethical situations, but practitioners more often rely on practical circumstances and their own personal values in deciding what they *will* do.[9]

Despite the dedicated efforts of those who write ethical guidelines for professional practice, a lot of what we do depends on the situation and on the counselor. Counseling has been described as "an ethical balancing act" that requires more than good will, the ability to follow rules, and the inclination to stay out of court. In counseling, issues come up every day that are not prescribed in the official standards of one's profession. No other field is like ours, "so utterly dependent upon the ethical strength of its practitioners," wrote one counselor. "The issue is not so much the ethics of *therapy* as the ethics of the *therapist*. Is he or she honest, trustworthy, sensitive, knowledgeable, courageous, open-minded, modest, and rigorously self-reflective? The last seems particularly important."[10]

CHRISTIAN ETHICS

How does all of this apply to Christians? If you are a professional counselor, you are likely to accept and attempt to abide by the ethical standards of your profession. With minor exceptions this is not difficult. A survey of Christian psychologists found that the ethics of most practitioners were highly consistent with the ethical principles of the American Psychological Association.[11] The APA statement of ethics, like those of the other mental health professions, has been carefully written and contains little that a Christian would challenge.[12]

Even so, the Christian counselor assumes that he or she has a higher standard of ethics, one that is more stringent, more definitive, and more demanding than that of one's profession. The non-Christian builds his or her ethics on the world views that come from a fragmented pluralistic society. With no outside source of authority or morality, counselors look in vain for clear fence posts on which they can stake their standards.[13] In contrast the Christian counselor must operate both as a member of a profession and as a part of the body of Christ where the fence posts are much more explicit.

In molding our ethics, Christian counselors are guided by God's Word (divine revelation), God's people (the community of believers), and God's character (the divine nature that calls believers to be like him).

God's Word. Many Christians, including all evangelicals, believe that God's Word, the Bible, is the only authoritative and completely accurate guide for faith and practice. As such, it is the highest authority for both doctrine and morals. It guides our ethics through its specific commands and precepts, general principles, examples, and overall world view.[14] Of course this book does not deal specifically with every ethical question that the counselor faces, and it is well known that Christians differ in their ways of interpreting Scripture. Nevertheless, the Bible speaks directly to many of the ethical issues that we face in counseling (and in life). Its principles and precepts give guidance in other situations that are not mentioned specifically on its pages.

> All Scripture is God-breathed and is useful for teaching, rebuking, correcting and training in righteousness, so that the man [or woman] of God may be thoroughly equipped for every good work. (2 Tim. 3:16–17)

Biblical ethics assumes that the Scriptures are more than a description of human nature, a listing of moral principles, or a guidebook for behavior. The Bible calls for commitment and obedience. The Christian counselor, who seeks to be guided by God's Word, has an obligation to submit to the teachings of Scripture, even if these conflict with the mores of one's society or profession.

God's People. Many Christian counselors are members of professions; all Christian counselors are members of the body of Christ. Even if we work alone in an office, with no other counselors for miles around, we are never simply in private practice. We are part of the church, a community of fellow believers to whom we are responsible and from whom we should receive support, encouragement, and perspective, and render accountability.[15]

In practice, many counselors feel alienated from the local church, especially from congregations that criticize Christian therapy and its practitioners. But the Christian counselor needs to be actively involved with a group of other believers, including those who are not counselees or fellow counselors. This involvement provides a moral context[16] that supports and guides Christian counselors as they face daily ethical decisions in their work.

In the Old Testament we read of a time, centuries ago, when the people had no leader and "everyone did as he saw fit" (Judg. 21:25). This lack of direction and accountability can lead to confusion and chaos, some of which we see in our society today. One therapist wrote, for example, that in the end "you're really alone, and you really have to answer to yourself. You're responsible for yourself and no one else." When this type of thinking prevails, the individual's standards are built solely on his or her feelings, attitudes, perceptions, wishes, and desires. Subjectivity rules. There is no accountability and little to prevent confusion and even anarchy. In contrast, if we are to have social stability, the individual, including the individual Christian, cannot be the center of his or her own decision making, values, and ethics. We need the church to be "a community of ethical accountability."[17]

Sadly, as I suggested earlier, some churches have refused to accept that responsibility or have failed to recognize its importance. As a result, the professionals in their congregations and communities have been left to find accountability and most ethical guidance among professional colleagues—many of whom have no Christian perspective.

God's Character. Mother Teresa's church has not left her on her own. This humble nun in India, one of the world's most admired people, is surrounded by a community of fellow believers, the Sisters of Charity. Their work does not involve therapy or counseling, as we define those terms, but these women are healers. Like most counselors, they seek to bring people to wholeness and health.[18]

Numerous writers have evaluated the work and impact of Mother Teresa and often they reach a similar conclusion. This remarkable woman has a godly character that touches and permeates the lives of all with whom she comes in contact. Her life shows that character is not simply a collection of personality traits. Character is that difficult-to-define core of an individual that guides behavior and makes one predictable and consistent. Personality traits may be inborn; character, in contrast, is molded and developed over a lifetime. Others, including those in our Christian communities, may contribute significantly to character development, but ultimately each of us becomes a person of character when we allow God to work in our lives to develop Christlike qualities—such as goodness, kindness, compassion, faithfulness, patience, and humility. These attributes do not develop solely from introspection or increased knowledge of God. Godly character unfolds and is refined when we combine our understanding with activity. We need to develop the practice of godliness.

Godliness, writes Jerry Bridges, is Christian character that springs from a devotion to God. This is more than an intellectual devotion. It is a "devotion in action," a devotion to God that results in a life that is pleasing to God.[19]

Books on counseling rarely mention godliness or character in the counselor, but these are essential if we are to maintain the highest and best standards of right and wrong. Christians are called to be holy, even as God is holy (1 Pet. 15, 16). That, of course, is an impossibility for finite human beings, but it gives us a high goal and standard for living.

How does this apply to ethics? Most counselors encounter ethics when they are faced with a dilemma and have to answer the question "what should I do?" Recent writers, advocates of "virtue ethics," suggest in contrast that more emphasis needs to be put on the question "who shall I be?" Ethical decisions involve much more than cognitive debate about issues; what a person decides and what he or she does comes from one's individual perceptions, personal values, experiences, personality, biases, and the orientation of one's discipline. Ethical decisions go beyond the boundaries of rules, principles, or difficult decisions. Ethical decisions arise from one's character.

Conclusions such as these have led some writers to argue that the pursuit and development of virtues is not optional for counselors. Each of us must strive for greater fidelity, prudence, discretion, perseverance, courage, integrity, public spiritedness, benevolence, humility, and hope. These have been called *professional virtues*. They are marks of the character that needs to be developing in all genuine counselors.[20]

The development of professional virtues or the growth in godly character does not ensure that we will make impeccable, always correct, ethical decisions. We are all human beings with limitations and imperfections. But godly character gives us a better awareness of God's nature, wisdom, and world view. Godly living gives us a greater sensitivity to the guidance of God's Holy Spirit. Professional virtues lead to the maturity, wise professional judgment, and discretion that counselors need. All of this, in turn, contributes to the likeliness of our making wiser, better ethical decisions.

PRACTICAL COUNSELING ETHICS

Books on ethics often deal with complex social issues that make headlines in newspapers and sometimes creep into our counseling rooms where they surface in individual lives. Decisions about racial discrimination, family instability, divorce, abortion, feminism, and the mistreatment of women, all are discussed in the pages of ethics books and all come up in counseling. Also included are issues such as contraception, reproductive technologies, addictive sexual behavior, homosexuality, juvenile delinquency, substance abuse, civil disobedience, homelessness, poverty, biomedical decisions, and more.

On occasion our counselees even struggle with "faraway" topics that seem more removed from daily life: ecology, war, capital punishment, euthanasia, infanticide, or world hunger. People who are involved in counseling, including those who read this book, can feel overwhelmed about all of these social issues. None of us has the time (and most of us don't have the desire) to develop expertise in each of the areas. It is more realistic to have a general knowledge of the issues and to read more in depth when one or more of the social topics surfaces in our counseling work.[21]

In his thoughtful book *Mere Morality*, Lewis Smedes makes a bold but surely accurate statement that has bearing both on social issues and on ethics: "I believe that God does reveal to us what he expects us to do, and that what he expects us to do is the sort of thing that people must do if they are going to live as human beings." Smedes acknowledges that life is exceedingly complex, but he suggests that the simple Ten Commandments give us the most basic guidelines for making ethical decisions. The commandments reduce to two fundamental issues: We should be just and we should act in love. Everything we do should be fair; if it is not fair, it is not right. And everything we do should be loving and helpful, or at least not hurtful. Ultimately, if it is not loving, it is not right. "Justice and love are absolute, unconditional, unequivocal. They are global, universal, all-embracing commands. They pin us down at every corner, grip us at the center, allow us no qualifications or evasions. Justice and love cover every conceivable human situation. They are the be-all and end-all of the moral life."[22]

It is not always easy to make a just decision, especially when two alternatives seem equally fair. Sometimes it is difficult to determine what would be the most loving thing to do. In situations like these we proceed as best we can, seeking to be guided by God's Word, by other believers who may help with our decisions, and by the knowledge that God's Holy Spirit works within those who are growing in their godlikeness. We can also find guidance in professional codes of ethics.

A Code of Ethics for Christian Counselors. A code of ethics is a set of standards that guide ethical behavior. These written standards express the moral convictions of a group of individuals, such as Christian counselors, who in turn seek to make ethical decisions that are guided by the ethical code. No ethical code can cover every ethical situation that one might encounter. It is not always easy to apply the code and sometimes disagreements arise over the ways in which a code should be interpreted. Nevertheless, an ethical code can be useful in setting standards and guiding counselors, writers, speakers, researchers, and others who are involved in mental health activities.[23]

Within recent years, several individual Christians and groups of counselors have attempted to write a code of ethics based on biblical values, instead of relying primarily on survey data or on the pluralistic perspectives of our society. Christian codes of ethics seek to build on a world view that is consistent with biblical truth. Surely the best and most complete of these ethical codes is that produced by CAPS—the Christian Association for Psychological Studies. This code of ethics for Christian counselors appears as Appendix A at the end of this book.

In many respects, the CAPS Code of Ethics is similar to the ethical codes developed by secular professional organizations. But in many ways the CAPS code is unique. In contrast to the professional codes of ethics, only the CAPS code includes a statement about God's Word, the Bible, being the foundation for professional behavior. Only the CAPS code mentions the community of believers, the church, and requires that the professional be related to a local body of believers. Only the CAPS code includes a commitment to God and to godly living as a part of one's Christian calling to service. Furthermore, the CAPS code is unique in its emphasis on love as the basis for professional service and on its concern for the integrity of the family.[24]

No code of ethics is perfect, but at present the CAPS code is the best available guide written specifically for Christians in psychology, counseling, and related areas of service.

Ethics in Christian Counseling

Some Ethical Questions for Christian Counselors. Whenever I am invited to speak to some group, when I think about writing another book or when I ponder my possible involvement in a new project, I ask myself a variety of questions: Is the proposed activity or project Christ-honoring and consistent with what the Bible teaches? Is it consistent with my life goals? Does it make best use of my abilities, training, and spiritual gifts? Could (or does) somebody else do it as well as I can or better? In accordance with Proverbs 15:22, do people who know me well, such as my wife, fellow church members, or professional colleagues agree it should be done? Is it feasible in terms of things like time, finances, schedule, or my energy level? If I do this, how would it affect my marriage and family? What are the advantages of doing it? What are the disadvantages? What are my motives for doing it? Is it possible that I might be manipulated by others if I do this, and if so, is that okay? Do I feel like doing it?

I don't ask all of these questions if I am making a minor decision, such as whether I could give a five-minute devotional to a small group of believers. But I do try to ponder and honestly answer each of these questions if I am facing a major choice point in life.

Perhaps we need something similar to guide our ethical decision making. Table 2–1 lists suggested questions that might be helpful to guide counselors in difficult ethical situations. You may want to refine the list or add additional questions.

Some decisions can be made quickly because the issues are clear. There is no need to go through a list of questions when a decision is clearly in violation of biblical principles or involves a flagrant disregard for another person's rights and best interests. At times, however, several alternatives appear to be equally desirable, or what appears to be the wisest decision may not be feasible. At those times, decisions are more difficult and going through the questions in Table 2–1 could be helpful.

What do you do if there are two alternatives? You have to choose one, but in either case there will be violation of a scriptural principle? The Bible, for example, says that we are his witnesses, charged with the task of making disciples. Surely that involves talking about Christ. The Bible also instructs us to be in subjection to civil laws, some of which tell us not to talk about Christ, at least in public schools. What, then, does a Christian counselor do if he or she works in the public school system or in the counseling center of a state university?

Ethical Decision Making: Some Guiding Questions

1. What is the decision that needs to be made?
    Try to state this clearly.
2. What additional information do I need?
    Try to get as much accurate information as possible.
3. What guidelines does the Bible give for making this decision?
    Try to determine what the Bible says about the issue. Remember that some issues are not specifically discussed in Scripture, but there may be general guidelines that apply. Examples of these guidelines: genital sexual behavior must be limited to married partners of the opposite sex; the tongue should be controlled; "whatever you do, do it all for the glory of God."
4. What guidelines does the ethical code of one's profession give to help with this decision?
    Christian counselors should give special attention to the CAPS code of ethics, but this should be in addition to professional ethical codes.
5. What are the alternatives in this decision?
6. Is it possible to determine what is the most *just* and fair thing to do?
7. What is the most loving thing to do?
8. How would each person involved be affected by the different alternatives?
    The rights, responsibilities, and consequences for each of the affected parties should be evaluated. This question may take some time to answer and the parties involved may have different answers.
9. In what ways might my personal biases, beliefs, values, attitudes, personality traits, and opinions be influencing the decision?
10. What do other believers and/or other professionals think should be done?
    Consultation with others can broaden your perspective and reduce idiosyncratic responses. In soliciting the opinion of others, however, take care that you do not betray confidences.
11. What do you feel is the right thing to do?
    Be cautious here. Feelings are variable and are not the best basis on which to make significant decisions. But sometimes a decision "feels right," after we have evaluated all the alternatives. At times the feeling could be the inner prompting of the Holy Spirit, so feelings should not be ignored. But always test your feelings against the Scriptures and the counsel of other dedicated believers. Sometimes feelings are good warnings to "go slow" until more clear-cut evidence becomes available.

Table 2–1

Assume a young counselee is struggling with life direction, values, guilt, and a search for meaning in life. The counselor knows that Christ can meet that young person's need. Does the counselor keep silent or mention Christ?

In a conclusion that not all Christians would accept, Norman Geisler argues persuasively for what he calls "graded absolutism." Not all moral laws are equal, he suggests. The New Testament clearly teaches that we should obey the law and submit to government authorities (Rom. 13:1–2; Tit. 3:1; 1 Pet. 2:13). But what do we do if the law tells us to do something that clearly violates biblical principles? When the local authorities forbade the apostles to preach, Peter responded that "we must obey God rather than men" (Acts 5:29). Apparently Peter saw the instruction to preach the gospel to be a higher moral law than the directive to obey the authorities. There are many unavoidable moral conflicts like this, according to Geisler, and Christians must always yield to "higher moral laws," such as the love for God taking precedence over love for people, or the precedence of showing mercy over always telling the truth. Because of her desire to protect persecuted Jews, for example, Corrie ten Boom did not tell the truth to the Nazi interrogators.[25] On occasion each of us might face issues that call for a similar kind of decision.

ISSUES IN COUNSELING ETHICS

Should a counselor ever counsel a relative?

Should a professor who teaches counseling agree to counsel one of his or her students?

If a counselee tells you about a crime he has committed, should you tell the authorities?

Is it okay to mislead somebody as part of a research project, even if you intend to tell the truth later?

Should you continue to counsel a person whom you dislike?

What do you do if a counselee wants help to continue with sexual behavior that you feel is morally wrong?

Should you continue to work with a counselee to whom you feel sexually attracted? If so, do you tell the counselee about your sexual feelings?

On occasion, most counselors face ethical questions such as these. Each is complex, but several excellent books now deal in depth with the more prevalent ethical issues in counseling.[26] The remainder of this chapter will give a more general overview of six issues and attempt to show how the preceding principles could apply in practice to issues of competence, confidentiality, informed consent, finances, sexuality, and the discovery of unethical or immoral behavior in others.

Competence. Who is competent to counsel? In his much discussed and controversial book, Jay Adams argued that pastors are the most competent counselors. His lectures and articles have repeated this message often: "A good seminary education, rather than medical school or a degree in clinical psychology, is the most fitting background for a counselor."[27]

Most professionals would disagree and so, I suspect, would most pastors. The problems that people bring to counselors are diverse and no one person, including a well-trained pastor, is competent to handle them all.

Ethical codes agree that no counselor should attempt to provide services outside his or her area of expertise. To do so, or to claim that we are experts in areas where we are not highly adept, is to open ourselves for trouble. False claims about our competence could leave us uncertain about how to proceed in the counseling. But we also face the reality that people who don't get better sometimes are inclined to file lawsuits and bring charges of incompetence, even against counselors in the church.[28] For this reason one should never use terms such as *professional counselor* or *psychologist* unless one has the academic degrees and, in many cases, the state license to practice. Such false advertising implies that we have academic and legal competence that, in fact, we do not have. It is safer, wiser, more honest, and ethical to stay within the limits of one's training, experience, and legal-professional areas of competence.

Perhaps it is surprising that a survey of professional psychologists found almost one fourth (22.8 percent) had practiced outside their areas of competence, at least on occasion. Some had used and interpreted psychological tests even when they had not been trained in the test's use. Over half (59.6 percent) acknowledged that they had done counseling when they were too distressed personally to be effective.[29]

These findings and the entire issue of competence raise other difficult ethical questions.

- Suppose you recommend that a counselee should shift to a more competent counselor but your counselee is unwilling to make

the change or is unable to pay the new counselor's fees? Or what should you do if you feel inadequate to give help but no alternative counselor is available. In these cases, is a partially competent counselor better than no counselor? Perhaps the questions in Table 2–1 could help in such cases
- How does a pastor act if the available professionals are competent psychologically but incompetent in dealing with the counselee's spiritual issues? In this case, two counselors are both partially competent. If they cannot work together, who does the counseling? Probably the best counselor in such situations is the one whose training and expertise will be more helpful in dealing with the immediate and most pressing problem. That counselor should be honest in mentioning his or her limitations to the counselee and should seek input and guidance in the areas where competence is lacking.

Competence is more than a matter of general overall skill and ability. For each counselee, the counselor must determine who is most competent to deal with this person at this time and in this geographical area.

Confidentiality. Every counselor knows that keeping information confidential is of crucial importance in counseling. Without this, many counselees would not come for treatment or they might withhold valuable information that has to be considered if the counseling is to succeed.

It is now widely agreed, however, that some information cannot and should not be held confidential. Counseling students often hear about the murder of Tatiana Tarasoff who was killed by a patient while he was being treated by a California psychologist. The psychologist knew about the patient's obsession with Tarasoff and had determined that the patient was dangerous, but the information was kept confidential. Even though the psychologist was the first to inform the police after the murder, Tarasoff's parents sued the psychologist and his employer because the victim had not been warned. The court ruled that a counselor must use "reasonable care" to protect an intended victim when the counselor "determines, or pursuant to the standards of his profession should determine, that the patient presents a serious danger of violence to another." In nonlegal terms this means that a counselor might be committed to keeping confidences but this does not excuse the counselor from warning an intended victim.[30]

A related ethical issue has come with the AIDS epidemic. When it is known that a counselee has AIDS but is unwilling to reveal this to his or her sexual partner, what does the counselor do? It is generally agreed that confidential information is revealed only when there are compelling reasons to do so, such as to protect the counselee or the community from danger, to comply with a court order, or to pass on information at the counselee's request. But is the possibility of AIDS infection one of these compelling reasons that would cause the counselor to break confidences?

One recent survey found that almost 60 percent of marriage and family therapists would never or rarely pass on this information,[31] but the writers of journal articles tend to disagree. Most conclude that if you are a counselor who learns that a counselee with AIDS is endangering others, you have two choices. Either you inform the counselee's sexual partner(s) or you face the possibility of a lawsuit based on a legal application of the "failure to warn" theory.[32]

Ideally, information that you obtain in counseling or from test results should be kept confidential and revealed only when the counselee gives you permission to do so. If a counselee has information that should be shared outside the counseling room, you can often encourage and support the counselee as he or she shares that information directly. Suppose, for example, that a man has been having an affair and has picked up a venereal disease as a result. To protect his wife from infection, to bring psychological and spiritual healing, and to renew marital stability, I suggest she should know about the man's unfaithfulness. It is better if he tells her, with your support, rather than having her learn about the affair in some other way.

Today, it is standard practice at the beginning of counseling to talk about the limits of confidentiality. Explain that information shared in counseling is kept confidential except in those rare situations where it is necessary to reveal shared information so that lives can be protected or so the counselee can be kept from self-harm. These issues can be discussed, often very briefly, before counseling begins.

Informed Consent. Most people come to counseling voluntarily, but this does not mean that the counselor has complete freedom to use counseling approaches that could go against the counselee's wishes or values. Some Christians are skeptical of secular counselors because there is fear that the nonbelieving counselor might use methods or push values that go against the counselee's Christian beliefs. Other counselees are afraid that a counselor might be manipulative or take away one's freedom to make decisions.

I have a friend whose counselor recommended an intensive, weekend group therapy session. My friend, who is a Christian, was not informed that the "treatment" would involve nude therapy. Regardless of how one might look at nude therapy (pun intended), it is unethical for a therapist to involve a client in such a group without first revealing what will take place and securing the counselee's prior consent.

Qualified counselors do not seek to manipulate their counselees, in part because manipulation is disrespectful and partly because it almost never brings lasting change. To respect the counselee and to be genuinely honest, counselors need to give clear, easily understood information about their values, their beliefs, and their approaches to therapy. This would imply that the Christian counselor has an ethical obligation to be clear about his or her beliefs and spiritual goals at the beginning of a counseling relationship.[33] Table 2–2 gives a sample statement that could be presented verbally at the beginning of counseling or given in written form to potential counselees. Christian psychologist Darrell Smith has prepared a written consent statement that is reproduced at the end of this book in appendix B.[34]

Informed consent assumes that the counselee's consent to "go ahead" with the counseling must be based on knowledge (that is why it is called *informed* consent), must be voluntary, and must be rational. And the counselee can withdraw consent at any time.

What does a counselor do if he or she is approached by a minor who wants counseling but there is no parental consent? What if a counselee is too disturbed emotionally to give consent?[35] Can a counselor withhold test information or a diagnosis without the counselee's consent? These are questions that aren't very exciting when they appear in a book, but they can lead to significant struggles when they come up in the counseling room.[36]

Finances. Someone has suggested that the most basic ethical obligations for counselors can be summarized in three words: competence, confidentiality, and consent.[37] These are the issues we have discussed thus far, but for many counselors difficult ethical decisions center around the topic of compensation. This is especially true for Christian counselors whose livelihood depends on client fees but who are reluctant to use a collection agency if fees are not paid or who hesitate to terminate the therapy of a person who cannot afford to pay.

Sample Statement of Counselor Values and Orientation[1]

My name is _____. I am a professional counselor with training in _____, and I specialize in marriage and individual counseling. I want to share some information about myself and what I do in counseling so you can make a fully informed decision about using my services.

First and foremost, I am a Christian counselor. As a Christian counselor I believe that hiding our beliefs and trying to do value-free counseling is both unwise and impossible to do, so I want you to know what my important values and beliefs are.

Like most counselors, I recognize that personal problems can come about because of physiology, social-environmental influences and psychological pressures. I also believe that many problems can be spiritual in nature, resulting from either not understanding biblical truth or from sinful behavior. I also believe that individuals are created in God's image and can only feel complete and fulfilled through a relationship with God. Thus, Christian counseling, as opposed to other kinds of counseling, is very concerned with the spiritual as well as the emotional and physical needs of clients. The main goal of Christian counseling, like the goal of Christian living, is to enable clients to move toward greater emotional and spiritual health by becoming more like Jesus Christ.

As a Christian counselor, I am not limited to psychological techniques or to my own human effort and wisdom. I believe that God is the real authority in counseling and he is the one who gives us the resources to change. I believe counseling can involve praying about the client's difficulties and looking to the authority of the Bible for guidance. In this way, I seek to encourage clients to build a dependency on God. The client can find forgiveness for the past, strength and comfort for the present, and hope for the future by trusting the Lord to daily meet needs and heal emotional wounds. I don't manipulate clients or force religion on to them, but in all that I do, I try to reflect the character of Jesus Christ and to love my clients with the same kind of unconditional love that God offers them.

Adapted, with permission, from a statement used at Iowa State University in research by Julia A Pecnik and Douglas L. Epperson, "Analogue Study of Expectations for Christian and Traditional Counseling," *Journal of Counseling Psychology*, 1985 (32), 127–30.

Table 2–2

Ethically, fees need to be discussed at the beginning of counseling and prices should not be raised without giving reasonable notice. Most professionals set fees based on their training (psychiatrists usually charge higher fees than psychologists), their level of experience, and on the "going rate" in their geographical areas. Often the fee structure is at least partially based on a counselee's ability to pay.

Most counselors, especially those who are Christians,[38] do not want to cut off counseling if a person cannot pay. Do we see these people without charge? If someone in private practice has only two or three such persons, giving free counseling is not likely to create financial hardship for the counselor, but what does one do if a larger number of people cannot or will not pay?

Professional counselors often are criticized for their high fees, and sometimes this criticism is justified. Counselees and critics fail to realize, however, that the counselor does not keep all of the money that is paid. Costs for insurance, overhead, answering services, and missed appointments (where the counselor has no income for an hour) can all reduce professional income more than some realize.[39] The professional, therefore, seeks to be fair and compassionate in charging fees, but firm in insisting that fees be paid as agreed and on time. If he or she is to survive financially, there can only be a limited number of nonpaying or low-paying clients.

Sexuality. Sexual intimacies with clients are unethical. Every code of ethics makes a statement like this and almost all counselors, secular and Christian, agree. Most agree, in addition, that there should be no sexual contact between a counselor and his or her supervisor or between a counselor and a former counselee.

But what we believe does not always translate into consistent practice. In confidential surveys, non-Christian counselors, Christian counselors and pastoral counselors all admit to having engaged in sexual intimacies, including intercourse, with their counselees. The percentages vary, depending on the survey, but it appears that between 5 and 7 percent of counselors get involved sexually with counselees, at least on occasion. Repeated surveys also show that the vast majority of counselees are harmed, often significantly, by sexual experiences with their therapists.[40]

If erotic behavior between counselors and counselees is considered to be by almost everyone unethical and if it is so harmful, then why is it so prevalent and why does it exist even among Christians? The answers, of course, are complex but they could be divided into two broad categories, vulnerable counselees and vulnerable counselors.

People who come for counseling often have low self-esteem, frustrating relationships with other people, and a desire for some kind of direction. Many are insecure and lonely. In therapy, talk is often about intimate issues, including sexual issues, and a bond of trust and closeness builds between the counselor and counselee. In the midst of their struggles and pain, some of these counselees are easily manipulated and led. They are moved by the counselor's warmth, understanding, support, and affirmation. A few may be starved for affection and closeness with another human being. These people respond readily to hugs or other expressions of care and in time there can be movement into sexual intimacies.

This is more likely when the counselor is vulnerable. If he or she is attracted to a counselee, has an unsatisfactory marriage or feels lonely, sexual involvements are more likely—especially if the counselee is needy, seductive, or manipulative. As intimate details of the counselee's life are discussed in therapy, any counselor could be aroused sexually.

Most often, it seems, these "affairs in the consulting room" seem to evolve slowly, without any prior planning and often to the surprise of the parties involved. "I thought I was invulnerable and that it would never happen to me," said one counselor. "We were just good friends," said another. "I was a good listener and he needed somebody to listen to. I don't know what happened. I guess it was the right chemistry. We fell in love and eventually ended up in bed."

Counselors need to remind themselves, and each other, that every person is vulnerable and that all of us should be careful to maintain accountability to one or two trusted colleagues. Also, counselors must to set limits on their time and counseling relationships, give attention and effort to building their own marriages and close relationships apart from counseling, avoid potentially compromising situations, and be aware of "warning signs" that could indicate vulnerability. The latter include working late to avoid contact with the family, thinking often about some special counselee, seeking intellectual and social stimulation apart from one's mate, and failing to maintain a consistent personal devotional life.[41] The biblical warning is clear. "If you think you are standing firm, be careful that you don't fall!" (1 Cor. 10:12).

Ethical Violations. How does the counselor respond if he or she learns that another counselor is engaging in unethical counseling behavior? If we ignore the situation, the unethical counselor's clients could be harmed, perhaps seriously. If, instead, we report the ethical violation, we risk doing serious damage to the career of a colleague, especially if we act on the basis of information that was wrong. If we gossip about the situation and tell one or two friends, everybody is hurt and we engage in behavior that is disparaged in Scripture (Prov. 16:28; Rom 1:29; James 3:5–10).

In a survey conducted several years ago, graduate psychology students were asked what they *should* do if they discovered unethical behavior in a colleague or friend, and what they *would* do.[42] About half of the students said they would overlook the situation and do nothing even though the APA ethical statement clearly says what they should do:

> When psychologists know of an ethical violation by another psychologist, and it seems appropriate, they informally attempt to resolve the issue by bringing the behavior to the attention of the psychologist. If the misconduct is of a minor nature and/or appears to be due to lack of sensitivity, knowledge, or experience, such an informal solution is usually appropriate. Such informal corrective efforts are made with sensitivity to any rights to confidentiality involved. If the violation does not seem amenable to an informal solution, or is of a more serious nature, psychologists bring it to the attention of the appropriate local, state, and/or national committee on professional ethics and conduct.[43]

This sounds very much like Matthew 18:15–17. If we have a complaint against another believer, we are to go in private to discuss the disagreement. Only then do we involve other people, first one or two colleagues, then a local church.

This biblical guideline is for believers, however. Even when Christian counselors are at odds with each other over an ethical issue they might prefer to take it, not to one's local church where the ethics of counseling may not be understood, but to a representative sample of the church—perhaps a group of fellow Christian counselors who are familiar with counseling ethics.

Some writers have suggested that the decision to ignore an ethical violation is, in itself, an ethical violation. Of the complaints that come to professional ethics committees, only about one in four involves a counselor complaining against a colleague.[44] The complainer has to be able to substantiate his or her charge in front of the committee and in the presence of the alleged violator. All of this can take time and energy that could be devoted to other activities. Sometimes the person complained against responds by charging the complainer with harassment. All of this can lead to anger, charges and counter charges, and efforts to find evidence to support one's complaints. Clearly it is best if all of this can be avoided.

Conclusion

Several years ago I felt that a colleague was engaging in behavior that was not unethical but it did seem inappropriate. After a lot of prayer and hesitation, I went to see my colleague to express my concern. He was a little defensive, but the conversation was cordial and the behavior stopped—at least publicly. But from that time until we moved away from each other, I felt there was tension between us. At times I have wondered how that tension could have been avoided.

We can avoid uncomfortable conversations and tense confrontations if each of us strives for excellence in our ethical behavior. For the Christian counselor this is not an option; it is demanded by our professions and by our God.

CHAPTER THREE
LIABILITY IN CHRISTIAN COUNSELING
Welcome to the Grave New World*

George Ohlschlager, J.D., L.C.S.W.

ON APRIL FOOL'S DAY IN 1979, twenty-four-year old Kenneth Nally pointed a shotgun to his head, squeezed the trigger, and violently ended his life. One year less a day later, Nally's parents filed suit for wrongful death against their deceased son's church and four of his pastors alleging "clergyman malpractice" and "outrageous conduct in failing to prevent [their son's] suicide."[1]

---

*Christian counselors cannot ignore the legal implications of their work, especially in a country and in a period of history when lawsuits are becoming more and more prevalent. To assist in our understanding of the Christian counselor's liability, we

Thus began a landmark suit that ushered in a new era of Christian counseling liability. For most of the 1980s the controversial case of *Nally v. Grace Community Church of the Valley*[2] wound its way up and down the California judicial system, with decisions by the appeals and state supreme courts alternating back and forth in support of either the aggrieved parents or the embattled church. It was finally and mercifully laid to rest in 1989 by the United States Supreme Court, which denied review of the California Supreme Court's final judgment. This case and others we shall examine in this chapter exemplify the grave new world of Christian counseling liability. Welcome to a brief exploration of this alien land.

This chapter presents a selective review of the burgeoning data of psychiatric and psychotherapeutic liability applied to Christian counseling ministry.[3] The limits of this chapter require me to focus on the facts and trends of legal and, to a lesser degree, ethical liability. My intent is not to present the comprehensive scope but rather give the reader a representative view of a few key issues in the field. While this legal focus is primarily descriptive, it is also predictive about future liability trends and, to some extent, prescriptive about preferred boundaries between law and ministry and clinical practice. For the sake of understanding, I explain legal concepts and minimize the jargon of law.

This chapter comprises three parts. The first presents current issues, data, and trends of the legal regulation of Christian counseling. The second part reviews the *Nally* case to give counselors a better view of how law interacts with ministry in the adversarial realm of the court. Part 3 assesses the epidemic of sexual misconduct in counseling, considering the various civil and criminal remedies being imposed by states to control this problem. Finally, this chapter concludes with a proposal for a preferred legal standard and with thoughts on integrating the law with Scripture as a guide to ethical and effective Christian counseling.

---

turn in this invited chapter to the expertise of a professional counselor—a licensed clinical social worker— who has an M.A. in counseling psychology from Trinity Evangelical Divinity School, an M.S.W. from the Graduate School of Social Work at the University of Iowa, and a J.D. from the University of Iowa College of Law. George Ohlschlager is associate director and cofounder of The Redwood Family Institute in Eureka, California, and teaches part-time in the graduate psychology program of Sierra University. He is currently coauthoring a book (with Peter Mosgofian) on legal issues and Christian counseling. The author's analysis in this chapter applies to legal issues in the United States, and many of his conclusions can apply to readers from other countries.

THE LEGAL REGULATION OF CHRISTIAN COUNSELING

Over the past quarter-century professional clinicians, including ministers and pastoral counselors, have faced a steadily increasing risk of lawsuit. Two major projects—the Hogan study of American psychotherapy malpractice litigation and the American Psychological Association Insurance Trust Study—show this increasing liability risk.

The Hogan Study

Daniel Hogan performed a valuable service to the legal and mental health professions by completing a comprehensive survey of psychotherapy malpractice litigation in the United States from the nineteenth century to 1977.[4] Three hundred cases were analyzed for their relevance to psychotherapy and mental health care. Over 80 percent of these cases were appellate decisions, coming from the courts that establish the case law foundations of our American legal system.

The key finding of the Hogan study was the dramatic rise in the incidence of malpractice litigation. Two-thirds of all decisions since 1850 were decided since 1960. One-third of all decisions were reported during the 1970–77 period.[5] This finding supports the widely reported assertion that a "malpractice crisis" exists in many fields and has become the subject of much social and political concern.[6]

Overall, plaintiffs won 31 percent of all suits, defendants won 45 percent, and 24 percent were nonfinal (the issue of defendant liability was not reached for various reasons). During the 1970–77 period, however, plaintiffs won 39 percent while defendants won only 42 percent. Among cases not appealed, plaintiffs won verdicts half the time.[7] Trends in case outcome clearly favor client-plaintiffs over counselor-defendants. Taken together, the above findings strongly suggest that counselors who harm clients will be sued much more frequently and will lose these lawsuits more often than in the past.

If you counsel in New York or California, you practice with a much higher risk of suit. Nearly half the cases came out of these two states, with Texas, Pennsylvania, Illinois, Missouri, and Massachusetts showing a smaller but consistent incidence of suit.[8] Hogan attributed the concentration of suits in New York and California to their urbanization, extensive mental health services, large populations of both mental health professionals and lawyers, and asserted that both states "have reputations for radical therapies with an orientation to sex and physical contact."[9]

Case settings reflect the national trend away from hospital to community-based treatment. While 74 percent of all actions came from hospitals versus only 10 percent from private and community settings during 1950–59, the 1970–77 period showed hospital-based actions had fallen to 60 percent while private and community settings increased to 17 percent of total suits.[10] Patients/clients or their representatives brought 77 percent of all actions, while third parties (people harmed by patients or patient relatives) brought 21 percent of the suits. Less than 2 percent of the suits were state-initiated criminal actions or actions to revoke professional licenses. Plaintiffs were far more successful against private and community-based defendants (43 percent vs.14 percent) than against hospitals and other institutions (32 percent vs. 44 percent).[11]

Mental health professionals were named in 32 percent of all actions. Hospitals defended 20 percent of the suits and governments at all levels defended 33 percent. Among practitioners, non-psychiatric physicians comprised half of all those sued while psychiatrists were sued 35 percent of the time. Psychologists were named in 5 percent of the suits, nurses in 4 percent, lawyers in 2 percent and an amalgam of social workers, para-professionals, marriage and family therapists and others in the remaining 3 percent of the suits.[12]

As part of his study, Hogan classed liable behavior according to negligent diagnosis, treatment, and care. Suits for negligent diagnosis and treatment are increasing while negligent care suits, confined to institutional settings primarily, are in the decline. Diagnosis of a mental disorder that led to commitment to an institution comprised 41 percent of all misdiagnosis suits. Failure to diagnose mental illness or potential danger and improper release from an institution as a result made up 29 percent of the actions. Inadequate or no treatment allegations comprised 28 percent of the maltreatment suits. Another quarter of the suits involved negligent electroconvulsive or drug treatment. Sexual misconduct was charged in 10 percent of the suits. Some of the other allegations included physical assault, failure to obtain informed consent, failure to consult or refer, negligent use of psychotherapy, and negligent handling of transference and countertransference dynamics.[13]

Regarding type of harm alleged, accidental injuries, usually in a hospital setting and often in conjunction with drug treatment, was most often cited at 20 percent. Loss of liberty involved 11 percent and deprivation of constitutional rights was noted in 9 percent of all cases. Suicide was the issue in 9 percent and another 9 percent of the cases noted accidental death. Emotional distress comprised 7 percent of all suits, economic loss in 5 percent, and sexual or marital harm was alleged in 4 percent. Some of the myriad other harms noted were self-inflicted injury, injury to reputation, loss of companionship, loss of health, insanity, alienation of affection, invasion of privacy, pregnancy, and abortion. Sexual abuse assertions were the most successful of lawsuits, with plaintiffs prevailing in 66 percent of these actions.[14]

APA Insurance Trust Study

A few years ago the Insurance Trust of the American Psychological Association analyzed malpractice suits nationwide against psychologists from 1976 to 1986.[15] The most significant finding affirms the Hogan study data: Malpractice suits are increasing at a geometric rate against psychologists and, by implication, all mental health professionals. Suits against psychologists more than tripled from 1976–81 to the period 1982–86. From an average of 44 actions filed annually during the initial period, the last period, on average, saw over 150 suits filed each year. A total of $5.4 million was paid against claims for the years 1976 to 1983; in 1985 alone, the insurers paid out $17.2 million.[16]

Sexual misconduct was the most prevelant cause of action, with 22.5 percent of all actions filed over the eleven-year period of the study. This, however, fails to reveal the major increase in these lawsuits. From roughly 9 percent of the actions filed during the early years of the study, sexual misconduct actions comprised nearly 50 percent of all suits filed at the end of the study. This increase in lawsuits for sexual misconduct is also reflected in the data from psychiatry.[17]

Following sexual misconduct in descending order of frequency are claims for incorrect treatment (18.5 percent), loss from evaluation (11.8 percent), client death (10.5 percent), breach of confidentiality (8.5 percent), improper diagnosis (7.2 percent), fee disputes (7.2 percent), defamation (5.3 percent), civil rights violations (3.6 percent), bodily injury (3.0 percent), assault and battery (1.3 percent), and failure to warn (0.6 percent). It is significant that "failure to warn" suits—reflecting the duty to protect third parties from the homicidal actions of clients—reveal the lowest incidence of suit. This certainly is contrary to the explosion of negative commentary nationwide that predicted dire consequences to counselor-client confidentiality following the landmark 1976 *Tarasoff* decision in California.[18]

Social and Systemic Trends in Legal Liability

Trends in society, in the ministry and the clinical professions, and in the field of law have all contributed to the growing risk of lawsuit for clinical professionals and pastoral counselors.

Trends in American Society. Modern American society has been described as being both psychological and litigious.[19] To the degree these attributions are true, a paradoxical dilemma has been created for the helping professional. Increasingly, many human and social problems are thought to have a psychological base, and demand for psychosocial services has dramatically increased in a generation. At the same time, professional service recipients are more educated and consumer oriented, more aware of their legal rights, and more skeptical of professional authority and power. Excessive psychological attributions and high expectations of psychosocial change combined with awareness of legal rights and a skepticism about therapist curative powers is indeed a volatile mixture for potential suit.

This secularization of American life is also seen in the emphasis on legal rights and individual liberty that grows at the expense of communal values, cooperative dispute resolution, and reliance on traditional institutions—the family, church, neighborhood, and community.[20] Rather than own these community values and institutions as allies, all too often American citizens see and oppose them as barriers to happiness and freedom. More and more, religion and spiritual truth are relegated to an individualized and highly private experience in the secular society.

As a result, the Christian message is pushed to extreme, polarized roles in social and political life. On one hand, in the name of pluralistic tolerance, Christian values are allowed little to no role in informing or challenging public policy and values. On the other hand, in the self-centered culture of narcissism, private beliefs become more important and are asserted over and against traditional values and the historical institutions of society. This fundamental societal rift is fertile ground for adversarial conflict and litigated dispute resolution.

Finally, the secular society has demanded alliance with government as the ultimate protector of rights and the only sufficient power to curb real and perceived abuses by other large and powerful institutions.

"A new social order has evolved that started with a reliance by citizens on government for the solution to certain economic, social and cultural problems and has grown to include pressures on government to mitigate almost every risk any individual might be asked to bear."[21] The church is a target that is increasingly seen as a threat against which the government must protect its citizens. As quoted by insurance executive Al Davidson, "Today, people are just as quick to sue the church as a secular organization."[22] Some clergy and churches will face a hostile adversary "looking for reasons to vent their frustration and anger against such overarching authority figures [as the church]. The Grace Community Church suit startles us with this reality."[23]

Trends in Ministry and the Helping Professions. At its worst, the American church has given secular society ample reason to believe it must be protected from erring and harmful ministry over this past decade. Our increasingly biased national media rivets attention on the worst aspects of our fallen ministers, such as the anti-Christian exploits of Jim Bakker and Jimmy Swaggart. When further reinforced by Elmer Gantry stereotypes on television, the secular world begins to believe a grotesque caricature of the Christian life. A societal counterreaction is unavoidable.

Though depicting only a very small minority and showing a very great contrast to the majority of godly ministers, this moral epidemic in ministry shouts an invitation to secular legal regulation and redress of harm. This process, already started and quietly growing, will likely transfer growing control of ministry to the state unless the church itself can take effective control of its erring ministers. If the Christian church does not assertively police itself, the behavior of a few will attract the legal regulation that could excessively constrain all the rest.

The clinical professions are not immune from this secular drift in society. Although greatly advancing our understanding of human and social behavior, these professions have also largely cut themselves adrift from the moral and spiritual values that have guided and defined Western culture.[24] The rejection of a Christian value base disserves many seeking help as it leaves the clinical professions discomforted and confused about spiritual issues. Hence, many counselors espouse a feeble neutrality regarding values or open the door to counterfeit religion in response to client (and their own) need. "Subsequently, given their largely autonomous functioning, limited moral development, and inadequate decision-making skills, professionals are left to make judgments based upon highly subjective and frequently self-serving moral ideals."[25]

Also, unlike the scientific foundations of medicine or the common law and constitutional heritage of American law, no single theoretical or empirical base is universally accepted to guide the development of psychotherapy and helping ministry. More than two hundred distinct forms of counseling and psychotherapy have been identified,[26] some that promote ethically questionable, even plainly harmful behavior that is the material of lawsuits. The counseling consumer is further confused by the myriad titles, degrees, licenses, and other sanctions that attach to the various mental health professions.

> Members of the public who find their way to these "therapists"—[some] who are, by and large, uneducated, uncredentialed and unethical—may be very displeased with the results.[27]

Many in the Christian church have certainly been displeased with both the clinical professions and the secular drift in society. The conservative church, especially, has led the charge of wholesale rejection of psychology and psychotherapy as part of its larger resistance to the intrusion of secularism.[28] The biblical call of separation of the church from the larger culture must be heeded (2 Cor. 6:14–7:1), but sometimes that separation is pushed to extremes that deny church members access to constructive societal resources and genuinely risk harming people.

Rejecting all that the mental health professions offer, without right discernment of what is beneficial and what is not, forces some churches to set themselves up as expert and comprehensive providers of every kind of spiritual and emotional care. This often results in exaggerated claims of competence and curative power, spiritualized misdiagnosis that denies many medical, genetic, and psychosocial problem factors, and a failure to refer to and work collaboratively with clinical professionals. Dependent and needy parishioners who rely exclusively on these often insular church communities do so to their own, sometimes deadly, peril.

This growing reactionary process of hyperseparatism within segments of the church predicts a troublesome future. Unless challenged and transformed from within the church, this will lead to further legal action from which the entire church will suffer. "Because of their fervent attitudes against secularization and their fear and rejection of psychology, many of these conservative churches cut their constituents off from professional help. It is the strategy of pastoral care and counseling in these churches that is most vulnerable in this age of increased charges of clergy malpractice."[29]

Trends at Bar and Bench. A critical and often overlooked fact about our litigious society is the explosive growth in the number of lawyers in America. The population of lawyers has doubled in a generation and will approach one million around the turn of the century. As legal competition steadily increases, lawyers on the economic fringe will more aggressively pursue litigation in fields that were once ignored. The American Bar Association sponsored a seminar in May 1989 on how to conduct litigation against the church and religious institutions.[30] This aggression by lawyers is reinforced by the growth of the contingent fee arrangement that, for the legal consumer, effectively removes a traditional economic barrier to litigation. With payment for services only when a claimant wins and receives damages, lawyers must aggressively pursue recovery to survive professionally.

This systemic reality also creates pressure to relax traditional barriers in law that impede claimant success. As will be shown, it is not easy, as a matter of law, for a client-claimant to win a lawsuit. Some legal theorists have attacked the protective barriers of traditional tort law, advocating simpler ways that client harm may be compensated for by professional service providers. After extensive review of the literature on harmful outcome in psychotherapy, Furrow argues for strict liability in therapeutic malpractice.[31] In this system, evidence of therapeutic harm alone would trigger damage awards. The intervening requirements of showing therapist negligence and causation of harm— essential elements of proof in a malpractice action—would be forsaken. Fortunately, no American court has adopted or seriously considered this change in American law. Furrow has provided the theoretical rationale, however, and such a system could tempt lawmakers in the future if the incidence and seriousness of counseling harm is not abated.

Judges, of course, are influenced by all these things. Considering the growth and power in modern society of government, business, transnational organizations, and the media, it is easy to understand how courts have become the protectors of individual rights and liberties. Without some effective system of redress, individuals harmed by the operations of these massive and increasingly global institutions would have no real ability to avoid and challenge institutional power. When the power of the organized church becomes abusive, American courts are now more willing to consider new ways to protect people from such abuses. Dennis Kasper, a Christian lawyer who gives workshops on church liability and protection, states that the "courts, already predisposed toward individual liberty, generally unfamiliar with the needs and requirements of institutional religion, and at times perhaps offended by what secular members of our society might view as religious excesses on television, have been willing to apply against churches and religious organizations legal remedies that did not exist in the past."[32]

Principles and Trends of Christian Counseling Liability

American law is derived from several, diverse sources. The foundational source is the Constitution of the United States which declares in Article VI, "This Constitution . . . shall be the supreme Law of the land. . . . " Each of the fifty states also has a constitution, ultimately subject to the federal charter. Statutes are another form of law enacted by Congress and the various state legislatures. The executive branches of the federal and state governments, including regional, county, and municipal governments, issue administrative regulations that implement statutory law.

Finally, the judicial branch of federal and state governments issues court opinions that define and advance the meaning of law when contested by affected parties. Each state has a supreme court, and a federal appeals court stands atop each of the thirteen regional circuits that comprise the federal judiciary. The United States Supreme Court is the final court of appeal for all federal and state courts, hearing a small percentage of the thousands of cases appealed to it each year.

The law that impacts Christian counseling ministry comes from all of these sources, as well as from the common law tradition we inherited from England.[33] This tradition of Anglo-American legal history had exempted church and clergy from liability based on the centuries-old doctrine of charitable immunity,[34] buttressed in America by the religion clauses of the First Amendment to the Constitution.[35] This historic protection is now being substantially eroded by a rash of lawsuits and regulatory actions all across this nation. America's courts are accepting lawsuits by parishioners, counselees, and their families that have claimed a variety of harms suffered in pastoral care and counseling ministry. This section reviews the primary bases of this contemporary expansion of liability.

The Malpractice Tort. The primary area of law that defines liability in counseling ministry is tort law. A tort is a noncriminal, civil, or private wrong, independent of contract, for which the law allows money damages as redress for injuries suffered.[36] Guided by a cardinal legal principle of rule by analogy, tort liability in Christian counseling follows the body of law developed from medical, psychiatric and psychotherapeutic liability. The field of tort law is divided into two major branches: (1) negligent tort, also known as malpractice or unintentional tort, and (2) intentional tort. Malpractice is considered a less severe form of wrongdoing compared to intentional tort, while intentional tort is considered less severe than criminal wrong.

Malpractice comprises two-thirds of all psychiatric and psychotherapy-related litigation in the United States.[37] It is defined legally as an

> act or omission by a professional practitioner in the treatment of a patient or client that is inconsistent with the reasonable care or skill usually demonstrated by ordinary, prudent practitioners of the same profession, similarly situated.[38]

Malpractice liability exists when it can be proven that a counselor owed a legal duty to his or her client, breached that duty by failing to meet the requisite standard of care, and by that failure the client suffered some demonstrable harm. A lawsuit can fail at any of these points of proof, making malpractice difficult to prove by a client-claimant in spite of its predominance as the legal basis for counseling liability.

The legal standard of care is established by expert testimony according to respected standards from the school or model of therapy one uses, taking into consideration the experience and nature of the defendant's practice. Specialists are held to a higher standard of care than generalists, as are those using new or relatively untested therapy models. Those holding themselves out as expert or especially competent with certain kinds of problems are also held to a higher standard of care.

All psychotherapists licensed or sanctioned in some manner by the state or by national professional associations, including Christian counselors, are subject to malpractice liability. Furthermore, anyone holding themselves out to the public as a counselor, including nonprofessional and unlicensed therapists, may be held liable for malpractice (as well as to the state for unlicensed practice).[39] The one group that remains exempt from malpractice liability is the ordained clergy, who counsel as a function of their ministry. Every malpractice action brought against clergy over the past decade, including the landmark *Nally* case, failed to establish a legal cause for clergy malpractice.[40]

Though the courts declined to establish clergy malpractice for numerous reasons of law and public policy, the overarching concern was that such cause would violate First Amendment constitutional protections of ministry freedom. Recent opinion by the U.S. Supreme Court,[41] however, may have seriously damaged historic protection of Christian ministry, paving the way for a new round of litigation in the 1990s that could establish a legal basis for clergy malpractice. These issues will be reviewed later.

Intentional Tort Liability. Though clergy malpractice has failed to date as a basis for suit, intentional tort has at least partially succeeded as a cause by which pastoral counselors have been sued. Some American courts have accepted suits for alienation of affections, invasion of privacy, and intentional infliction of emotional distress[42] A unique legal paradox exists here, however, because due to the requirement of proving the mental state of intentionality, these torts are harder to prove than malpractice. "This general rule does not apply, however, when the wrongful conduct is committed by a clergy counselor. In that situation, the rule is clearly the converse."[43]

In the case of the pastoral counselor, liability for intentional tort is easier for courts to accept than is malpractice liability. This is because the wrongful conduct of the minister is much more easily separated from the religious beliefs of the church. Courts are showing little trouble in holding pastoral counselors liable for outrageous and immoral conduct that is easily distinguished from historic and well-recognized religious standards. Courts simply assert that the First Amendment is not implicated by this kind of behavior. This avoids the constitutional challenge that blocks the courts from applying malpractice liability to clergy and church.

A leading case in this regard is *Destefano v. Grabrian*.[44] The plaintiff-husband sued his Catholic priest and his archdiocese for a sexual affair between his wife and the priest. The affair was initiated while the couple were in marriage counseling with the priest and which allegedly led to an eventual divorce between the couple. The Colorado Court of Appeals held that the priest's conduct was not actionable under tort law. The Colorado Supreme Court reversed this rule, in part, rejecting the constitutional defense by the priest by asserting that "every Catholic is well aware of the vow of celibacy required of a priest . . . [S]exual activity by a priest is fundamentally antithetical to Catholic doctrine. As such, the conduct . . . is, by definition, not an expression of a sincerely held religious belief."[45]

Constitutional and Civil Rights of Mental Patients. Although tort law comprises the bulk of psychotherapeutic litigation, constitution-based litigation is the fastest growing type of suit over the past quarter-century.[46] A revolution in patient and client rights has reshaped mental health treatment in America and should be understood by every pastor, chaplain, and Christian counseling practitioner who works in a hospital, in residential treatment, or any form of restrictive treatment environment.

Three events in the 1960s signaled the transformation of American mental health care. Congress passed the Community Mental Health Centers Act in 1963 and provided states with funding to establish a national network of community-based centers for noninstitutional mental health treatment. In 1964, the Federal Civil Rights Act was passed, attaching rights and creating liabilities (along with many other groups) with respect to mental patients. Finally, a federal appeals court in 1966 ruled that a mental patient could not be held involuntarily if a less restrictive alternative were available through which safe and essential treatment could be delivered.[47]

The right to treatment is also an important constitutional and civil right. In a case from Alabama,[48] a federal appeals court required the state to provide treatment to its nondangerous, involuntarily confined mental patients or it must allow their release. The court applied Fourteenth Amendment due process law that barred restriction of fundamental freedoms without some quid pro quo, or reciprocal obligation by the state—in this case, the duty to provide treatment and decent living standards to involuntary mental patients. The U.S. Supreme Court, in *O'Connor v. Donaldson*,[49] essentially upheld this rule and its reasoning under the Fourteenth Amendment, making the right to treatment or release applicable to all states.

Another major constitutional right in this arena of law is the right to refuse treatment. Rooted in historic common law rights to autonomous control over one's own body and life, this right denies the application, without patient consent, of certain high-risk and invasive therapies.[50] The legally competent patient can refuse psychosurgery, electroconvulsive treatment, various kinds of drug treatments, and aversive behavior therapies.

In spite of the many benefits these legal developments have brought to mental patients, many problems have also been created. Thirty years of deinstitutionalization on a mass scale has directly contributed to our national disgrace of homelessness. Also troubling is the systemic failure to provide effective aftercare for significant populations of chronically mentally ill persons released from our nation's hospitals.[51] Psychiatrist and author Seymour Halleck echoes the concerns of many mental health professionals in decrying a "new legalism" in mental health treatment that rigidly asserts "freedom values over health values," often to the detriment of the patient.[52] Fear of litigation has resulted in the practice of "defensive psychiatry" that resists innovation, rewards caution, and often avoids altogether the most needy patients who indicate high legal risk.

Professional Licensure. Increasingly, the most common interactions with law for the Christian counselor revolve around the pervasive regulation of counseling through mental health licensure, certification and registration statutes. Every state regulates its mental health care system to some degree. Licensure of mental health practitioners—psychiatrists, psychiatric nurses and psychologists in all states, clinical social workers in all but one state, and marriage and family therapists in a few states—is a primary method of state regulation. The central justification by states for this regulatory scheme is protection of the public from incompetent and unethical clinicians and counselors.[53]

California has been a leading regulatory state in the licensing of its mental health professionals, and its model has influenced laws in many other states. No one, except those specifically exempted by statute,[54] can provide counseling and mental health services for a fee without being licensed. Psychiatrists are regulated by the Medical Board, psychologists by the Board of Psychology, and clinical social workers and marriage and family therapists by the Board of Behavioral Science Examiners. Each group defines the title, nature, education and intern preparation, functions, and limits, and professional requirements necessary to obtain and maintain licensure. These boards also prescribe ways to advertise and organize corporately as a professional service provider and denote the reasons and procedure by which a license may be suspended or revoked.[55]

The Legalization of Professional Ethics. A developing and controversial issue in California is the degree to which the state incrementally incorporates professional ethics into the statutory code of unprofessional conduct.[56] The failure of professional associations to effectively police their erring members is forcing a tense marriage of ethical codes with state statutes. This process of legalizing professional ethics codes, in effect, transfers control of the profession from the profession itself to the state. The state, then, uses its power to revoke or deny a license to someone who fails the statutory standard of professional conduct.[57] For states like California that are increasingly legislating comprehensive and mandatory licensing laws, this is a significant shift of power with major implications regarding professional self-control for all mental health professions.

Paradoxically, this trend can benefit the individual practitioner. The courts are increasingly looking to ethical codes in litigation where clear standards do not otherwise exist by statute or judicial precedent. This process will protect the ethical practitioner who may otherwise be exposed to liability or sanction by the courts. A clinical social worker successfully resisted an order to breach confidentiality in a state that had no statute protecting privileged communication. The judge upheld confidentiality based on the ethical codes of the National Association of Social Workers and the American Association of Marriage and Family Therapists, the clinician being a member in both organizations.[33]

First Amendment Free Exercise after Smith. The free exercise of religion clause has protected Christian ministry from government control for two hundred years. U.S. Supreme Court decision making in this arena has been historically rooted in the thesis that while freedom of belief is absolute, freedom to practice that belief is not.[59] Over a century ago the Court upheld federal antipolygamy statutes against the Mormon church[60] and had since developed sound rules that effectively upheld societal interests while protecting core religious freedoms.[61] The Court's holding in 1990 in the *Smith* case, however, has turned its historic religious liberty analysis on its head. Ironically, as our nation celebrates the bicentennial of the Bill of Rights, the Christian church (and all religions in America) may rightly mourn the loss of fundamental freedoms it has enjoyed for two centuries.

Recently, Christian attorneys and law professors charged that the Supreme Court's decision in *Smith* was "a sweeping disaster for religious liberty."[62] The high court upheld denial of unemployment benefits following job loss for drug use where peyote was used sacramentally in the Native American Church. Bypassing its own free exercise precedent, the Court ruled, in effect, that the burden on religious practice is essentially irrelevant if the law at issue is generally applicable and neutrally stated. "In *Smith*, the Court held that only laws specifically directed at religion were laws 'prohibiting' free exercise; no special justification is necessary if law merely has the effect of prohibiting religious exercise."[63] The implications of this rule are so serious that these lawyers advocate amending the Constitution or pushing congressional action to restore fundamental religious freedoms that existed for two hundred years before *Smith*.

The Smith case, and the doors of state intrusion into counseling (and all) ministry that it opens, expresses well the gravity of the grave new world of liability we all face. *Smith* effectively removes the constitutional bar to state regulation of Christian counseling. Arguably, no constitutional barrier now impedes the courts from developing a clergy malpractice standard, something I suspect will be in place in some states by the new millennium. Legislatures now have a green light to attempt to regulate pastors and church staff with no substantial distinction from professional regulatory standards. Not only might the clergy exemption from licensing statutes be restricted or even eliminated, but pastoral counseling standards regulated under state licensing boards is conceivable. Although these changes may be difficult to make politically, the Smith decision renders them legally possible. After two hundred years, the ground rules that govern relations between church and state are very different now and the Christian counseling field cannot be ignorant or passive in the face of them.

A Brief Review of the *Nally* Case

After a decade of torturous litigation, Grace Community Church of the Valley, one of the largest churches in America, with over four thousand members, did prevail and "win" its lawsuit. Also vindicated were its four pastor-defendants, including the well-known senior pastor and author Dr. John MacArthur, Jr. Their commitment to stay the course in the face of adversity and to persevere to a conclusion that protects fundamental Christian ministry rights gives all of us just cause for thanksgiving. On the other hand, the events that led to this suit and the behavior of the defendants that influenced the tragic course of Ken Nally's life should give pause for a sober appraisal of the role, limits, and behavior of the pastoral counselor.

The Tragic Story of Kenneth Nally

In the early 1970s, UCLA student Ken Nally "converted to Protestantism,"[64] began attending Grace Community Church, and became involved in their extensive collegiate ministry. His conversion created much strain in his relations with his Roman Catholic parents and he often discussed his bouts with depression and the "absurdity of life."[65] He began a counseling or "discipling"[66] relationship with Pastor Rea in January 1978. Court records revealed that Pastor Rea had evaluated Nally as being distraught and depressed, stating that he couldn't cope and once said, "I just can't live this life."[67] After breaking up with his girlfriend late in 1978, Nally became even more despondent and began counseling with Pastor Thomson who concluded that suicide was a "vague possibility."[68] In February 1979, Nally told his mother he couldn't cope and she had him consult with a general practice physician who prescribed Elavil, a strong antidepressant medicine. Ken Nally attempted suicide by overdosing on the Elavil on March 11, 1979.[69]

After hospitalizing Ken following the overdose, Mr. and Mrs. Nally were told by hospital staff that their son would not be released without psychiatric consultation. Presumably concerned about the reactions of their friends, the parents instructed the hospital not to disclose the suicide attempt, but to state their son was hospitalized for the pneumonia he contracted following the overdose. The psychiatrist recommended hospital commitment, warning Ken and his parents that he was likely to attempt suicide again.[70] Both Kenneth and his father declined such action, seemingly more concerned with the stigma of suicide and psychiatric problems than with receiving help.

Upon release Nally stayed with Pastor MacArthur, who encouraged him to see the psychiatrist on an outpatient basis and also had him examined by a Christian physician who was a deacon in the church. This doctor believed Nally was a serious threat to himself and recommended psychiatric hospitalization in an Adventist facility. Mr. Nally phoned the psychiatrist about this recommendation and the doctor offered to come to the Nally home to assist in an involuntary commitment. Tragically, the Nallys refused this offer; Mrs. Nally is reported to have stated, ". . . no, that's a crazy hospital. He's not crazy."[71]

Eleven days before his death Nally counseled with Pastor Thomson, inquiring about the salvation of Christians who commit suicide. Thomson stated that once a Christian is saved, he's always saved, but that thinking about it that way was "wrong." Thomson then referred Nally to yet another nonpsychiatric physician for a physical exam, to whom Nally reported headaches and paralysis in his arm. Referral and contact with Christian counselors and psychologists was also made that last week of his life. After a desperate plea for marriage toward his estranged girlfriend and a final family conflict, Ken Nally left home and was found dead of self-inflicted gunshot wounds two days later at a friend's apartment.

The Legal Battle Between Parents and Church

In their allegations of clergy malpractice and outrageous conduct, the Nallys asserted that Grace Community Church was negligent in the selection and training of its spiritual counselors and that they "actively . . . discouraged [Nally] from seeking further professional . . . care."[39] They charged that the church's teaching of religious doctrine disparaged Nally's Catholic upbringing and "exacerbated [Nally's] pre-existing feelings of guilt, anxiety and depression." They also alleged that the church taught Nally, while they knew he was suicidal, the notion that he would go to heaven even if he committed suicide.[72]

Duty of Care? The key legal question is one of duty: Did the church owe Ken Nally a duty of care that obligated them to act in his behalf in a manner that would forestall or protect him from suicide? The trial court said no duty existed, but the Court of Appeals consistently answered this question in the affirmative.[73] California follows historic common law precedent that requires existence of a "special" relationship, one in which "the plaintiff is typically . . . vulnerable and dependent upon the defendant who . . . holds considerable power over the plaintiff's welfare."[74] The Court of Appeals reasoned that this psychological dependence would be no different whether the therapist were a licensed professional or a "nontherapist counselor." [40] On this basis the appellate court, in 1987, held that "the nontherapist counselor who has held himself out as competent to treat serious emotional problems and voluntarily established a counseling relationship with an emotionally disturbed person has a duty to take appropriate pre-cautions should that person exhibit suicidal tendencies."[75]

The California Supreme Court reversed this rule in 1988. It held that no special relationship exists between a nontherapist counselor and his or her counselee due to the noncommercial, noncustodial, and voluntary nature of the relationship. This court looked at the question of legal duty from a structural rather than psychological perspective. Relying on precedent that essentially holds that no duty to forestall suicide exists outside a medically supervised relationship,[76] it refused to extend such duty to "personal or religious counseling relationships in which one person provided nonprofessional guidance to another seeking advice and the counselor had no control over the environment of the individual being counseled."[77]

California's highest court argued that while foreseeability of harm may make referral "prudent and necessary" it is not sufficient to create a legal duty that the court thought could "stifle all gratuitous or religious counseling."[78] It noted the exemption of clergy from the state's comprehensive licensure of mental health professionals and asserted that "access to the clergy for counseling should be free from state imposed counseling standards, and that 'the secular state is not equipped to ascertain the competence of counseling when performed by those affiliated with religious organizations.'"[79] Though it did not address the weighty constitutional issues implicated in this case, the court suggested that the appellate ruling would not pass First Amendment protection under the free exercise clause.[80] Finally, the Supreme Court hedged its rule by noting, "Our opinion does not foreclose imposing liability on nontherapist counselors, who hold themselves out as professionals, for injuries related to their counseling activities."[81]

Supreme Court Justice Kaufman concurred with the majority's ruling but disagreed "that defendants owed no duty of care to the plaintiffs."[82] He argued that the church did owe a legal duty to Ken Nally but that they fulfilled it, primarily through Pastor MacArthur's encouragement to Nally to follow through with psychiatric care during those last desperate weeks of his life.[83] Key to Kaufman's assertion of duty was the way the church held itself out as a major counseling ministry to the larger church and community, one that was expert in treating any type of emotional problem. He reviewed facts, most of which were ignored by the majority, that showed the pastoral counseling ministry of the church to be a significant enterprise.[84] Evidence was taken on materials that claimed the "biblical" counselor was competent to counsel "every emotional problem," including addictions, severe depression, manic-depression, and schizophrenia.

Kaufman argued that a "special" relationship giving rise to the duty of care existed because the pastors "patently held themselves out as competent to counsel the mentally ill, and Nally responded to these inducements, placing his psychological and ultimately his physical well-being in defendants' care."[85] Contrary to the majority opinion, he asserted a psychological rather than structural basis for understanding the duty of care, arguing that the relations between a pastor and counselee show "elements of trust and dependence which closely resemble those that exist in the therapist-patient context."[86] The duty, in Kaufman's view, was established as a result of the counselor's claim of expertise and active solicitation of the counseling relationship that Nally trusted and became dependent upon.

Behavior Analysis

Although the case record reveals that many people contributed to this tragedy, the inescapable truth is that Ken Nally killed himself. Along the way the church erred, Nally's parents erred, and some of the doctors and helping professionals erred in their intervention. However, had these errors not taken place, it is not at all clear that Ken Nally would be among us today—he was very serious about dying. This knowledge tempers this critique.

Grace Community Church's biggest mistake was its exaggeration of competence and expertise in counseling ministry. Simply put, it misrepresented itself to the larger church and urban community in which it resides. At best, the church's claim to competently treat every kind of emotional disorder[87] was naive overstatement. At worst, especially if the church counseled against or even passively resisted referral to professional clinicians,[88] it was a noxious boast ripe for this kind of ministerial tragedy. Such claims are impossible for a community service that does not have an inpatient or even partial hospitalization capability.

Furthermore, claims of expertise with severe depression, bipolar (manic-depressive) disorders, and schizophrenia deny a mass of accumulated psychiatric research and treatment over the past two decades that show significant genetic and biological roots to these problems.[89] Included in this psychiatric data are promising results from many new drug therapies which are increasingly used in conjunction with professional and pastoral counseling.

Grace Community Church failed to adhere to the most basic ethical and biblical norms in this regard. The ethical codes of every major clinical discipline speak out strongly against misrepresentation and require practice that adheres to the limits of one's competence.[90] While the church has a valid argument against being judged by professional standards or even pastoral counseling ethics it does not ascribe to, it would be a grave mistake to push that argument and assert that the pastor need answer only to God or to one's employing church. This is an age of ministerial accountability and, especially now after *Smith*, neither the public nor the law will allow nor should the larger church permit such failed accountability.

The pastoral counselor is accountable before God, a responsibility made tangible through relationship and submission within the church (1 Cor. 12:12–26; 1 Thess. 5:12; Heb. 13:17). Accordingly, we are challenged to judge ourselves with sober humility, avoiding self-deceit by recognizing our limits and weaknesses and not falling prey to thinking of ourselves "more highly than [we] ought" (Rom.12:3; see Gal. 6:1–5). In fact, Paul's instructions in Galatians are set in a helping context, indicating that humble self-assessment that respects the limits of one's abilities is essential to the task of restoring the erring brother or sister in Christ.[91]

The church, some of the physicians, and Ken Nally's parents all failed to provide adequate suicide intervention. Neither law nor ethics, applicable in an outpatient setting, requires that a helper prevent suicide. Rather, appropriate action is called for to forestall such behavior so that a suicidal person might have opportunity to live. The physician[92] who, prescribed Elavil and failed to make a psychiatric referral was vulnerable to suit. The record also reveals a tragic and pitiful account of the plaintiffs.[93] Their failure to hospitalize their son, against the strongest medical advice and seemingly because they were more concerned about the stigma of a psychiatric disorder being attached to the family name, was a critical failure. Such actions, faced in hindsight, often compound the grief they may still experience and may have been a factor in the level of hostility and acrimony reported about this case.[94]

Pastors Thomson and Rea failed to take appropriate action on behalf of Ken Nally. We may concede that they were not as expert as they claimed and that they wouldn't be expected to competently evaluate the various clinical, social, and demographic factors that showed Nally to be a significant risk. Still, he did talk to them directly about depression, dying, and suicide. While it seemingly had to be pried out of them at trial,[95] both these counselors admitted to some awareness of a suicidal risk. After the nearly successful overdose attempt, the failure to consistently encourage follow-through with hospitalization, or even to participate with the psychiatrist to commit Nally involuntarily, were major errors of judgment. The Court of Appeals especially noted, even if a pastoral counselor were resistent to a psychiatric referral that might be hostile to the faith of the person referred, this church had access to a wealth of professional Christian resources throughout the Los Angeles basin.[96]

A few lights shine in the darkness of this tragic story. Pastor MacArthur behaved with commendable compassion and good judgment concerning Nally in the final weeks of his life.[97] Bringing Nally into his home and under his wing exemplifies the best of pastoral care and ministry. His consistent encouragement to follow through with hospitalization and the psychiatrists revealed sound judgment about the seriousness of the crisis and the need for intensive intervention beyond what the church could provide.

His continued bashing of psychology and failure to discern the good from the bad in professional counseling is troubling,[98] especially if Grace Community Church continues its exaggerated claims and misrepresentation in counseling ministry. In the Nally case, however, it may be argued that apart from the caring actions by MacArthur, the California Supreme Court may well have judged against the church. Even Pastors Thomson and Rea, in spite of their poor counseling intervention and questionable courtroom behavior, demonstrated care and concern for Ken Nally in many ways.

Legal Analysis

The California Supreme Court respected the historic boundary between church and state and was right, in my opinion, to protect Christian ministry rights by refusing to impose a broad duty upon pastoral counselors to assess and refer suicidal parishioners. As the court correctly reasoned, such duty, expressed as an onerous rule of malpractice liability, would have a "chilling effect" by inducing a fear of suit in pastors that would inhibit rather than assist their ministry to the suicidal person.[99] Indeed, following the Court of Appeals decision, the Northern California District of the Church of the Nazarene distributed a letter to their pastors from their legal counsel that cautioned the church about the opinion and was a source of much concern in Nazarene and other churches on California's Northcoast.[100] Since the clergy is by far the most commonly approached resource by persons in family or emotional crisis, the court rightly held that inhibiting such relations would truly be bad public policy.[101]

Though correct in refusing to create a broad legal duty, the Supreme Court strained to exclude Grace Community Church from its own well-stated exception that liability could be found if pastoral counselors held themselves out "as professionals,"[102] with expertise beyond their true ability. The court's structural, commercial distinction between professional and nonprofessional counselor was not convincing when considered against the substantial evidence of an extensive, professional-like counseling ministry that the church offered to its congregants and the community-at-large.

The Supreme Court majority may have failed to properly apply its own exception to the facts of the Nally case and its holding could have declining influence as future precedent.[103] Instead, according to a historic process where a dissent or concurrence provides the seed for future case law development, Justice Kaufman's concurring opinion along with the opinion by the Court of Appeals may be more convincing in future cases that will face similar issues.

Justice Kaufman held that the church owed Ken Nally a duty of care because they assertively held themselves out to him as competent and expert to treat severe depression and suicide. The reality of Nally's spiritual bond and psychological dependence on the church, together with the church's exaggerated claims of competence, form a sound basis for a narrow legal duty.[104] Kaufman's statement of a limited duty is good law and worthy of respect, whether in a pastoral, parachurch or lay helping context, "Where, as here, defendants have invited and engaged in an extensive and ongoing pastoral counseling relationship with an individual whom they perceive to be suicidal, both reason and sound public policy dictate that defendants be required to advise that individual seek professional . . . care."[105]

Implications for the Church. These regulatory trends are critically important for the church and the pastoral counselor. Although clergy currently remain exempt from licensing statutes and are protected in ministry by the constitution, both *Nally* and *Smith* teach us that we can no longer assume that no standards apply except those derived from Scripture or church constitution. The degree to which the church is failing to adequately supervise and police its own ministers is already drawing the state, by both legislation and litigation, into this vacuum of accountability.

After *Smith*, the pace and force of this intrusion could quickly escalate. Sadly, the prediction that litigation against the church will increase in the future is probably quite accurate.[106] If this proves true it will be largely due to the failure of the larger Christian church to hold incompetent and harmful ministers accountable for their wrongdoing. These trends hold no fear for the ethical and biblically faithful counselor. Even though the legal margin for error will continue to narrow, the great majority of godly ministers can and should boldly pursue their service call.

SEXUAL MISCONDUCT IN CHRISTIAN COUNSELING

Like the explosive trends in the secular mental health professions, the church has begun to face an epidemic of spiritual, moral, ecclesiastical, and legal trouble due to sexual misconduct in counseling ministry. The legal response to this epidemic is also rapidly developing and it is difficult to predict when and how this problem will abate and how much influence legal threats will have on that control. One thing is very clear: Sexual misconduct has become the most troublesome of issues and its cases are the most frequently seen in America's courts, before state licensing boards and, increasingly, before the leadership councils of the church.[107]

What Is Sexual Misconduct?

Historically, sexual misconduct was defined primarily with reference to sexual intercourse between therapist and client or overt sexual foreplay that was clearly judged as intending sexual arousal. Problems of proving sexual misconduct by way of the malpractice suit required overt sexual contact if the plaintiff were to prevail.[108] Modern definitions have transformed the meaning of sexual misconduct to effectively include any behavior or expression that may reasonably be understood to intend some kind of sexual contact, solicitation, or innuendo. This inclusive definition is driven by professional ethics codes, current case law, and statutes that govern professional licensure and define sexual misconduct in therapy as criminal behavior, the new legal trend that will flower in the years to come.

California statutes influence development of statutory law in many states. The legislature of the Golden State has rendered illegal any type of sexual contact and misconduct short of contact, including asking for sex by any licensed therapist in the state. Essentially, any form of sexually expressed behavior by a therapist, whether actual sexual contact was engaged or not, is legally wrong.[109] The statutory code for unprofessional conduct by Licensed Clinical Social Workers tracks the codes regulating psychiatrists, psychologists, and marriage and family therapists. Its definition of sexual misconduct that can lead to license revocation and other legal action is becoming a normative definition across the United States. It renders liable the therapist who "has sexual relations with a client, or who solicits sexual relations with a client, or who commits an act of sexual abuse, or who commits an act of sexual misconduct, or who commits an act punishable as a sexual related crime if such act or solicitation is substantially related to [professional duties]."[110]

The Sexual Misconduct Crisis

The great majority of sexual misconduct in counseling is perpetrated by male therapists and pastors who victimize younger adult female counselees.[111] "The stereotypic case involves a male therapist striving to adjust to middle age and personal problems who, despite his training, misinterprets the client's overtures for purely emotional support and acceptance as efforts to establish a romantic or erotic connection. The confused client accepts the therapist's advances as a substitute for the type of caring or love she is really seeking."[112] As with all sexual misconduct this common pattern, no matter how innocently begun or assertively justified,[113] becomes a type of sexual abuse that almost always harms the victim and usually hurts the abuser in significant ways. While cases exist of female therapists abusing male clients, of homosexual misconduct and, most tragically, of minor children sexually abused by pedophilic counselors and ministers,[114] this section will review the predominant pattern of male abuser and female victim.

The Incidence of Sexual Misconduct. The various surveys on sexual misconduct done over the past twenty years indicate that between 6 to 10 percent of all psychotherapists in the United States have engaged in some form of sexual or erotic contact with their patients and clients.[115] These studies also reveal that from 40 to 80 percent of therapists who have crossed sexual boundaries with their clients have done so more than once; some of these repeat offenders have dozens of victims. While these figures are disturbing enough, considering the numbers of counselors nationwide, many believe them extremely conservative and that they do not begin to reveal the extent of this social and moral epidemic. The great discrepancies between incidence and reporting figures suggests the problem is far bigger than the survey numbers indicate.[116]

What little data that does exist about sexual misconduct in ministry certainly denies the church any finger-pointing at our secular counterparts. Many pastors and Christian leaders have anecdotes and (sometimes) horrific and tragic stories of clergy who have fallen under this plague.[117] The 1988 *Leadership* poll surveyed nearly a thousand pastors (with a 30 percent response rate) and an equivalent number of nonpastor subscribers to *Christianity Today* magazine.[118] The findings reveal a pervasive and painful problem in Christian ministry, one that a pastor revealed "covers the greatest agonies of my life." Twelve percent of the pastors and 23 percent of the subscribers admitted to extramarital intercourse. Nearly a quarter (23 percent) of the pastors acknowledged some form of "sexually inappropriate" behavior while in local church ministry. Among those people with whom pastors were involved sexually, 69 percent came from within their own congregations, *including 17 percent who were counselees.* Physical and emotional attraction was noted as the major reason for the misconduct by 78 percent of the respondent pastors while marital dissatisfaction was noted by 41 percent.[119]

The Harm Suffered. Significant personal, marital, vocational, and financial harm is suffered by the great majority of people who become involved sexually with another person in a counseling relationship. This is true for both victim and abuser alike, though the frequency and degree of the victim's harm is usually greater. A study of California psychologists[120] who worked with clients who had been involved sexually with former therapists reported that 90 percent of these victims had suffered adverse effects. Eleven percent required hospitalization and 1 percent had committed suicide. Direct assessment of therapeutic abuse victims also reveals significant and pervasive levels of personal and social harm. Increased depression and emotional disturbance, impaired social adjustment, increased drug and alcohol abuse, divorce and marital conflict and inability to use subsequent therapy effectively are the common harms reported.[121]

No doubt the extensive evidence of serious harm to victims of therapeutic sexual abuse is a key reason why this is the most successful cause of action against counselors. After reviewing the limited evidence on this harm that existed fifteen years ago, Masters and Johnson asserted that it should be viewed and prosecuted as a form of rape.[122] Feminist analysis[123] also recognizes the rape (as well as an incest) analogy and decries the sexist standards in both the predominant male abuser/female victim typology and also in the ineffectual systemic response to sexual misconduct by the mental health professions. The charge of a "conspiracy of silence"[124] that works to deny, minimize, and ultimately protect male-dominated professions and ministry cannot and should not be dismissed by the church in view of the manifold evidence regarding this epidemic. Again, as in all other areas of ministerial and professional misconduct, failure of the professions and the church to control its harmful members invites the legal control it detests.

The Legal Response to Sexual Misconduct in Counseling

By legislative mandate, all licensed mental health professionals in California have available a small booklet for clients entitled "Professional Therapy *Never* Includes Sex."[125] As a consumer-oriented response to the sexual misconduct epidemic, the state hopes to educate and embolden victims to overcome the dismal reporting rate of such abuse and get the help they need.[126] Four types of victim response are noted.

Liability Under Professional Ethics Codes. Every major mental health professional group, including those that regulate pastoral and Christian counseling, condemn sexual activities with clients as unethical.[127] The code of the American Association of Pastoral Counselors states that "pastoral counselors do not engage in sexual misconduct with their clients." The National Association of Social Workers Code of Ethics asserts that "the social worker should under no circumstances engage in sexual activities with clients." Commenting on the language used in this prohibition, the NASW Task Force on Ethics stated that it "deliberately used the strongest language of absolute prohibition, 'under no circumstances' . . ." in view of the "great damage" done to sexually exploited clients.[128]

Many but not all therapists and counselors belong to these professional associations that exist to advance the profession, set standards for membership and conduct, and discipline its erring members. A victim can file a complaint with the association which may, based on evidence of violation against its ethical code, take various disciplinary actions, including removal of the offending member from the association. This is not the same as license revocation; the erring therapist might still practice even if removed from professional association. This option is recognized as the weakest in terms of punishment and protection of the public from further harm.

License Revocation Under Administrative Law. As states increasingly license and regulate mental health professionals, the threat of license revocation becomes an increasingly powerful tool for compliance with statutory standards of professional conduct. Proof of sexual misconduct by a licensed professional almost certainly leads to revocation of that license and an inability to practice in a growing number of states. The problems of proving sexual misconduct in this arena are less for a victim since there is usually no statute of limitation and the standards of proof are less stringent than those required in a courtroom. While the entire process may take a year or two to resolve and does not pay any money damages to the victim, one is far more able in this way to stop an offending therapist from continuing practice and hurting others.

Civil Liability Under Tort and Related Law. More and more victims are filing and winning lawsuits against sexually abusing counselors, including pastoral counselors. The growing success of these suits against therapists is reflected by the widespread insurance industry refusal to cover liability for sexual misconduct. The victim who prevails in a civil suit is the recipient of money damages and this fact makes such lawsuits the most restorative legal action for the victim.

The problems for victims in civil lawsuits revolve around proof. In the well-known case of *Roy v. Hartogs*,[129] the defendant psychiatrist was nearly successful in denying sexual contact and blaming the victim for her own distress. The case was won by the plaintiff-victim only after three former sexual abuse victims of the psychiatrist came forward and testified against him. Not only must the victims prove each element required under malpractice—duty, breach of duty, harm and proximate cause—but they must also prove they did not consent to sexual relations. Some courts have limited this defense,[130] but it remains a formidable barrier to claimant relief.

A few states have legislated a stronger framework for civil action to overcome some of the common law barriers in traditional tort law.[131] While none of these statutes abolish the consent defense, they do increase the likelihood that victims will succeed in suits against sexually abusing therapists. Not only should we anticipate many more states creating statutory causes in the 1990s, but due to the *Smith* decision, it is probable that legislatures will also include pastors and church-based counselors as defendants in these actions. Certainly, the harm suffered by pastoral counseling victims is no less than by any other counselor or clinician; clergy status will not and should not protect this behavior.

Criminal Liability: The Future Is Fast Arriving. Wisconsin, Minnesota, Colorado, and California have all criminalized sexual misconduct by therapists.[132] California's new law makes it a crime for a licensed therapist to have sexual contact with a client during therapy and for two years after the close of therapy. This controversial two-year post-termination bar of sexual contact was passed as a legislative compromise to forestall therapeutic termination for the purpose of engaging in sex that was perceived by participants to be legally safe. A first offense is punished as a misdemeanor; second and subsequent offenses may be felonies with fines up to $5,000 and a year in state prison.

The criminal laws and penalties in the other three states are much more stringent than California's. Colorado law applies to anyone doing psychotherapy and defines therapy so broadly that pastoral counselors would easily come under this rule. Wisconsin's statute explicitly includes any "physician, psychologist, social worker, nurse, chemical dependency counselor, *member of the clergy* or other person, whether or not licensed by the state who performs or purports to perform psychotherapy" (emphasis mine).[133]

All these states regard sexual contact as felonious behavior and have prosecuted offending therapists, some of whom are now imprisoned. Sexual penetration in Colorado is aggravated sexual assault and can lead to an eight-year prison sentence. The same act in Minnesota, criminal sexual conduct in the third degree, is punishable by up to ten years in prison with fines up to $20,000. While offending clergy would probably escape criminal prosecution in California (though subsequent legislatures may amend this law to eventually include the clergy), pastors and Christian counselors, whether on paid staff or in lay ministry, are clearly liable in these other states. Criminal sanction is, no doubt, the harshest and most serious response by the state to the sexual misconduct epidemic.

A Plea for Sexual Control in the Ministry

The church could and should lead the fight for sexual self-control in counseling and psychotherapy.[134] No matter the doctrinal or theological stripe in the church universal, there is near unanimous condemnation of sexual exploitation. It might be easy to conclude that, like the poor, the sex-offending counselor will always be with us. Even so, that should not stop the proclamation that every Christian counselor, through Christ Jesus, has the power to avoid the pervasive sexual temptation that we all find so frustratingly familiar. There should also be no doubt that if the church will not proclaim sexual self-control and take authority over its erring ministers, it shall be done for us and to us by the state. As regretful as it is to say, I must admit that the church will deserve the state's control in this arena if it cannot control itself.

CONCLUSION

God reveals that law is good and that two fundamental purposes are at work in the revelation of law to humankind.[135] "We know that the law is good if a man uses it properly. We also know that law is made not for good men but for lawbreakers and rebels . . ." (1 Tim. 1:8–9a). Assessment of counseling liability is necessarily a study of those boundaries of right and wrong that warn the lawbreaker in us all. This aspect of law is imposed by God through the agency of the state to restrain evil by threat of punishment for wrongdoing (see Romans 13:1–5). The complex and rapidly developing system of Christian counseling liability merely expresses the simple cardinal rule that has governed professional liability throughout history: *Do no harm* in the work of your ministry. As citizen of both church and state the Christian counselor, whether pastor or clinical professional, is duty-bound to know and resist overstepping this complex web of wrongful boundaries.

Scripture also reveals the guiding power of law that beckons every Christian to the highest good in loving service to God and others. This is that law written in the heart of the regenerate believer "who loves his fellow man [and] has fulfilled the law. . . . Love does no harm to its neighbor. Therefore love is the fulfillment of the law" (Rom. 13:8b,10). This is the law that reveals and challenges the very best of Christian service beyond mere avoidance of harmful wrongdoing. This is the law to which the psalmist expressed faithfulness and delight.

> Your laws endure to this day,
>   for all things serve you.
> If your law had not been my delight,
>   I would have perished in my affliction.
> I will never forget your precepts,
>   for by them you have preserved my life. . . .
> Your word is a lamp to my feet
>   and a light for my path.
> I have taken an oath and confirmed it,
>   that I will follow your righteous laws.
>   (Psalm 119:91–93, 105–106)

The helper whose heart toward God and his law reflects this will do no harm to others and need never fear the punishing threat of the law of the state.

The Fiduciary Trust of the Christian Counselor

A superior legal framework for defining the rules and understanding the relationship between Christian counselor and client is the fiduciary trust. This is a trust far more consistent with the biblical norms stated above than is the law of malpractice or contract. Rapidly evolving from its historic association with financial trust on behalf of clients by lawyers and other money managers, it is being applied to a broad range of professional services, including those provided by mental health professionals.[136] Rooted in ancient Roman law, the fiduciary is one who is bound to a special duty of service due to the trust and confidence placed in them by another and the power to abuse that trust with devastating consequence. This fiduciary duty is to act always in the best interests of the people served, never exploiting them nor taking advantage of that trust for one's own interest.

The *Destefano* case cited earlier (see page 53) is also significant due to the Colorado Supreme Court's recognition of fiduciary law as a cause of action against clergy misconduct. Even though the court agreed that no malpractice liability existed against the sexually offending priest, under fiduciary law the priest "had a duty, given the nature of the counseling relationship, to engage in conduct designed to improve the Destefanos' marital relationship."[137] Breach of fiduciary trust has been argued in at least one other case against the clergy[138] and it is likely that we will see this cause increasingly argued against the church and its ministers.

Frankel asserts that, as traditional social controls weaken and abuses of the power of service providers increase throughout society, reliance on fiduciary law will inevitably increase.[139] For a number of reasons, I believe this developing trend in law can bless, rather than curse the church and its Christian counseling ministry. First, fiduciary duties are synonymous with the biblical call to hold the interests of those served above those of the servant. Jesus asserted that loving God and our neighbor as ourselves is the greatest of the commandments (Mark 12:28–31; Luke 10:25–37). Furthermore, in his kingdom, the one who would rule or be great is the one who most humbly serves the rest, who gives up his or her life for the good of others (Matt. 20:25–28; Luke 22:25–30). Paul's great challenge to imitate Christ's humility is seen in the call to

> Do nothing out of selfish ambition or vain conceit, but in humility consider others better than yourselves. Each of you should look not only to your own interests, but also to the interests of others. (Phil. 2:3–4)

Secondly, even though for the foreseeable future fiduciary law will compete for the court's attention with many legal theories of counseling liability, if (or when) it becomes ascendant it will simplify the understanding and application of legal duty to Christian counseling. The fiduciary definition is broad enough conceptually to include the many biblical, ethical, and legal duties that are being attached to Christian counseling. A fiduciary standard is also far more consistent with the actual moral and ethical rules that guide Christian helpers in their day-to-day ministries. Such a standard would be far more useful, then, to a pastor or Christian counselor in assessing liability by knowing that it is intimately related to their biblical, moral, and ethical boundaries.

The pressure on the church of significantly increased liability risk and the imposition of legal standards that inaccurately reflect the nature of true counseling ministry makes the value of a fiduciary standard all the more attractive now. Assuming, as we must following *Smith*, that these liability trends will continue and lawsuits will increase against Christian counselors, it is critical for informed counselors and the church-at-large to take control of this standard-defining process. Courts, lawyers, and legal theorists are advancing these standards already and the church may disagree with their premises and values and be quite displeased with the results. Fiduciary trust as a unifying concept and law friendly to biblical standards could give a factional church the grace to overcome some of its historic internal disunity. Such law might also pave the way to mutually agreed liability standards for Christian counseling and viable twenty-first century relations between church and state that are as nonintrusive as possible for the church and all its gospel work.

Law, Ethics, and Excellence in Christian Counseling

Archibald Hart makes a strong case for a durable ethical code to guide the Christian counselor beyond mere knowledge of right and wrong in specific situations. Many things that are not wrong in a given situation may still need to be avoided due to the cumulative risks or long-term consequence of harm. A code of ethics is essential to guide the counselor through the many complex and confusing dilemmas faced in helping ministry. Hart recommends a code that tangibly fulfills principles of responsibility, accountability, confidentiality, and integrity. "A healthy concern for morality is not enough to maintain a ministry of integrity. . . . All told, we need great wisdom and a clear code of ethics so as not to become obstacles to the gospel but rather to uphold a ministry of honesty, integrity and reconciliation."[140]

The escalation of legal liability in Christian ministry makes Reeck's call for Christians to formulate and assert their own ethical code imperative to ministry self-control.[141] Beck and Matthews argue that an ethical code for Christian counselors could spur development of a broad organization that could advance the Christian counseling field.[142]

Such a code might provide a model for conflict resolution which would reflect Christian values and current legal duties. A biblical code of Christian counseling ethics wedded to the law of fiduciary trust is needed by the diverse population of Christian counselors across the theological spectrum. We must do it or it will be done for us and to us by those who hold dear neither Christ nor God's law.

The grave new world of state intrusion into Christian counseling has indeed arrived and will be a familiar if unwelcome neighbor from now till kingdom come. Though this is troublesome on numerous levels, especially considering the rapidly increasing risk of lawsuit, it is in no way fatal to the ethical counselor who genuinely follows the example of Christ. The counselor who is humbly committed to Christ, to a practical biblical ethic, and to Christian counseling excellence has nothing to fear from any of these current legal trends. More than that, the Christian counselor may even be able to embrace these trends in a spirit of suffering love that sees God's perfect law imperfectly expressed through the state that is an instrument in his hands. He is the Lawmaker, the Judge of judges, and his Supreme Court will have the final, victorious review of all things.

CHAPTER 4

THEORY IN CHRISTIAN COUNSELING

I NEVER EXPECTED TO SPEND most of my teaching career in a theological seminary. The idea was first suggested to me shortly after I started work as a young assistant professor at a liberal arts college in Minnesota, but I shrugged off the thought. My training was in clinical psychology. I was happy teaching undergraduate psychology students, I didn't have a seminary degree, and I knew very little about ministers or the ministry. Only a couple of times in my whole life had I ever been in a pastor's home. What, then, did I know about teaching prospective pastors to counsel?

This thinking began to change when my wife and I went as chaperones and faculty representatives on a college choir tour. Almost every night after the concert, we would be taken to stay in the home of the host pastor where the conversation invariably turned to the minister's counseling role. Very quickly my eyes were opened to the needs and challenges of pastoral counseling. More than anything else, those late-night discussions stimulated my interest in writing about Christian counseling and several years later I accepted an invitation to teach in a graduate school of theology.

Before I arrived on campus to take a seminary job that would last for twenty years, the dean sent a copy of the academic catalog and indicated that, among others, my duties would include teaching the introductory course in pastoral counseling. Imagine my surprise when I discovered how the course had been taught to that point. Apparently there was little emphasis on helping troubled marriages, counseling lonely or anxious people, grief counseling, or any of the other issues that pastors might face. Instead the seminary students read a textbook on personality theory and learned about such things as the id, ego, superego, collective unconscious, archetypes, psychic energy, somatotypes, parataxic distortions, paradoxical intention, ego-ideal, functional autonomy, two-factor learning, reinforcement, and even penis envy—to name a few. One of my first decisions as a new professor on campus was to throw out those theoretical terms and to make the basic counseling course more practical.

This was not meant to imply that I thought theory unimportant. Courses in theory were among the most interesting parts of my training, and with my undergraduate students I had always enjoyed teaching about the views of Freud, Jung, Rogers and the more modern theorists. But theory can be dull and can seem irrelevant, especially to people who are busy counseling every day. Few practitioners have time for what one book has called "therapy wars"[1] between theorists, each of whom claims to be right in contrast all of the others who are assumed to be wrong. I would guess that some readers will skip this chapter because they think it is likely to be boring and unnecessary. For you who are still reading, congratulations! The following pages will try to show that theory is very significant, even to practical people who want to be effective Christian counselors.

Maps, Lenses, and Paradigms

John D. Krumboltz is a Stanford professor who won an award from the American Psychological Association for "outstanding contributions to the scientific foundations, the professional stature, and the practice of counseling psychology." As a part of his acceptance speech, Krumboltz made some interesting comments about theory.

> A major puzzle for me has been the role of theory in counseling. Why do people think theories are so important? What good are they? Why do psychologists get upset with colleagues who prefer a different theory? Since I don't understand this puzzling situation, I will explain it to you.
>
> We counseling psychologists are in the business of helping our clients solve immensely complicated problems that involve their lifetime histories, their personal values and skills, their interrelationships with numerous others, and their hopes and fears for the future. Their problems are so complicated that our poor feeble brains cannot possibly comprehend the multitude of factors that impinge on every sentence they utter. In order to get a handle on the complexity, we resort to using theories, which are intellectual crutches that help us hobble through the forest without bumping into the trees.[2]

In a more serious vein, Krumboltz goes on to suggest that a theory is an attempt to help us better see some part of reality. It is like a map that gives useful but limited information.

No one map can tell us everything we need to know. A road map is useful for a motorist but not much help to an engineer or a geologist. A map showing the average rainfall in different parts of the world may be of little interest to a sociologist but very useful to an agronomist. Every map is constructed to give *some* useful information but to leave off facts that the user would consider nonessential. Often, maps even distort reality in order to illustrate a point. A road map, for example, may show the freeways in bright red, the lesser roads in black, and the largest cities surrounded by stars—none of which actually exists. Some maps are more accurate or more useful than others and all good maps are updated periodically. At times a map reader uses more than one map to get the desired information.

Probably you already see the parallel between maps and theories. No one theory can tell us everything we need to know. A theory about learning disabilities may be useful for a remedial reading teacher but of less help to a psychiatrist who, in turn, might be more interested in theories about the causes of homosexuality. Like maps, some theories give more information than others and at times a theory might even distort reality to illustrate a point.

Freud's theory of psychoanalysis, for example, said very little about physiological influences on behavior, but included detailed descriptions and discussions of ids, egos, psychic energy, and other "concepts" that don't exist in tangible form and may not exist at all. Even so, these words, like stars around the major cities on a road map, can give useful information. Some theories, again like maps, are more accurate or more helpful than others and all theories need to be updated periodically if they are to stay useful. Often the theory user relies on more than one theory to get information and to guide his or her counseling.

While some like to compare theories to maps, others liken theories to camera lenses[3] or binoculars that bring different issues into focus while others remain blurred. Computer users compare theories to different windows on the screen that allow the keyboard operator to bring up some things from the databank of information while others are kept hidden temporarily.

Professor Krumboltz puts all of this into perspective when he concludes that a theory is "a distorted, inaccurate oversimplification" that allows us to derive answers to innumerable questions but that has unpredictable usefulness. With these shortcomings, he adds, surely we would not expect counselors to get into arguments or to stake their professional careers on issues of theory. "Yet discussions of theoretical orientations seem to dominate many of our professional deliberations. We sometimes inquire of colleagues, 'What is your theoretical orientation?' Something about the way in which the question is asked makes it seem to be a vitally important issue. The very term 'theoretical orientation' sounds high powered. But as we have seen, the question really inquires about how a person distorts reality."[4]

These words are insightful and they serve the useful purpose of warning us not to get caught in endless arguments over theory. But theory should not be dismissed as no more than how a person distorts reality. Theories are built on world views, many of which are deeply entrenched. Since counselors differ in their views of the world, they also differ in their ways of looking at human behavior and in their approaches to making changes through counseling.[5] These philosophical and perceptual differences have led some writers to avoid using words like "theoretical orientation," and instead to think in terms of perceptions and the ways in which each of us sees the world.

Shifting Paradigms

A recent article dealing with research in missions made some interesting observations about science and perception.[6] Starting with the Old Testament account in Numbers 13, the author suggested that Moses gave the twelve spies a research assignment. They were to go into the promised land to discover "whether or not the people who live there are strong or weak, few or many."

When they returned, the spies all agreed with the facts about what the land was like, but the data was perceived and interpreted in different ways. Two members of the team, Caleb and Joshua, believed that God would allow the land to be possessed even though the cities were large and fortified. The other ten concluded that victory would be impossible. Moses agreed with the ten and the decision cost the Israelites forty years in the wilderness.

What does this have to do with counseling and theory? To Moses and his associates, the facts were unambiguous but the differences came in how these facts were interpreted and used in making a decision. The two groups of spies each looked at the situation from a perspective. To use modern language, they each had *paradigms*—ways of viewing and interpreting the world. Perceptual paradigms often are unconscious and heavily influenced by past learning, but they influence how we see the world, how we view problems in our clients and how we make decisions or therapeutic interventions.

Some time ago I was present in a meeting where two Christians—one a psychiatrist, the other a missiologist—discussed their strong differences of opinion about psychopathology. These men considered a number of cases with which they were both familiar. In each of these, the psychiatrist saw biochemical disorders, multiple personalities, and psychological malfunctioning. The missiologist concluded that in every case the individual involved was demon possessed or otherwise influenced by satanic forces. The two men were both committed believers and their debate was friendly, but neither did much to change the other's opinion. As Christians they had a similar viewpoint but they had different paradigms for interpreting abnormal thinking and behavior.

Like theories, paradigms change. Some are more popular than others and individuals sometimes shift from one paradigm to another. This usually happens, for example, when a person is converted to

Christ. The world and its problems, sin, forgiveness, the purpose of living, the direction of history—these are among issues that the convert begins to see in a new light. The believer is introduced to a biblical world view that is a different paradigm from the humanistic viewpoints of most non-Christians—including most psychologists. The believer sees and understands life in a way that differs from the nonbeliever (1 Cor. 2:9-16). Paradigms and ways of thinking may be among the old things that are replaced by the new when one becomes a Christian (2 Cor. 5:17).

In an important book published over two decades ago, Thomas Kuhn[7] argued that all scientific advancement occurs when there is a "paradigm shift." This often occurs when an outsider or a small group of young "rebels" begins to question the old ways of seeing and doing things. The new group is criticized and sometimes ostracized by the old guard, but in time the new paradigm defeats the old and ushers in a new period of science. All of this may involve struggle but struggle often is the essence of growth.

Nearly every day the newspapers describe an ongoing political and economic paradigm shift in the Soviet Union and in what was once the communist empire. Within recent years, shifting paradigms have concerned writers in a number of academic fields. In a book titled *Powershift*, futurist Alvin Toffler described what he sees as a paradigm shift in our viewpoints about "knowledge, wealth, and violence at the edge of the 21st century."[8] Management expert Peter Drucker[9] has discussed paradigm shifts in politics, economics, and business. Leslie Newbigin[10] has addressed the impact of paradigms on theology and missions, and the previously mentioned article on Moses in the wilderness suggests that paradigms must be understood and sometimes altered if there is to be progress in research.

We who are Christian counselors claim to see the universe and the problems of our counselees from a biblical paradigm. Like Caleb and Joshua, we have a paradigm that includes a belief that God meant what he said in the Bible, that he is all-powerful and all-knowing, that he does have the power to change lives. Part of the Christian's purpose in life is to understand the biblical paradigm and to help others change their paradigms about events in their lives.

Often, however, Christian counselors claim to see the universe from a biblical paradigm but in practice counsel from a more humanistic perspective.[11] They may be sincere Christians but their counseling shows no awareness of sin, spiritual warfare, the transforming power of the Holy Spirit, the influence of prayer, or the Word of God that is more cutting and powerful than any two-edged sword (Heb. 4:12). Perhaps much of our work has remained too entrenched in traditional psychotherapy paradigms or in the scientist-practitioner model of counselor education. If we are to be more effective as individual Christian counselors, we need to take a fresh look at our counseling paradigms, methods, goals, and theories.

WHY WORRY ABOUT THEORY?

Christian counselors are busy people who deal with complex problems, some of which come in the form of crises that demand our immediate attention. We don't have time for reading esoteric theories, especially when we have piles of more pressing things to read. Theory development might be fine for professors in ivory towers but for those who have daily involvement with human needs, why should we bother about theory?

There can be four good answers.[12] Theory has a practical influence on counselees, counselors, educators, and researchers.

Theory Influences Counselees

When they come through your door, each of your counselees brings problems and frustrations; but they also bring expectations about what you will do and whether or not your counseling will be helpful. Counselees have their own paradigms—ways of viewing themselves and the universe—and they probably have preconceived views about counselors, including you. Stated differently, each counselee comes with his or her own theory about counseling. Often the theory is poorly formulated, it might be inaccurate or biased, and it may not even be conscious, but these theoretical expectations determine how the counselee will act, at least in the beginning. If the counselee's expectations differ from those of the counselor there can be difficulties in relating and the counseling will not proceed smoothly, at least until these differences are seen and discussed. The counselee's theory, therefore, influences his or her behavior and affects the therapeutic process. Counseling might even fail if the counselor is unaware of the counselee's expectations, is too directive in trying to change these expectations, or is unwilling to adapt to the counselee's perspectives.

Some people, for example, assume that counseling involves getting tested and being told what to do about a problem. Since few counselors think that way, there could be an initial conflict over expectations. American or Canadian students who visit a campus counselor expect that counseling will help, assume that it will not be too directive, and are willing to discuss their personal problems freely, even with a stranger. Asian students, in contrast, might be less willing to talk about personal issues, especially with a stranger before whom they want to "save face." If they have grown up in a culture that admires age and authority, they might expect the counselor to be older and the source of wise information. Clearly, a person's expectations about counseling depend on one's culture, age, viewpoints, and past experiences, including experiences with previous counselors. These influences all contribute to the personal theory that the counselee brings to the counseling room.

Theory Influences Counselors

Most theories dealing with therapy tend to fall into one of two categories, insight therapies and action therapies.[13] Insight approaches, including psychoanalysis, client-centered therapy, and rational-emotive therapy, try to help people think differently. Often the counselor looks past the symptoms in search of underlying thoughts, unconscious assumptions, unexpressed feelings, or other hidden dynamics that are creating the symptoms. Action therapies, such as behavior therapy, skills development approaches, or nouthetic counseling, focus on helping people change their behavior and do things differently. The counselor's perspective, which may be some combination of the insight and action approaches, molds how he or she views symptoms, makes interventions, relates to the counselee, and measures progress.

In place of insight and action approaches, Corey and his colleagues suggest that counseling theories can be classified into moral, compensatory, medical, or enlightenment approaches.[14] Each of these makes an assumption about whether the counselee is responsible and should be held accountable for the problem. Each approach also makes assumptions about who is primarily responsible for finding a solution and taking steps to deal with the problem. This is illustrated in Table 4–1.

In the *moral model,* counselees are assumed to be responsible for both creating and solving their problems. The counselor motivates the

Four Theoretical Models[15]

		SOLUTION Who is responsible for solving the problem?	
		Client **IS** Responsible	Client is **NOT** Responsible
PROBLEM Who is responsible for causing the problem?	Client **IS** Responsible	MORAL model	ENLIGHTENMENT model
	Client is **NOT** Responsible	COMPENSATORY model	MEDICAL model

Table 4–1

counselee to take responsibility and gives both encouragement and guidance as counselees change. Reality therapy, rational-emotive therapy, person-centered therapy and nouthetic counseling are grounded in this model.

In the *compensatory model,* counselees are not held responsible for causing their problems but they are expected to expend the effort and do something about changing the situation. This includes people who were raised in an abusive or otherwise dysfunctional family. These people are victims of the past, but they can do something to change. A contemporary example of this model is seen in analyses of "toxic faith."[16] According to Stephen Arterburn and Jack Felton, many people grow up in families or churches where they learn pathological views about God and about religion. This sick religion can influence their whole lives unless they are able to understand and move beyond the power of their poisonous religious backgrounds.

The *medical model* sees people as victims of disease or other circumstances who are treated by an expert who takes responsibility for the treatment. This approach tends to foster dependency and leaves counselees at the mercy of somebody else, but there is less of a tendency for counselees to heap blame on themselves. An example of this approach might be the person who is depressed because of a chemical imbalance and is treated with drugs prescribed by the psychiatrist.

The *enlightenment model* might apply to people who have addictions or other problems that have risen, in part, from their own past mistakes and unwise decisions. These people often feel trapped and in need of help from others to get free of the self-created problems.

Which of these four models is most descriptive of your approach to counseling? Depending on the problem and the counselee, you may not always stick with one approach, but in general your counseling is likely to be in one of these four categories. Where you are in Table 4-1 has a bearing on what you ask, look for, assume, and do in your counseling. An awareness of these issues helps counselors to better understand their own work. This helps us to function better even if our clients expect us to use a different model.

Theory Influences Counselor Education

Much of our knowledge about counseling comes from our teachers and supervisors. Those teachers have values and viewpoints that concern not only how counseling should be done, but how counseling should be taught and how well-trained students should counsel. The counselor-educator molds the student's behavior, points out "errors," reinforces "good therapy," and serves as a role model of an effective counselor. The supervisor or counseling teacher decides what will be taught in a counseling program and determines whether counselor education will be "expressive" or "instrumental."[17] Expressive approaches encourage students to "get in touch with themselves," or to "deal with their own psychological baggage so they can be better helpers." Such training might put minor emphasis on techniques and specifics. Instrumental approaches, in contrast, focus more on methods and on what the counselor does. There is less emphasis on who the counselor is or on how his or her personal concerns can affect counseling.

All of this suggests that students should choose their teachers carefully and that teachers should be aware of how their own theories are influencing students.

Theory Influences Research

Perhaps you don't do research or read research articles, but books on counseling (including this one) are filled with conclusions that are based on empirical investigations. Each researcher is influenced by theoretical viewpoints that largely determine the issues to be studied, the questions to be investigated, and the methods that are used. Behavior theory, for example, seeks to change behavior so it is not surprising that research dealing with this theory attempts to determine when and how old behaviors are replaced by behavior that is new. Behavior theory tries to be strongly empirical, so research is carefully designed and precise measuring instruments are likely to be used. Psychoanalytic research, in contrast, is more likely to use clinical observation that has nothing to do with making measurements and applying statistics. "The improvement of counseling research hinges on the improvement of counseling theory," write Stefflre and Matheny, "Research cannot be better than the theory from which it derives."[18]

WHAT MAKES A GOOD THEORY?

If so much of our counseling work is guided by paradigms and theories, it is important that we select our theories carefully and try to find a theory that is the best possible. What makes a good theory?

Many years ago I wrote about this in what probably was my first professional article. According to a much younger Collins writing at a "relatively early point in my thinking," a good theory should have "clear and explicit language; should give a description and explanation of human behavior; should give practical techniques for the guidance of researchers and practitioners; and should be able to make predictions about human behavior."[19] Now, twenty-five years and several publications later, I can still agree with this early perspective.

Theories differ in their structure and their content. The *structure* of a theory refers to the ways in which it is put together. The best theories are clearly written, explicit, relatively free of technical jargon, and precise enough to be useful and testable.

That kind of theory involves much more than the dreaming and dogma of a theorist. Counselors who rarely have time to read a book or journal article are not good theory builders; and neither are academicians who never see a client.[20] Instead, good counseling theory is built on clearly developed philosophical presuppositions, on conclusions that come from a familiarization with the professional counseling literature, on the realities of practical experience, and on a healthy self-awareness in the theory builder. Good Christian theory goes further and builds on a foundation that is consistent with Christian doctrine and based in sound biblical hermeneutics.[21] In the opinion of psychologist Darrell Smith, "a comprehensive approach to counseling and psychotherapy integrates biblical concepts and principles with unique, complementary elements derived from many theories and methods of psychotherapy."[22]

As we have seen, theories are like maps; they are meant to be useful but they can't explain everything or tell us all we need to know. The *content* of a theory has to be limited, but counseling theory should at least deal with the basics of helping others. These basics include our assumptions about the existence and nature of God, the nature of the universe, and the nature of human beings; the causes of personal and interpersonal problems; the goals and methods of therapy; the role of the therapist and the nature of the counselor-counselee relationship; and who takes what responsibilities for change. A useful theory should guide counselors, stimulate discussion, suggest ideas for research, and be able to make at least some predictions about how behavior changes.

Christian Counseling and Theory

Books that summarize and evaluate counseling theory usually consider the theory's structure and content, but there is almost never any mention of God or theology.[23] Most theories of counseling could probably fit into one of the four models presented in Table 4–1, but each of these models assumes that there are only two major players in the counseling drama: the counselor and the counselee. There is no recognition of the power of Satan to create dissension and turmoil in people's lives and neither is there any awareness of God who is the only true agent of physical, psychological, relational, and spiritual healing.

Approaches to helping that depend more on the power of God than on the power of counselors tend to be ignored by secular therapists and dismissed by Christians who counsel. When students or counselees ask about inner healing or "prayer counseling," we tend to dismiss these as being of no proven value[24]—the work of psychologically unsophisticated Christians who tend to be hyperemotional and often naive about the dynamics of human behavior. We urge our secular colleagues to be more open and tolerant of Christian approaches while some of us show closed minds and intolerance when we encounter people who claim that their lives have been changed by interventions that are solely theological—without input from psychology.

Many Christian counselors would disagree with the theologies and the methods of those who practice inner healing and related approaches, and most of us would concur that these practitioners tend to be limited in their understanding of psychological issues.[25] But these people recognize the power of God to change lives and their people-helping activities are guided by their theological beliefs in ways that would put many of us to shame.

The New Testament describes the work of Apollos and of twelve men in Ephesus who were sincere and active believers but limited in their understanding of theological truth (Acts 18:24–19:6). Their helping ministries became more effective when their work was based on clear biblical theology. Could the same be said of us?

Good Christian counseling builds on theory that is solidly constructed first on the Scriptures and then on the established data of the social sciences. To ignore one of these sources of data while we focus on the other is to severely cripple the effectiveness of our theory building and our counseling.

Theoretical Agreements

If we assume that a good theory can guide our counseling, does it follow that a bad theory can undermine our therapeutic efforts? There is no research to support such a conclusion and neither has it been possible to show that one theory leads to results that are clearly superior to the others.[26] Within recent years, therefore, a "psychotherapy integration movement" has emerged with the goal of identifying and pulling together the common features that appear throughout different therapeutic systems.[27]

In one investigation, two methodical researchers went through back issues of fifty professional publications looking for the core "commonalities" among counseling theories and therapeutic methods.[28] Eighty-nine common therapeutic features were found and these were divided into five categories.

The first of these dealt with *principles of change*. Of the eighty-nine therapeutic commonalities, 41 percent dealt with ways to help people change. Of these, the therapists most often agreed on the importance of letting people express their feelings, helping counselees learn and practice new behaviors, enabling them to understand the reasons for their symptoms, helping them see new insights, and guiding as they learned new ways of relating to others.

Twenty-one percent of the common features dealt with *therapist qualities*. Most often mentioned were positive personal qualities, warmth and positive regard for counselees, empathic understanding, and the ability to cultivate hope. Improvement seems more likely when a therapist can stimulate hope and encourage counselees to expect that things will get better.

Good counseling does not drift from topic to topic. The experienced counselor has an idea where he or she is going and what the counseling seeks to accomplish. These are issues that relate to *treatment structure*. Also included are adherence to a theory, focusing on explorations of the counselee's "inner world," providing a rationale for the counseling methods, and working in a specific "healing setting," such as an office or a church.

The fourth category of commonalities concerned the *therapeutic relationship*. More than half of the surveyed articles (56 percent) stressed the importance of a close working alliance between the counselor and counselee. When counselees experience open conversation with another human being without getting hurt, there is a greater willingness to risk open relationships apart from therapy.

Surprisingly, only 6 percent of the commonalities concerned *client characteristics*, such as having positive expectations about the therapy. Perhaps the mere fact that a person would come to counseling makes people feel better and increases their faith that in time they will get well.[29]

The conclusions of this research can have value for Christian counselors, but you will notice again that the theological dimension is ignored. If the study was repeated using published articles about Christian counseling would the results be different? In addition to the above five categories would there be a category labeled *religious variables*? Perhaps not! Most of us acknowledge that we work under the direction of the Holy Spirit but our approaches tend to be built around secular intervention strategies.[30]

Integrative Therapy

To date, the most complete evangelical approach to Christian counseling has been proposed by Darrell Smith who has sought to create a therapy "that is theologically sound, theoretically open, and methodologically rich and varied." Commenting on the debates over therapeutic effectiveness, Smith argues that it is "time to bury the polemic hatchet and to begin to build unitedly and wisely upon the foundations of Scripture and the scientific bases of counseling and psychotherapy" that have already been laid.[31]

Smith defines his integrative therapy as "a comprehensive, multi-dimensional approach to counseling and psychotherapy that unifies biblical truths with complementary psychological concepts, principles, and methods derived from a variety of theoretical orientations. While disciplined and systematic, it is open to all sources of truth regarding human personality and behavior and is loyal to the tenets of evangelical Christianity."[32] Christian counselors will not all agree with Smith's theory and conclusions, but his approach and careful documentation will be a pacesetter for Christian theorists in the next few years.[33]

What About Eclecticism?

When surveys have asked professional counselors to state their theoretical orientations, eclecticism is by far the most often selected category.[34] Counselors recognized that no single theory can account for the complexities of human behavior and neither can one theory give guidance for all of the therapeutic approaches needed to help people in distress. As a result, many counselors select from a variety of existing theories or therapies and use an eclectic form of counseling.

Some counselors, encouraged by their teachers and textbook writers, assume that each of us should form our own personal theories of counseling. In this way we can counsel using approaches that are consistent with our personalities and personal preferences. But the resulting theories often are more accurately called *syncretism* than *eclecticism*.

Syncretic theory is the product that comes from picking and choosing from a variety of theories and approaches. Like bargain hunters at a discount clothing sale, we grab for what looks good or might fit with our personalities, bypass what we don't like, and toss back some things after a closer look. This is a haphazard, nonsystematic, undisciplined, and highly subjective approach that often tries to combine elements that don't fit together.

A lot of the grabbing is for techniques. Some counselors rummage about, often at workshops and skills-development training seminars, looking for cookbook or paint-by-numbers approaches to counseling. Apparently this is what attracts attention and sells.[35] But the result is as many theories as there are therapists. "Each operates out of his or her unique bag of techniques; on the basis of his or her particular background of training, experience, and biases; and case by case, with no general theory or set of principles for guidance. Essentially, it amounts to flying by the seat of one's pants."[36]

In contrast, genuine *eclectic theory* involves the careful selection and orderly combining of compatible ideas and methods that come from a variety of sources. The eclectic takes time to understand both the methods proposed by a theory and the rationale behind those methods. The resulting eclecticism does not grow out of ignorance, laziness, or a superficial understanding of counseling theory. Careful eclecticism—some would prefer to call this *professional eclecticism*[37]—is the result of careful study, thoughtful reflection, and experience in cautiously trying new techniques. The true eclectic knows how to operate within the framework of at least two or three existing theories, but chooses instead to develop a creative synthesis of concepts and methods from different approaches. This synthesis is tested in the counseling room and is continually open to being refined. Developing a reasoned eclectic perspective is a process that goes on for a lifetime.

Conclusion

Several years ago I read an article on evangelism in which the author asked if Jesus would ever use one of the existing approaches to evangelism, such as sharing the Four Spiritual Laws. The article concluded that Jesus would not have used any prepackaged evangelistic approach because he wouldn't have needed them. But most of us do need help, and until we are experienced and sensitive enough to respond effectively in each situation, we may need to rely on more structured approaches for telling people about the gospel. The same could be said for counselors. For most of us, many years pass before we can say, with confidence, that we really know what we are doing in therapy. Until that time, it can be much more helpful and effective to work within the framework of an established theory. Gerald Corey and his colleagues state this concisely:

> Practicing counseling without an explicit theoretical rationale is somewhat like flying a plane without a map and without

instruments. We do not see a theoretical orientation (or a counseling stance) as a rigid structure that prescribes the specific steps of what to do in a counseling situation. Rather, we see theory as a set of general guidelines that counselors can use to make sense of what they are doing.[38]

Where does this leave Christian counselors, especially those who aren't well acquainted with existing theory but lack the time or inclination to expand their knowledge in this area? Many books are published every year in the field of Christian counseling, but many of these are self-help books or volumes that are heavy in their presentation of techniques but much lighter in the discussion of theory. Carefully developed Christian counseling theory is almost nonexistent, although there are signs that this will be changing as several writers bring books into print.

What do we do while we wait? Christian counselors, especially those who are professional therapists, tend to forget that the church has been in the business of caring for centuries. We may agree that a good Christian theory could be helpful but from this it does not follow that we must flounder in our care-giving. We can seek the guidance of the Holy Spirit to lead us as he has guided those who lived and counseled in less complex, bygone eras.

In addition, we can continue to read broadly, in the counseling, pastoral care, and theological literature. In this way we become better informed and able to understand our counselees and how they can be helped.

We can give continued attention to our own personal and spiritual growth, recognizing that good helpers are spiritually alive and seeking to grow in their knowledge of God and his attributes.

And we can learn from others, including more experienced colleagues whose theoretical approaches to counseling may be better established. The experiences and perspectives of others can often help us clarify paradigms, sort through theory and find useful approaches that will enable us to be more effective people helpers.

CHAPTER FIVE

EFFECTIVENESS IN CHRISTIAN COUNSELING

SOMEPLACE IN MY CHILDHOOD, I developed an interest in other countries, travel, and international issues. As a college undergraduate, I joined the reserve navy to "see the world" and took several summer training cruises to Europe. I traveled around North America and, after receiving a master's degree, finally had opportunity to live and study overseas.

I was accepted into two one-year training programs, both in England. One of these was at Tavistock Clinic, working for a year with Dr. Hans Eysenck. The other had an emphasis on social psychology and was centered in the heart of London. I chose the latter, not for some exalted academic or professional reasons, but based on the fact that Eysenck's program would have kept me at the clinic for a full twelve months. Part of my reason for living abroad was to travel and to experience Europe; the study gave me an excuse for going there.

Sometimes I wonder how my thinking and career direction might have changed if I had spent that year with Eysenck. I once heard him give a lecture in London in a large hall packed with an overflow crowd. I don't remember the lecture's content, but I remember the man's humor and hard-hitting critique of the counseling profession. Even then, Eysenck was questioning the effectiveness of psychotherapy.

In 1952 (several years before my trip to England), Eysenck published his controversial findings about psychoneurotics who improved within two years, whether or not they had been treated psychologically.[1] The paper aroused a storm of controversy. Even today it is cited often by critics of psychotherapy, including Christians who question the effectiveness of psychological treatment.[2] It has been cited by Eysenck himself, who sticks by his original conclusions.[3] And the paper has stimulated four decades of aggressive research, including one reanalysis of Eysenck's original data—a reanalysis that challenged the controversial 1952 study and reached different conclusions.[4]

Does psychotherapy do any good? Is it a myth to think that psychological change can come through counseling? Do people who pay for counseling really get their money's worth? Is self-therapy or talking to a friend likely to be more helpful than professional therapy? Is Christian counseling really effective? Is its effectiveness different from counseling that has no Christian emphasis? These questions about the value and usefulness of counseling are controversial, important, and difficult to answer.

Questions about counseling effectiveness are *controversial* for several reasons. If therapy is not effective, as many critics claim, then our whole society is being duped into paying millions of dollars annually for a worthless or near worthless product. If therapy and personal counseling are ineffective, how do we help innumerable people who are plagued and sometimes immobilized by the inner turmoil and intense pressures that characterize our stress-filled society? Within the Christian community, controversy and concern has arisen over the rapid rise and impact of Christian counseling—especially when that counseling draws on the writings of secular psychology.[5] Even if its effectiveness can be demonstrated, is the counseling movement a subtle force that undermines the effectiveness of the church? Are we really involved in the promotion of "psychoheresy" as some have claimed?

Questions about effectiveness are *important* to pastors, congregations, clients, potential counselees, and counseling students. Several years ago, a journalist named Martin Gross wrote a book arguing that the church's influence was fading and being replaced by modern psychology. "As the Protestant ethic has weakened in Western society, the confused citizen has turned to the only alternative he knows: the psychological expert who claims there is a *new scientific standard of behavior* to replace fading traditions."[6] Psychologists, psychiatrists, and other counselors have become the new spiritual leaders, according to Gross. With increasing frequency, professional counselors are taking over the caring and compassion that once were viewed as the responsibility of church leaders.

This conclusion raises disturbing questions about the influence of professional counseling in the church. If counseling is effective, as its advocates claim, it will have significant future impact on local congregations. It becomes important, then, for us to know if counseling really works and to know whether the psychologically trained counselor is more, or less, effective than the seminary-trained pastoral counselor.

Questions about effectiveness have stimulated powerful rhetoric, but solid answers have been harder to find. Research evaluating psychotherapy and counseling is very *difficult* to design and carry out. How, for example, does a researcher define and measure effectiveness? How can a researcher be sure that change in a counselee comes because of the treatment and not because of something else—such as changing family circumstances? Is it ethical to treat some people but to withhold treatment from others so we can have a better research design in studies of counseling effectiveness? How can we keep the researcher's bias from influencing the data? How can we be sure that our research measures the counseling and is not being influenced by the personalities of the different therapists or the different clients?

Despite these and other difficulties, significant empirical studies have been done and when all of this research is compiled and reviewed, one conclusion is clear: "Most of the existing data do indicate some effectiveness for the psychotherapies that have been evaluated in comparison with some type of untreated control group."[7] A review of 475 published research reports concluded that "the average person who received therapy is better off at the end of it than 80 percent of those who did not."[8] A similar conclusion was reached following another exhaustive overview of research in therapy effectiveness:

> Many psychotherapies that have been subjected to empirical study have been shown to have demonstrable effects on a variety of clients. These effects are not only statistically significant but clinically meaningful. Psychotherapy facilitates the remission of symptoms. It not only speeds up the natural healing process but often provides additional coping strategies and methods for dealing with future problems. Psychologists, psychiatrists, social workers, and marriage and family therapists as well as patients can be assured that a broad range of therapies, when offered by skillful, wise, and stable therapists, are likely to result in appreciable gains for the client.
>
> The effects of therapy tend to be lasting. While some problems, such as addictive disorders, tend to recur, the gains many patients make in therapy endure. . . .
>
> *Not only is there clear evidence for the effectiveness of therapy, relative to untreated patients, but psychotherapy patients show gains that surpass those resulting from pseudotherapies and placebo controls.*[9]

In this chapter we will look at some of the issues in counseling effectiveness. Details about research studies will be cited in the notes at the end of the book; our emphasis here will be more practical. We will consider how our knowledge of effectiveness can be translated into counseling behavior that in turn will build excellence in Christian counseling.

WHAT IS EFFECTIVENESS?

Many years ago, social psychologists compared church attenders with non-attenders to see if the groups differed on issues such as prejudice and compassion. The results were meaningless because the researchers made the mistake of lumping very different people together. Church attenders, for example, include dedicated followers of Jesus Christ, minimally involved people who go to church because it is socially acceptable, "seekers" who know nothing about religion but are looking for some answers to their struggles, and bored, disinterested people who go because of habit or to please a spouse or girlfriend. Obviously, church-goers are not a homogeneous group that can be pulled together and meaningfully compared with an equally diverse group of nonattenders.

The same is true of Christian counselors and non-Christian counselors. These are not two distinctively different homogeneous groups. Each group is diverse and so are groupings of counselees, counselor-counselee relationships, the problems that are brought to counseling, counseling methods, goals, and theories. If we ignore uniquenesses and lump groups together, as some early researchers tended to do, we get confusing results.

This has happened in many studies of the overall effectiveness of counseling. Assume, for example, that we want to compare a group of people who have been counseled by professionals with a comparable group who have not been counseled. You can guess the problem with this. The counseled group may have seen a variety of therapists whose styles, theoretical orientations, methods, and personalities are all lumped together as if they were unified. The counseled people, therefore, have not all had similar experiences. But the noncounseled people have had different experiences as well. Some may have gone to friends, pastors, physicians, family members, self-help books, or other sources of help that may have been as effective (or more effective) than the professional treatment.

Because of these difficulties, recent researchers have become more careful about making comparisons between groups. Now there is less emphasis on large group comparisons or on overall effectiveness and more focus on specific questions such as the following.

- What are the goals of counseling and how do we know when the goals have been reached? Veteran psychotherapy researcher Hans H. Strupp writes that counselees should expect (1) improvements in their interpersonal functioning, (2) increased self-esteem, self-confidence, security, self-respect, and feelings of personal worth; (3) a greater interest in living, energy, and life satisfaction; (4) a greater sense of self-confidence and mastery; and (5) a significant reduction in the problems and symptoms that were brought to counseling.[10] A Christian counselor's goals might include more positive counselee attitudes toward the church, faith in Jesus Christ, and clearer thinking about personal and theological issues. If these kinds of goals can be measured,

we can more easily determine whether or not the counseling has been effective.
- Who are the people most likely to benefit from counseling? When we can answer that question, we can better predict who will change if they see a counselor.
- Are trained counselors better able to help people reach goals than untrained people?
- What characteristics in counselors are most likely to help people reach their desired goals?
- Which methods bring positive change and which do not?

For counselees to reach their goals, we need to know which counselors, working with what kinds of clients, under what circumstances, using which techniques, can bring about which changes. This presents a massive challenge: to establish a large base of high quality research. Happily, this process already is well under way. Researchers have learned much about effective therapists, effective clients, effective therapeutic relationships, and effective methods. These are the issues that we discuss in the remainder of the chapter.

EFFECTIVE THERAPISTS

Two terms periodically appear in articles about therapeutic effectiveness. The first of these, *spontaneous remission,* describes the fact that many people seem to get better without any professional counseling. There are several explanations for this. Whenever we have problems, most of us apply a little self-counseling—reading articles, writing in our journals, looking into Scripture, thinking about the problem, and praying. Each of these is helpful, and so is talking to relatives, friends, or other nonprofessionals who offer help. Often, crises pass and problems fade with time. The problems that once were so severe seem to disappear "spontaneously" without the help of more formal counseling.

The second term, *deterioration effect,* recognizes that counseling sometimes makes people worse rather than better. This may be due to therapist and/or counselee anxiety, a poor counselor-counselee match, faulty diagnosis, or the use of ineffective or ineffectively applied methods. When there is lack of progress, the counselee can get discouraged, making the initial problems worse. Some evidence suggests, however, that when the effect of counseling is negative, the fault is most likely to lie with the counselor.[11]

Effectiveness in Christian Counseling

Consider counselor burnout, for example. This word was first applied to counselors less than twenty years ago but those who work with people have long recognized the sense of emotional exhaustion, loss of energy, and cynicism that comes from intense involvement and prolonged contact with others who are in need. When their case loads go up, the effectiveness of therapists goes down, especially if there is no apparent way to reduce the pressure. Counselors who work in agencies where there is little control over case load (this would include pastors who work without assistants) are more likely to burn out than professionals in private practice who are better able to control their counseling loads.[12]

Assuming they don't burn out, what makes a counselor effective? Researchers have uncovered some interesting conclusions:[13]

1. The sex of the counselor does not make a great difference in effectiveness, although some evidence suggests that women counselors have a slight edge over men. When the counselee and counselor are of the same sex, the results tend to be better. And counselees respond best when they are able to choose whether to have a female counselor or one who is male.[14]

2. Is counseling better if the counselor has gray hair? The counselor's age probably is more important in oriental cultures (where the elderly are highly respected) than in North America. Evidence thus far suggests that age similarity between counselor and counselee is more important for effectiveness than the age of the counselor alone. Older clients especially are inclined to prefer same age or older therapists largely, it seems, because older people are more concerned about the credentials and the sense of professionalism that more experienced counselors bring.[15] How does this apply to you? If you are otherwise qualified, your age isn't likely to hinder counseling, especially if you are not far removed from the counselee in age and are not counseling the elderly.

3. There is no conclusive evidence of differences in effectiveness between psychiatrists, psychologists, social workers, or similar mental health professional groups. One study did find that counselors with training in psychology "seemed to have a greater positive effect than those trained in psychiatry or education."[16] Overall, professionals and paraprofessionals have been found to be equally effective, especially when the treatment is short-term and highly structured.[17]

4. The personal qualities and characteristics of the counselor continue to be emphasized in the literature. One study gave a questionnaire to former clients, four months after their counseling had terminated.[18] Seventy percent or more of those who considered their counseling to be successful listed the following five items as "extremely important," or "very important" in causing the improvement:
   a. the personality of the therapist,
   b. his or her helping the counselee to understand problems,
   c. encouragement to gradually face the bothersome problems,
   d. being able to talk to an understanding person, and
   e. the therapist's helping people to greater self-understanding.

5. Pastors do much of the counseling, at least in the United States, perhaps more than psychologists, psychiatrists, and social workers combined. Parishioners and other counselees are as satisfied with pastoral counseling as they are with other professional counselors. But as a group, pastors feel underprepared for their counseling responsibilities, feel incompetent to counsel, and often function at a low level of effectiveness.[19] There is no empirical evidence that training in Clinical Pastoral Education (CPE) increases counseling effectiveness, although this observation does not negate CPE training; we only can conclude that it has not yet been proven to be effective.[20]

Sadly, for those of us who tend to be conservative theologically, there is some evidence that theologically conservative pastors are less effective than theologically liberal pastors, even when differences in educational level are controlled statistically. Seminary training per se is unrelated to counseling effectiveness although training in counseling courses does increase effectiveness.[21] Of course, all of these conclusions report differences between groups (e.g., conservatives versus liberals; CPE-trained versus those without CPE training). There are likely to be many exceptions within individual counselors.

6. Some evidence supports the conclusion that positive outcome is more likely when counselors express their intentions to counselees and explain what the counseling is expected to accomplish. Effectiveness is greater still when counselees are able to respond in accordance with these intentions.[22]

7. Effectiveness is greater when the counselor emphasizes support rather than interpretation or insight; occasionally makes some self-disclosures; shows attentiveness and genuine interest in the counselee;

is able to give direction and a sense of coherence to each session; shows acceptance of the client's beliefs and values; engages clients on an emotional level; and communicates accurate empathy, warmth, reassurance, genuineness, and positive regard. These and related research findings "suggest that the therapist most likely to achieve a positive outcome is active, optimistic, expressive, straightforward yet supportive, involved, and in charge of the therapeutic process but also able to encourage client responsibility."[23]

8. Effectiveness is greater when counselors are psychologically healthy themselves and when counselees perceive that their therapists are trustworthy, credible, and experts.[24]

Several years ago one of my students, whose name was also Gary, counseled a young woman who apparently assumed that I was her counselor. She had read one or two of my books, wanted to be counseled by the book author, and was easily confused because the student counselor used my office every week on my day off. Several weeks into the counseling, after the counselee had made considerable progress, the mistake in identity was discovered—to the genuine surprise of both the counselor and counselee. The woman wanted to drop out of counseling immediately.

"Why would you do this?" Gary asked. "Hasn't the counseling been going well?"

The woman agreed that progress had been good and decided to complete her counseling. My former student was (and is) a good counselor, but the incident made us all wonder how effectiveness might be related to the counselee's perceptions of the counselor's expertness and experience. In counseling as in other fields, our reputations do make a difference in our effectiveness.

Effective Counselees

"No matter how wisely therapists select their intervention strategies and no matter how abundantly they demonstrate those qualities that correlate positively with outcome, therapy will not be effective if the client is not ready or able to benefit from those techniques."[25] This observation by Linda Seligman is a concise summary of research on the role of the counselee in counseling effectiveness. You can work hard to increase your effectiveness and to approach excellence in counseling, but your best efforts can be undermined by unmotivated, uncooperative, unwilling, or unconcerned counselees. People cannot be forced to change through counseling, and sometimes they resist even gentle persuasion.

The research on counselees could be divided into six categories. Once again we must take care lest we reach conclusions that are not accurate. Observations that apply to a group may not be relevant to some members of that group. It is well established, for example, that less educated people and those from lower socioeconomic levels are least likely to benefit from counseling. Often they fail to keep appointments and they drop out sooner. But this does not mean that poor and poorly educated people can never be helped. On the contrary, if a counselee is motivated to change and willing to work at therapy, he or she will show improvement that is every bit as effective as that shown by other counselees.

1. *Counselee Background.* In our society, people who seek counseling tend to be college educated, white, from middle to upper socioeconomic levels, and somewhat aware of what is likely to happen in counseling. Women are more likely than men to seek counseling, to stay with it, and to improve. Young adults between ages nineteen and twenty-two benefit more from therapy than those who are older or younger.[26] Despite these variations, there is no evidence of different improvement rates based on client age, sex, or race. These issues have no bearing on outcome when clients are motivated and when their counselors are competent.

As we might expect, people with long-term problems are less likely to improve than counselees whose problems are acute, based on specific situations, and relatively recent. Prognosis for improvement is also better in people who have had few prior episodes of emotional disorder and little or no prior therapy.[27] In sum, healthier people are more likely to benefit from counseling. This is not surprising because something similar is seen in the treatment of physical illness. People with healthy bodies are most inclined to respond to treatment and to bounce back when they do get sick.

2. *Felt Need.* Psychic distress, inner conflict and an awareness of one's own helplessness or weakness are all significantly related to therapeutic outcome. In general, the more distress one feels, the more likely will that person seek and stick with counseling, at least until the distress is reduced. Most likely to improve are clients who feel distressed but who recognize that this distress can't all be blamed on other people. Counseling is often effective when a person feels inner

turmoil but acknowledges his or her own responsibilities both in helping to bring on the problems and to do something about them.[28]

3. *Expectation.* People who come for counseling have differing attitudes and expectations. Every marriage counselor has seen this in couples where one person is motivated and expects things to get better but the spouse doesn't have much hope or desire to see things change. Frequently a self-fulfilling prophecy occurs. Those who expect to improve most often do; those who expect to stay the same show little change.

One team of researchers has divided counselees into four groups based on their *readiness* for counseling.[29] For maximum effectiveness, each group is assumed to benefit from a different type of counseling.

High-readiness counselees are motivated to change, relatively independent, active, marked by a variety of interests, able to take a broad perspective on their problems, generally competent in relating to others, and possess "adequate self-control and a good sense of themselves." These counselees could benefit most from counselors who listen, provide minimal direction and support, and help clients take responsibility for making changes in their lives.

Counselees with moderately high readiness are a little less able to cope without help. These people tend to respond best when the counselor emphasizes understanding and support but gives limited direction. A client-centered approach to counseling might fit best.

Moderately low-readiness counselees need a lot of support, teaching, and direction. The counselor and counselee are actively involved, grappling with issues in a team approach. Reality therapy, would fit well here.

Clients with low readiness need strong direction and a firm awareness of the counselor's control. Empathy and support are important but the client is likely to drop out if he or she feels that nothing is being done. Rational-emotive therapy, behavior therapy, or nouthetic counseling might be most useful with these counselees.

It is difficult to get a precise and accurate appraisal of the counselee's readiness and expectations about counseling, but many counselors (and several researchers) have determined that some kind of expectation evaluation near the beginning of the counseling is important if treatment is to succeed. For example, it can help to ask the counselee what he or she expects. This gives opportunity to set more accurate expectations and to stimulate realistic hope. When the counselor and counselee have similar expectations, the counselee's readiness improves and effectiveness is more likely.[30]

4. *Counselee Beliefs.* Articles by mental health professionals and secular training programs often ignore the issue of counselee religious beliefs. But this can be of crucial importance in the success or failure of counseling with Christians and other religiously oriented counselees.

Evangelical and other conservative Christians, for example, tend to avoid and mistrust professional counseling because they fear that their faith will be misunderstood, unappreciated, ridiculed, or eroded. Pastors and other spiritual leaders sometimes reinforce beliefs that a secular counselor will (a) ignore spiritual issues, (b) treat spiritual beliefs and experiences as pathological or merely psychological, (c) fail to understand spiritual language and concepts, (d) assume that religious clients share the norms and behavior standards of the culture concerning issues such as premarital sex, divorce, cohabitation, or homosexuality, (e) recommend behaviors that the counselee considers wrong such as abortion or viewing of pornography, and/or (f) make assumptions, statements, interpretations, or recommendations that discredit and disagree with Scripture.[31]

Research on the effectiveness of religious counseling is almost nonexistent. It is known that deeply religious people prefer like-minded counselors and are more willing to cooperate with counselors who understand and appreciate religious issues. Widespread fears of being misunderstood or manipulated into changing values can get in the way of counseling if a professional counselor shows no awareness or comprehension of theological language and beliefs. When a committed Christian counselee seeks help from a non-Christian therapist, there is likely to be a period of caution and unwillingness to trust the counselor. Until this tension is resolved, counseling effectiveness is likely to be hindered.

5. *Counselee Personality.* Sometimes research confirms what we already suspect. It is not surprising, then, to read that people who stay in counseling and improve tend to be more dependable, sensitive to their environments, less anxious, in touch with their feelings, able to express their thoughts and emotions, not inclined to be defensive, high in "ego strength," and able to take responsibility for their lives and their problems rather than blaming problems on other people and situations. When counselees have a determination to participate in the counseling and do whatever is needed to make changes, improvement

is more likely.[32] Stated succinctly, better adjusted people stay in counseling and get better.

As we all know, few of our counselees fit such positive descriptions. People who come for help more often are anxious, highly dependent, inclined to blame others, defensive, entangled in depression or guilt, dissatisfied with themselves, bogged down with frustrations, lacking in energy, feeling hopeless, and sometimes unable or unwilling to verbalize and express their deepest struggles. For counseling to be effective, these people must be helped to change some of their defeatist attitudes and must see quick evidence of at least minimal improvement. Some counselors who begin with a focus on acceptance and active listening also try to point out reasons for hope, even before the first session ends. This begins to help counselees change their perceptions.

6. *Perception.* Another review of the articles and books on counseling effectiveness concluded that outcome depends largely on how the counselee views the counselor and counseling. "What has emerged as the most consistent process predictor of improvement is the patient's subjective perception of the therapist-offered relationship."[33]

Counselors, like teachers, often are involved in helping people change perceptions of themselves, their problems, and their situations. This process will be more successful and lead to more effective outcomes if the client has a positive view of counseling, of his or her counselor, and of the counselor-counselee relationship.

MATCHING: THE EFFECTIVE THERAPEUTIC ALLIANCE

Have you ever been consulted by a counselee whom you disliked? It isn't easy to form a warm and empathic counseling alliance with everybody. Some people are more pleasant to work with than others and, as might be expected, we tend to be more effective working with clients whom we like. One study showed that therapists felt less confident of their abilities to help disliked clients, were more inclined to think that disliked clients probably wouldn't get better, and tended to judge these people as being "difficult patients" and more in need of therapy.[34] In contrast, counselors and counselees who like and respect one another are more satisfied with counseling.[35]

It seems logical to assume that a good working relationship between counselor and counselee is necessary if the counseling is to be effective. When there are similar goals, values, perceptions, backgrounds, expectations, and beliefs, there can be better rapport in counseling, greater hope in the counselee, more effective modeling of behaviors by the counselor, and often more successful therapy.[36] All of this is accepted widely, although researchers have more difficulty in precisely demonstrating the value of a good counselor-counselee match and making suggestions about ways to improve matchmaking in counseling.[37]

Several years ago, Jay Adams convened a conference of several Christian counselors who had written in this field. Our interactions together were cordial, lively, and consistently stimulating, but characterized at times by considerable disagreement. One of the debates concerned the importance of a relationship in counseling. One side argued that counseling methods are more important than building relationships. The opposing view held that a close counselor-counselee relationship also is of great importance if counseling is to be successful.

Counselors still disagree on these issues, but most practitioners and most researchers would argue in favor of a good therapeutic alliance if counseling is to be effective. Even when the relationship is good, however, counseling will not be of maximum effectiveness unless there is also a good choice and use of counseling methods.

EFFECTIVE METHODS

In the years following Eysenck's famous study, hundreds (probably thousands) of researchers have done carefully designed studies that have demonstrated the overall effectiveness of psychotherapy. More recent research has put greater emphasis on finding the reasons for this effectiveness. Does improvement depend primarily on the therapist, the counselee, the methods used, or on some combination of these and other influences?

One analysis of fifty professional publications concluded that a good therapeutic alliance was the most important factor in effectiveness, followed by the opportunity for catharsis, the client's having positive expectations about the counseling, beneficial therapist characteristics, and having the counseling done within the confines of a clearly defined theoretical rationale.[38]

Other research has focused on more specific issues such as the value of interpretation (its value has not been documented[39]), length of therapy (long term is not necessarily better than short term), place of treatment (that doesn't seem to make much difference), and whether one school of therapy is more effective than another. There is little support for the superiority of one school of therapy over another; much depends on the therapist and on the counselee's problems. In general, the cognitive and behavioral approaches appear to be better than the humanistic and psychoanalytic approaches, although part of these differences may depend on the fact that cognitive-behavioral approaches are easiest to investigate and to support scientifically.

Someone has estimated that over four hundred different psychotherapies currently exist, but methods or strategies such as the following appear to be common to them all:[40]

- Establishing and maintaining a therapeutic relationship;
- Giving support by way of suggestions, structure, confirmation, acceptance, reality testing, and communication of a sense of confidence and optimism;
- Giving information and education;
- Reducing anxiety, depression, and other painful feelings;
- Decreasing specific maladaptive behaviors;
- Helping people change misperceptions;
- Helping clients make sense of their concerns and put them in context;
- Expanding emotional awareness; and
- Enhancing personal effectiveness.

Most Christian counselors would add religious counseling techniques to the list; these include praying with counselees, making references to Scripture, urging the confession of sin, focusing on religious imagery, or encouraging involvements with groups of believers. Christian counselees expect their counselors to use such methods, but to date there is no evidence that these religious treatments are any more (or less) effective than nonreligious methods.[41]

Most counselors might agree that their work involves three changes: helping people experience their feelings, master their thinking, and regulate their behavior,[42] but no clear research evidence indicates how this should be done.

Consider, for example, whether a counselor should be directive or experiential. The answer, it seems, depends on the counselee and the problem. Research in this area indicates that the directive approach (a structured, therapist-guided form of treatment) is best suited for people who are:

- willing to take direction from others and/or unable to establish their own direction;
- primarily motivated to achieve specific goals;
- severely disturbed, dysfunctional, or fragile;
- in crisis or experiencing situational problems; and/or
- having difficulty setting limits and boundaries, especially in therapy.

In using directive methods, the counselor assumes an authoritative attitude, makes specific suggestions, and sets programs for change.[43]

In contrast, experiential (more client-centered, minimally directive) approaches are better for people who:

- can establish their own direction;
- are functioning acceptably even though they fall short of their potential;
- are not in crisis;
- are guided by broad, far-reaching goals; and
- can establish appropriate interpersonal boundaries, in and outside of therapy.

Catharis, ventilation, reflection of feelings, praise, encouragement, and support are all involved.

Religious Psychotherapy

Psychologists W. Brad Johnson and Charles R. Ridley evaluated a broad group of Christian approaches to counseling and perceptively divided them into four groups, depending on their assumptions.[44]

The *accommodation assumption* is based on the idea that counseling will be most effective, at least with religious clients, when established psychological principles are used but adapted to Christian values. These approaches—represented by writers such as Backus, Crabb, Malony, McMinn, Minirth and Meier, and (according to the article) Collins—assume that treatment outcome depends on the therapist's skill in modifying and using a secular technique. "This means that the therapist must have sensitivity to the client's unique religious values. Therapist sensitivity entails the ability to identify and support the client's values. It also involves recognition of one's own values without imposing them on the client or negating the client's values if they are contrary to those of the therapist." Johnson and Ridley add that "such would appear to be a demanding challenge."

The *hope assumption* holds that religious therapies go beyond secular approaches by instilling and mobilizing hope. Hope is assumed to be essential and indispensable for change. Effective counseling moves clients beyond their feelings of hopelessness and despair, helping them to "reframe" or get a more positive view of themselves and their situations. In this view—seen in the writings of Clinebell, Vande Kemp, and Vayhinger—level of training or therapeutic orientation are of less importance than mobilizing hope. Even untrained people can succeed in helping others find hope.

The *truth assumption* rests on the belief that the Bible, God's Word, contains divinely established standards and guidelines for emotional wholeness. Violation of these propositional truths creates tension, irresponsibility, guilt, and the kinds of problems people bring to counselors. When a counselee understands and applies these truths to life, changed attitudes, behaviors, perceptions, and emotions will result. Counselors who work with this assumption—Adams, Drakeford, Mowrer, Seamands, Solomon, and Tournier, for example—are responsible for knowing and clarifying propositional truth. The counselee, in turn, must accept divinely given truth and integrate this into his or her lifestyle and daily behavior. Failure to integrate these principles is assumed to indicate irresponsibility, resistance, disobedience, or spiritual immaturity. The counselor gives direction but change is assumed to depend on the client's commitment to adopting religious values into life.

The *active agent assumption*—best represented by Adams, MacNutt, Sanford and Sanford, and Stapleton—presumes that a divine agent (God the Father, Jesus Christ, or the Holy Spirit) intervenes in counseling to bring change. Secular therapists and treatments don't have access to this agent. "Counseling is the work of the Holy Spirit," according to Jay Adams. "Effective counseling cannot be done apart from him . . . because unsaved counselors do not know the Holy Spirit, they ignore his counseling activity and fail to avail themselves of his direction and power."[45]

Although some advocates of this view assume that the Holy Spirit only works through one method (such as inner healing, imagery, or prayer counseling), others believe that the Holy Spirit is sovereign and works as he wills. The counselor is "a conduit for change, and the need for the therapist's skills is secondary at best. Basically the role of the therapist is to prepare the client to receive the intervention. The client, on the other hand, needs to become receptive to the healing, often by relinquishing unhealthful attitudes or misconceptions about the divine agent. But, neither the therapist nor the client claims responsibility for the healing. It is totally the work of the divine or higher power. Similarly, neither the therapist nor the client claims responsibility for nonhealing with the exception of a nonreceptive client. Nonhealing also is regarded totally as the work of the divine or higher power. In this case, it is often said that 'this is as God wills.'"[46]

Table 6-1, based on an earlier, nonpublished draft of the Johnson and Ridley article, places all of these approaches on a continuum of responsibility. The authors assume that some counselors draw on more than one of these assumptions. Adams, for example, appears to accept both the truth and the active agent positions; Malony and Propst are among those whose work includes the accommodation and active agency positions. Many Christian counselors might attempt to draw from all four assumptions.

Responsibility in Four Approaches to Treatment

Greatest—————-Therapist Responsibility—————-Lowest

Accommodation	**Hope**	**Truth**	**Active Agent**
(therapist responsible)	(client responsible)	(client responsible)	(God responsible)

Adapted from W. Brad Johnson and Charles R. Ridley, "Sources of Gain in Christian Counseling and Psychotherapy," (1991), in press.

Table 6-1

Even with this useful four-part classification, there still is limited research on the comparative effectiveness of any one of these approaches as compared to the others. Again, apparently much depends on the counselee and the problem. And it is probable that many counselees would resist all four approaches and opt, instead, for nonreligious counseling.

EFFECTIVE RESEARCH

We end this chapter on effectiveness where we began—with comments about the difficulty of doing research on counseling. Perhaps the word *research* appears more often in this chapter than anywhere else in the book, but the quality of these studies has been criticized, especially the quality of research in religious counseling. Writing in the somewhat technical language of a professional journal, Clara E. Hill concluded that we "have not yet figured out how therapist techniques and the therapeutic relationship (e.g., working alliance, transference) interact to influence treatment outcome. We also need to know how extratherapeutic events combine with in-session events to produce change (e.g., how support systems reinforce or hinder change). . . . Relatedly, further work needs to be done on the quality or competence of therapist interventions."[47]

Does this have practical relevance to those of us who want to be effective Christian counselors, committed to excellence? We may see the value of research and recognize the difficulty of trying to apply social science tools to religious methods, especially to those methods that are based on the truth and active agent assumptions. We may skim the research journals on occasion and look at the findings. But for many practitioners, research reports are boring and largely irrelevant to the day-to-day practice of counseling.[48]

Some among us might be willing to attempt quality research in Christian counseling, but funds for such work are limited and, as Everett Worthington, Jr., has noted, "research on religious counseling is a risky undertaking, only occasionally acceptable to some of the major counseling journals."[49] Many times our fellow Christians aren't enthusiastic about such research either, especially if there is any suspicion that the results might question the efficacy of some dearly held religious interventions.

Nevertheless, there is need for quality research in Christian counseling. Those of our numbers who persist at this sometimes thankless task are to be applauded and encouraged. They are doing a good and important work.

CONCLUSION

We have come a long way since the early work of Eysenck. In this chapter, our brief journey through the effectiveness research has shown that therapy works, but this conclusion cannot and need not be based solely on enthusiastic endorsements from people who claim to have been helped. Instead, many professionals and graduate students are doing research and looking carefully at what we do in counseling and trying to discover how we can do it better.

The critics of counseling, including those who demean Christian counseling, have challenged us to demonstrate that our methods are effective. While the critics point to our weaknesses and sometimes dismiss our approaches, our colleagues are doing the hard work of investigating our methods, counseling relationships, and therapist characteristics. In time, their efforts are likely to validate and refine what we seek to accomplish in our work as effective Christian counselors.

CHAPTER SIX
GROWTH AND TRAINING IN CHRISTIAN COUNSELING

SEVERAL MONTHS BEFORE THIS BOOK was completed, a group of forty educators gathered at a hotel near Chicago for three days of interaction and discussion of professional papers. Most of those participants would identify themselves as evangelical Christians, most are professional therapists, and all are involved in training the coming generation of Christian counselors. During the days of that conference, the participants talked about the selection of students, the quality of course work, and how training in counseling could be supervised. Most of those educators appeared to go back to their campuses with fresh ideas, renewed enthusiasm, and a rejuvenated commitment to work toward excellence in counselor training.[1]

One of the conference speakers was C. Stephen Evans, a professor of philosophy at St. Olaf College in Minnesota. Evans is among a new breed of evangelical writers in Christian counseling who are bringing renewed vitality into the field.[2] His paper at the conference on training dealt with wisdom and how this could be instilled in Christian counselors. We must start by finding wise people to be our students, Evans suggested, and we must be committed to fostering wisdom in our trainees and ultimately in ourselves.

When they apply for admission to graduate programs in counseling, most new students are selected on the basis of their past grades, recommendation letters and test scores. But Evans argued that admission committees should look at applicants more closely. "A Christian graduate school of psychology," he said, "should strive to recruit and select students who are wise people, or at least people who are growing in wisdom and have the potential to be truly wise." These are people whose past course work goes beyond psychology and includes philosophy, literature, history, theology, biblical studies, sociology, anthropology, and other liberal arts subjects. Potentially wise students often have had hardships, suffering, loss and adversity—all of which can stimulate maturity. To this we might add the increased breadth of experience that comes from travel, especially travel to countries overseas. We should look for students who have had the right kind of mentors and role models, Evans added, and we should seek people who are spiritually growing.

> Look for students who genuinely seem to care about Christ and Christ's kingdom, and who wish to understand their whole lives through the framework of their faith. We should look for people who seem aware of their weaknesses, and who seem to have learned from their mistakes; the people who are trying to deal with their weaknesses. What we need to discern, and what is so terribly difficult to discern, is whether the insights a person seems to possess into the nature of God have actually made a concrete difference in the person's life. Does a person seem to be committed to a life of prayer and service? Does he or she utilize the disciplines of the Christian life? Are the fruits of the Spirit recognizable? I know this seems like an impossible task, since we often find that we don't really know people we have lived with and worked with for years. Nevertheless, I think it

would be useful to find out as much as possible about what kind of church experience an applicant has had, as well as getting some feel for the individual's own personal spiritual autobiography.[3]

Evans realizes that his selection criteria are ideal and difficult to use in choosing students. Almost as difficult would be instilling wisdom in counseling trainees. To do that, he suggests, we must select highly competent faculty members who model wisdom and who foster mentoring relationships with their students. We must encourage these students to be involved in local churches, to have networks of supportive Christian friends, and to have time for spiritual reflection and the development of spiritual disciplines. Faculty members must strive to develop solid psychology and counseling courses that are supplemented by a much broader perspective. "Psychologists learn too much psychology and not enough other things," Evans believes. "When a psychologist, especially an applied psychologist such as a therapist or counselor, addresses human problems, those problems do not fit neatly into the syllabus of a standard course in the psychology program."[4]

How well do we select and train Christian counselors? There is not much research to answer that question, although one survey of Christian graduate training programs in counseling found that training in spiritual disciplines and explicitly Christian techniques was almost nonexistent.[5] Things have not changed much since a writer noted in 1980 that Christian mental health professionals "often have a tendency to ignore, or at the very least, feel embarrassed about, so called 'spiritual approaches to mental health.'"[6]

So what? These issues of recruitment and training may seem far removed from the people who read this book, unless you are a professor or student. Practitioners have already gone through their training and many would like to forget the difficulties and uncertainties of graduate school. If this describes you, your focus is likely to be on helping counselees. You may have little time or motivation for thinking about counselor training.

I would suggest, however, that every counselor, even those whose work is far removed from the classroom, must be concerned about excellence in training and professional growth. The reputation of our professions and the ability to continue our work depends in part on the quality of the young professionals who come out of our graduate schools. Excellence in pastoral counseling largely builds on the quality of seminary courses that prepare new candidates for the ministry. Lay counseling programs must be of the highest quality if nonprofessional people helpers are to make a genuinely positive difference in the lives of others. Christian counseling has been under attack within recent years and some of the criticisms are valid. The most productive response to this criticism is not fighting back, but showing quality, excellence, competence, and clear Christian values in our work. These attributes must be imprinted into students during their training and modeled by professors and practitioners.

Christian counseling is a diverse field, although training and service tend to fall into three categories—each of which is needed and none of which is superior to the other two. *Professional counselors* are people preparing for careers in counseling. Their training is the most intense and prolonged of the three groups and occurs most often in universities, graduate schools, clinics, and hospitals. *Pastoral counselors* are in various forms of ministry. For most, counseling is only one of several responsibilities although theologically trained men and women do much, maybe most, of the counseling in North America. Their training usually comes from seminaries. The third group of counselees are lay people whose training usually includes one or several courses although some in this group may have no training at all. These might be called *paracounselors* in the same way that we have paramedics and paralegals. Paracounselors may be the most trusted and the most often consulted people helpers. Their training often takes place in college classrooms, schools, churches, or other community locations.

Each of these three groups is important and necessary. Each needs the other two. Each should be trained and stimulated to work at the highest level of excellence. Each can benefit from the input and teaching of more experienced practitioners, most of whom are not graduate school or seminary professors.

And what about training for those of us whose formal education has been completed? For all of us, there is need for continuing education. The fact that you are reading this book and this chapter attests to your desire to grow in your knowledge and excellence. Whatever our work, growing individuals cannot ignore training and education issues.

Growth and Training in Christian Counseling

In this chapter we will look at three topics: training counselors (at all three levels), supervision of counselors-in-training, and continuing education for people who already are in the counseling field. Each of these can have a practical bearing on our work as counselors.

TRAINING IN CHRISTIAN COUNSELING

Sometimes I think my training was not very good. I went to quality graduate schools, had a top-rated clinical internship, and learned from some of the leaders in our field. In those days my professors—almost without exception, highly capable men and women—knew less about counselor education than we do now. But even then I wondered how my competence as a clinician could be enhanced by hearing complex lectures, writing innumerable papers, or plowing through courses in advanced statistical methods. Like professional educators in the fields of medicine, theology, or law, people who teach counseling still struggle to find the best ways by which quality professional training can be accomplished. This has been the focus of numerous seminars, journal articles, and national conferences, including the recent conference on training Christian counselors.

Perhaps there always will be active debate surrounding issues of training. This can be healthy if it refines and leads to improved counselor education. Several observations from the ongoing debate are of relevance to practitioners.

1. *The classroom is not always the best place for learning, especially when the emphasis is on lecturing.* After I became a teacher, for several years I began most of my graduate classes with excerpts from a marvelous commentary on education, written by a West Coast philosophy professor. It was written twenty years ago, but it still has contemporary relevance.

> Suppose we enter a typical college classroom and encounter some students and a professor. What might they be there for? To "search for the truth"? Perhaps, but more often than not, unfortunately, we find students, at least, searching for the almighty grade. Or a bit better, but not much, searching for "the facts." After all, the professor has spent all those extra years in graduate school learning what the facts are, so his [or her] obvious function in the class is to communicate these facts to the students. On occasions the facts might actually be interesting,

or entertaining, and sometimes they might even prove useful later on from a strictly vocational standpoint, but most of the time they must be learned "simply because they're there." Students and professors together pretty much assume that education is concerned with "covering the ground" of a particular discipline. Thus, when we enter a classroom we should not be surprised to find an entire roomful of stenographers, not students, busily scribbling down whatever the professor has to say. If the professor is a bad one he duly reads his old graduate school notes to his students. If he is a good one and has thereby developed his own lecture material in which he is very interested, he still more or less presents it to the class to digest until time to regurgitate it on an exam. The best digesters with the most regurgitation get the best grades, of course, for after all, that's what education's all about. So who can search for truth when "the ground" must be covered?[7]

2. *Acquiring knowledge is important in counselor training,* but there is debate about what knowledge the student should get and whether this learning really makes much difference. Most would agree that counselors should have *knowledge of issues,* such as facts relating to the nature, causes, and effective treatment approaches for common maladies such as depression, anxiety, marital tensions, or low self-esteem. Some have suggested that prospective counselors who will work with hurting people need to supplement this knowledge about psychopathology with knowledge about "positive mental health topics," such as how to mobilize assets, prevent problems, improve environments, or stimulate support systems.[8]

Students also should acquire *knowledge of procedures* (including counseling skills, theoretical approaches to therapy, and how to make referrals), *knowledge of oneself* (including an awareness of our own personal limitations and assets for working intimately with counselees), and at least some *knowledge of culture* (including experiences that broaden one's life perspective and teach about cultural and social diversity). To this lengthy list, Christian counselors should also have *biblical and theological knowledge,* including a good grasp of Scripture, experiential and scriptural knowledge about the nature of God, and some awareness of the pastoral care tradition from which so much contemporary Christian counseling has come.

When I was a seminary professor, two of my faculty colleagues once had an interesting discussion about their work as counselors. One of them, a New Testament scholar, argued that his ways of helping people were no different from those of the counseling professor, except the counselor got paid. In earlier chapters we have cited research showing that psychologically trained and untrained counselors often are similar in their methods and effectiveness. But as my professor friends debated, the counselor suggested (I think correctly—but I was on his side of the debate) that the trained therapist, unlike his biblical-scholar colleague, brings something extra to the counseling relationship: the ability to draw on his or her specialized knowledge of problem dynamics and of helping skills.

California professor Eileen Gambrill would agree. Using the problem of agoraphobia as an example, she writes, "It is unlikely that a college professor of English who is friendly and supportive but who has no specialized training in working with agoraphobic patients could attain the same results with such clients as could a recognized expert in this area." But Gambrill is honest enough to add "however, to my knowledge, such a study has never been done."[9] There still is debate, then, about the extent to which factual knowledge can make a difference in attaining counseling excellence, and we still are uncertain about what the counselor really needs to know.[10]

3. *Effective counselors are skilled in relating to others.* I once heard about a man who took his doctorate in counseling from a university that required a few classroom courses and completion of a thesis, but no practical experience. It seems unlikely that this man would be a very effective counselor, despite his wealth of knowledge. Degrees and diplomas alone do not confer competence to perform counseling and psychological services.[11]

An estimated five hundred counselor-education programs now exist in the United States.[12] Add the many training programs that operate overseas and the lay counselor approaches worldwide[13] and we see the breadth of this training movement. To date there has been little quality research on the effectiveness of counselor education[14] but one trend is clear: There are consistent calls for "competency-based" training that emphasizes both skills and knowledge.

Graduates of professional-level counseling programs cannot be licensed to practice in most places, unless they have had significant supervised experiences in working with real counselees. Ideally, there would be simulated (role play) experiences early in training and later supervised involvement with actual counselees. This training must not be limited to listening and responding skills. The counselor should know how to encourage change in counselees, how to help people cope with difficult circumstances, and how to work toward bringing changes in stress-inducing counselee environments.

4. *Theory can be an important part of training.* As we saw in chapter 4, the educator's theoretical position has a bearing on how he or she teaches others to counsel. When students are given a theoretical framework in which they can work, counseling goals and methods more easily can be understood and applied. Within recent years a variety of counselor training models have been developed.[15] Most of these are based on theories that guide both trainers and their trainees.

5. *Training should be tailored to individual differences in students.* We don't all counsel in the same way and neither do we learn in similar ways. Most counselor education programs have ignored personality or behavior differences in students and have provided all learners with similar training experiences. Recently, however, there have been several calls for more individually tailored approaches to training.[16] This, of course, creates more work and difficulty for educators but individualized training is likely to be more effective for the students.

6. *Experienced counselors are not necessarily the best counselors and trainers.* Much depends on the kinds of experiences a counselor has had and on what he or she has learned from working as a therapist. Experienced counselors can draw from a greater store of knowledge and often are able to make counseling interventions more efficiently and simply.[17] But greater experience can also lead to declining standards of quality.

In medicine, for example, there is evidence that some physicians act routinely and sometimes even carelessly as they gain experience and move further away from the rigors of their training institutions. As we have more experiences, we realize increasingly that cases are complex and in some counselors this may lead to uncertainty and vacillation about ways of proceeding. It is well to remember, therefore, that in counseling, experience may not always be the best teacher.[18]

7. *Mentoring is an important part of counselor training, especially for beginning counselors who need good models.* This conclusion is cited repeatedly in articles about training but it is less often seen in

practice.[19] Maybe the professors are too busy or the classes are too large. But many students apparently go through counseling education programs and never watch one of their professors counsel, never are coached and encouraged by their instructors, never talk one-to-one about counselor anxieties or about how experienced counselors arrive at clinical decisions.

Training Christian counselors can be a demanding but fulfilling task. Our work is more likely to be successful and to stimulate counseling excellence if we can identify what we want our trainees to learn, what knowledge and skills they should possess, and how these can be instilled and evaluated. It is likely that our results will be best if students can learn from instructors and books, and go beyond this to utilize videotapes and other technical aids, observations of counseling and interactions with successful counselor-mentors, opportunities to know themselves through therapy or other growth experiences, and frequent practical experience with feedback from experienced and insightful supervisors.

This kind of ambitious program can be applied to professionals in training, but in modified forms it also can be useful in training pastoral counselors and paracounselors. In this type of education, local practitioners often are called to work as trainers or supervisors. [20]

SUPERVISION IN CHRISTIAN COUNSELING

Most of us who travel frequently take air safety for granted. Before we board the plane and buckle up we assume that airline mechanics have done their maintenance checks and that people in the cockpit are qualified to get us from where we are to where we want to go. As a passenger, I know almost nothing about how these airline people have been trained, but I can make some guesses. I suspect they have done a lot of classroom work, have viewed films, have seen demonstrations, and have taken tough examinations.

I wouldn't feel very secure or comfortable, however, if the men and women who service and fly the planes had never had any carefully supervised practical experience. Can you imagine trusting your life to a pilot who was highly knowledgeable about flying and about airplanes but who had never before taken the controls? Passengers assume correctly that nobody flies a commercial jet unless he or she has spent many hours under careful supervision, gaining valuable practical experience on simulators and in a variety of aircraft.

The application to counseling is obvious. Good training is not very helpful unless it is accompanied and followed by good supervision.

What is good supervision and why is this of interest to practitioners already in the field? It is surprising, perhaps, that questions like these are relatively recent and difficult to answer. A lot of counselors, including counselor-educators, don't give much thought to supervision—what it should accomplish, how it should be done, who is most competent to supervise. We "just do it," without much planning or direction.[21] Research on the effectiveness of supervision still is limited[22] and even now graduate programs offer few courses in how to supervise beginning counselors. All of this is changing,[23] however, and some educators have even suggested that there should be separate credentials for counselor supervisors.[24]

Already, some conclusions are clear:

1. *Good supervisors are first of all good counselors.* Research on supervisor characteristics is still limited, but most writers agree that the same respect, empathy, genuineness, concreteness and self-disclosure that are desirable in counseling should also characterize supervisors as they work with their supervisees. Even though supervision is different from therapy, the supervision experience can be a good model of what counseling should be like.[25]

2. Effective counselors are not necessarily effective supervisors. Supervision may focus at times on any hangups or blind spots that might interfere with a trainee's potential effectiveness as a counselor, but the goal of supervision is not therapy for the supervisee.[26] Instead, the supervisor seeks to provide a learning environment where trainees can be helped to improve counseling skills, increase knowledge, heighten sensitivity, and evaluate practice.

3. Supervision involves different styles, goals, and methods. One research report identified several teaching techniques and concluded that supervision is best when a variety of methods is used. Brainstorming, for example, involves the free and open discussion of novel ideas about therapy in a noncritical setting. Role play is more structured and allows the supervisor and trainee to try new and different approaches to problem solving. Guided reflection more often focuses on the trainee's cases and discusses how he or she could have done things differently. Sometimes this discussion will be based on the student counselor's case-notes, but at other times the supervisor and

trainee will discuss a counseling session that the supervisee has conducted and recorded on video or audiotape.[27]

Writing from a Christian perspective, psychologist Everett Worthington, Jr. suggests four models of supervision. In the *minimum intervention* model the church provides brief counselor training but there is little or no direct follow-up supervision. The *vertical supervision* model often is used by followers of Jay Adams's nouthetic counseling. There are four levels of trainees, each of which is guided by a senior staff member: those who (a) attend classes and receive didactic instructions, (b) observe more experienced counselors during actual counseling sessions and participate in case discussions, (c) are involved in counseling as junior members of a team, and (d) participate as senior counselors.

In the *professional training* model, each trainee is expected to attend didactic instruction classes. In addition to didactic training, the trainee also sees clients in role-play situations or in real life, and in audiotaped or videotaped sessions. Such sessions are either observed by a supervising professional, or the trainee and supervisor listen to and discuss audiotape or videotape recordings of role play or actual counseling sessions. After sufficient observation of actual and role-play counseling, and a favorable evaluation by the supervisor, the trainee is deemed to be a qualified counselor.[28]

Worthington adds that in reality there probably is a fourth approach: the *implicit trust* model. Here no direct supervision is ever made. If a supervisor asks a counselor how the counseling is going, the counselor's verbal report is assumed to be accurate. Like pilots without practical experience in flying, counselors without supervision sometimes see their counseling crash because of a pile of misinformation and harmful practices that severely injure both themselves and their counselees.

4. *There are ethical and legal aspects of supervision.* This is true just as there are ethical and legal implications of counseling. Supervisors ultimately bear legal responsibility for the welfare of clients who are counseled by trainees. Like counselors, supervisors have an ethical obligation to respect counselee confidentiality, to insure the highest levels of counseling care, and to insist on referral when cases go beyond the counselor's capabilities and levels of expertise.

Ethically, counselors should remain within the boundaries of their competence so they should not supervise if they have no training as supervisors. Other issues include who gets paid and how much when a supervisor oversees the work of a counselor who is also a supervisee, how the supervisor can be protected from litigation, and how the supervisor and supervisee can avoid power struggles.[29]

For anyone involved in training professional, pastoral, or lay counselors, issues surrounding supervision are likely to be of increasing importance. Educators, professional counseling associations, insurance agencies, and the people who write laws about licensing and certification are all calling for better supervision practices. If there is to be excellence in Christian counseling, there also must be high quality in our ways of supervising Christian counselors in training.

Continuing Education in Christian Counseling

What do you know about psychopathology? How well would you answer a questionnaire about the kinds of problems people bring to counselors? How well would practicing counselors score on a test of abnormal psychology? Would most of them be able to recognize the signs that potentially suicidal people show?

In an effort to answer questions like these, a University of Arizona researcher gave a test on basic knowledge of psychopathology to groups of clinical psychologists, graduate and undergraduate students, and clergy. The clergy (which included Catholic priests, Jewish rabbis, Eastern religious leaders, and ministers unaffiliated with any denomination) scored lowest. Even though a majority of people turn first to religious leaders in times of counseling need, this research joins others in showing that the clergy are not much different from educated nonclergy in their ability to spot suicide potential or in knowledge about depression, anxiety, guilt, stress, or other common human problems.[30]

This kind of research could bring cries of protest. Of course professional counselors are more knowledgeable than pastors about psychopathology—just as the reverse would be seen if the test covered basic theology. One survey of Protestant seminaries found that most only require one course in pastoral counseling,[31] so graduates have had little opportunity to learn about psychopathology or suicide. But survey results don't tell the whole picture. Many pastors are highly competent counselors whose knowledge and effectiveness would be as good or better than that of professionals.

At all three levels of counseling, however, there are people whose knowledge and helping skills are limited. Some have done little to keep abreast of new developments in the counseling fields since taking their initial counseling courses. Others have grown tired, discouraged, and burned out, and their effectiveness has declined. Some of our counseling colleagues live in remote areas where additional training and continuing education opportunities are many miles away. How, then, can we improve our knowledge, keep up to date, and continue to grow after we complete our formal training as counselors?

These questions bring us to the issue of continuing education, which can occur in several ways.

1. *Seminars and workshops.* Perhaps thousands of these are offered every year, geared for all levels of counseling expertise and competence. These programs may last from a half-day to several weeks in duration. Some are open only to Ph.D.'s, M.D.'s, or ordained ministers, but many are open to anyone who applies. Often the seminars are held in locations far removed from university or seminary campuses. Some, for example, are offered in conjunction with professional conventions or with denominational annual meetings. These training experiences vary in quality and usefulness, but most give up-to-date information, contact with counseling colleagues, and needed breaks from sometimes difficult counselees. The best workshops also give the continuing education credits that many states and professional organizations require practitioners to acquire annually.

2. *Courses.* Most often these are offered in academic or treatment centers although some, especially courses in lay counseling, are given in churches, at retreat facilities, or elsewhere in the community. When the courses are offered in affiliation with a college or seminary, academic credit is available that can be applied toward a degree.

Do courses improve our effectiveness as counselors? The answer, as all of us know, depends on the course and on the teacher. Some educational experiences are difficult to apply to our lives and our work. For example, courses on "integration" that form part of Christian graduate training programs may have little impact or relevance on the therapeutic work of practitioners after graduation.[32]

3. *Home study.* Reading books or journal articles, watching videos, listening to audio cassette tapes, or completing computer-based learning programs[33] can all be helpful in giving information. These and other instructional-based programs may improve knowledge but, as

we have seen, knowledge alone does not make a sensitive, astute, capable counselor. Excellence in counseling involves development of skills that are practiced, honed, and used repeatedly so the counselor does not become an unskilled (and therefore less effective) people helper.

4. *Peer review and peer accountability.* Within recent years, accountability has become a popular word. Almost everybody believes in its importance, but relatively few have others to whom they can be genuinely accountable.

There can be great value in reviewing one's counseling with trusted colleagues or with more experienced counselors who are able to give their observations and suggestions.[34] With the permission of counselees sometimes it is possible to have a colleague observe and evaluate one's counseling. Fellow counselors often can spot early signs of burnout, emotional depletion, impatience, insensitivity, unrealistic expectations (including unrealistic expectations of ourselves), rigidity, or other evidences of counselor stress. Others often see what we do not see or want to see. The support and encouragement of fellow counselors can be personally therapeutic and indirectly helpful for our counselees. On occasion there also can be value in going to another counselor for our own counseling. This can give greater insights into our work-related and other tensions and, in turn, we are able to return to our own counseling with a greater degree of effectiveness.

Interactions with other counselors can improve counseling quality and stimulate collegial accountability, but at times these experiences also trigger threat and resistance, especially in counselors who feel inferior to their peers. Sometimes, as a result, the people who most need peer interactions find reasons to drop out of consultation groups.[35]

5. *Nonprofessional input.* Involvement with other counselors can be stimulating, supportive, and satisfying, but too much involvement with colleagues can be stifling. To keep our perspectives fresh and growing, each of us needs to get away from counseling on a regular basis. We need to build relationships with family, friends, and fellow believers who are not counselors and may have no interest in our work. We need to develop and stimulate interests in activities, books, recreation, and other sources of diversion that have little to do with counseling. If at all possible, we should find opportunities for travel—especially in other countries. Few experiences can be more broadening and en-

lightening, especially for those who are able to learn from their travels and not get bogged down with attitudes of superiority or with criticisms of the way things are done in other societies. The counselor whose interests don't go much beyond helping others in a narrow geographical area is a counselor who is in danger of drying up, burning out, and becoming dull, regardless of the numbers and varieties of continuing education courses that might be taken.

Never forget that counselors are people-experts. Our abilities to understand and relate to complex human beings will be enhanced if we can avoid entrapment with the problems of others and if we can work to become multi-interested human beings ourselves.

Selecting Continuing Education

In most parts of the world, counselors have limited opportunities for continuing education; but in English-speaking North America we have more offerings than we can handle. How do we get information and make selections?

Seminars, workshops, courses, and other educational opportunities are usually advertised by brochures that come in the mail or by advertisements in denominational and professional publications. For Christian learning opportunities, watch the pages of magazines such as *Leadership, Christianity Today*, or *Moody*. The *Journal of Psychology and Theology* or the *Journal of Psychology and Christianity*, which include articles of interest to Christian counselors, sometimes list conferences and seminars as well. If you are part of a professional organization, watch for conference listings in trade publications. As a psychologist, for example, every month I receive a newspaper titled the *APA Monitor*. A recent issue listed over four hundred upcoming professional seminars and workshops with topics ranging from working with dysfunctional families or counseling alcoholics to a seminar on "entrepreneurial jump-starting" and another on counseling the Indo-Chinese client. Many of these same sources of information include useful articles, but look also for book notices or reviews of videotapes and other resources.

Over one thousand new books are published every week—more than even the Library of Congress can tabulate. Most of these are far removed from counseling issues, but many publications do have relevance for our work or could be read with profit by our counselees. How do we siphon out the mounds of psychological junk and spend our time and money on publications that truly are worth reading? Try to get past the flashy covers and "blurbs" on the dust jackets and back covers. These tend to be written by advertising people who are intent on selling books, but who often have no time to read. (Most authors, I suspect, have been amazed at what appears in the advertising that accompanies their books). Better selection criteria include the following questions. (Although these refer to books, you could ask similar questions about workshops, seminar speakers, academic courses, and other continuing education opportunities.)

1. *Who is the author and what are his or her qualifications for writing the book?* Television personalities and popular pastors are not always the best qualified to give advice on personal matters. Experts in one area of counseling may not be experts in every area.

2. *Who published the book?* Some publishers (including several Christian publishers) major in the sensational and seem to be minimally concerned about quality or accuracy. Others come from a theoretical or theological perspective that you may not want to absorb or recommend. Try to find trustworthy and reputable publishers. Browse in a bookstore and find out what kinds of books each publisher produces. The store manager may be able to help with your investigation.

3. *Who recommends the book?* If a recommender's name appears on the book cover or in the advertising, ask if this is a person whose opinion you value and trust. Book reviews in journals, magazines, and newspapers often give a more balanced evaluation of the book, but remember that reviews sometimes say more about the reviewer's personality and biases than about the book.

4. *What do your friends say about the book?* It is an axiom in the publishing industry that "word of mouth" is the best advertising. If somebody you know and respect has read and appreciated a book, that can be a good indication about whether you might do the same.

5. *Do the book's self-help techniques work?* This is harder to determine but important for counselor self-education. Even writers with good credentials may make sweeping generalizations that are not backed up by facts. (The previous sentence may be an example!) Seek to determine, therefore, if there is any convincing documentation to back up the book's claims.

I have a counselor friend who has limited time but a strong desire to keep aware of trends and developments in his field. He prays regularly about his own continuing education, asking God to lead him to educational opportunities and books that he should read, and to give him the wisdom to ignore the rest. This is an obvious, usually overlooked, and significant way to select the most effective means for continuing education.

LICENSING, CERTIFICATION, AND SELF-DISCLOSURES

During the time when I was writing this chapter, I had lunch with a young man who wanted to see a counselor about some vocational and insecurity issues.

"I'm an engineer," he said. "I don't know anything about counseling and haven't any idea how to find someone who is competent and also a Christian."

My friend is not alone in his dilemma. "Christian counselors" seem to be plentiful; *competency* in Christian counselors may be harder to find.

In a frightening description, lawyer Steve Levicoff describes how easily any one of us could create a diploma mill that gives meaningless but legitimate sounding degrees in Christian counseling or any other field.[36] Sadly, many people become victims of these diploma mills and sincerely believe that they are qualified and certified as Christian counselors. Their counselees don't realize that these counselors are incompetent and that their credentials are meaningless. As a result, considerable counseling harm can be done.

How, then, can potential counselees like my friend determine who is qualified to counsel and who is not? To answer, we must consider issues of licensing, credentials, and self-disclosure.

Licensing

I am a licensed psychologist. The license came from the state where I live and is available to any person who has a doctorate in clinical or counseling psychology from a government-recognized training institution, has completed several hundred hours of supervised counseling, and has passed the national licensing examination. The license shows that I have met the requirements of the state licensing agency, but does it mean that I am competent to counsel?

Not necessarily.

Licensing laws differ from state to state and vary from one country to another. But they all are designed to indicate who in the community has met minimum training standards and who, as a result, can charge fees for offering psychological services. In looking for a counselor, consumers can know that a licensed counselor at least has successfully completed a rigorous training program.

But that does not mean that licensees are effective as counselors. In the state where I live, I can have my license renewed without further examination so I could never see a counselee ever again, but still legally call myself a licensed clinical psychologist.

Some critics argue that licensing doesn't do much to protect the public against incompetence, but instead creates groups of self-serving professional monopolies. Often the people in these groups control licensure and protect their own self-interests rather than protecting the public from poor counseling services.

Many Christian counselors are licensed, most often as psychologists, psychiatrists, social workers, or professional counselors. We have to be licensed if we are to function legally as professionals. Since licensing comes from the state there are no people (to my knowledge) licensed as "Christian counselors" or as pastoral counselors.

Certification

Licensing and certification both seek to insure minimum standards for counselors, stem quackery, and protect the public from incompetence. But certification usually comes from professional organizations who seek to evaluate the competence of members. The National Board for Certified Counselors, for example, or the National Academy of Certified Clinical Mental Health Counselors, both offer examinations leading to professional certification of counselors.[37]

The value of certification, like the value of a license, depends on the certification agency and on whether or not certified people really are expected to show competence. If the agency has meaningless standards or if it exists to produce an elite group of "us versus them" counselors, then the certification is useless. Unfortunately, people who seek counseling don't know this and may be impressed when somebody advertises that he or she is a "certified Christian counselor."

Self-Disclosure

Are there better alternatives to licensing and certification as they currently exist? In most states, we take a test to get a driver's license and periodically we have to be tested again before the license can be renewed. Could something similar happen with licensed or certified counselors? This periodic reassessment could weed out people who have diplomas but have lost their counseling skills.

More realistic, perhaps, is the suggestion of an annual disclosure statement that counselors would file with the state if they are licensed, with the certification agency if they are certified, and with their counselees. Recent writers have noted that the practice of self-disclosure seems to be gaining in popularity in view of the growing consumer movement.[38]

What would appear on the disclosure statement? That is being debated, but several topics have been suggested including these:

- a statement of the counselor's degrees and other training, including the field of study in which the degree was granted;
- a statement of counseling goals and philosophy, accompanied, perhaps, with some indication of the proposed length of treatment and anticipated outcomes;
- a summary of counselor beliefs and values;
- a fee structure; and
- a report of the number of clients seen during the past year and the average number of counseling sessions per client.

Could Christian counselors take the lead in producing such statements? Some may resist making such disclosures, but the process could be voluntary (unless licensing and certification groups required disclosure statements for continuation of credentials). The procedure could be of great help to counselees and could benefit more competent counselors who are willing to be open about their work.

Conclusion

Excellence and quality in Christian counseling can be no better than the quality of those who of us who are Christian counselors. And the quality of Christian counselors often depends on one's training and efforts at continuing education.

Several of my friends are in the magazine industry. Every month or every quarter they have to produce new and fresh material for their readers. Pastors have an even greater challenge: to come up with new sermons, sometimes several times every week.

My magazine friends (and, I suspect, most pastors) almost never get away from looking for ideas, anecdotes, material that they can put into the next publication. "My mind is like an idea file," a magazine editor said to me recently, "and the file drawer is always open."

Maybe Christian counselors need similar attitudes toward the quality of their work. Always keep your mind open for ways of making improvements. If we do that, we will see increasing quality in Christian counseling as we move into the future.

CHAPTER SEVEN

TRENDS IN CHRISTIAN COUNSELING

SEVERAL MONTHS BEFORE I was scheduled to speak at the Australasian Congress on Christian Counseling in Melbourne, I began reading about Australia and New Zealand. I had visited both countries previously and knew the importance of a foreigner's being well informed before speaking to Australian audiences.

The writings of one fascinating author, a pastor named John Smith, were especially helpful in giving me insights into the people who live in the land "down under." At the beginning of his analysis of contemporary Australian culture, Smith tells about a young man whom he met in the inner city.

> A kid came to me once on the street—a switchblade packing kid from an inner-Melbourne suburb. Offering me a wee chink of

possibility he said, "Okay, mate. Tell me what God's like and I will talk to you." His response was a concession: it was obvious that he didn't particularly want to talk.

At the time, I was studying the Lord's Prayer at Bible college, so the answer came readily. In my terrible ignorance of his environment I said, "Well, son, God is like a father."

His eyes filled with hatred as he bitterly declared, "If He's anything like my bloody bastard old man, you can stuff Him up your jumper." I found out later that his sister had been raped by their father, a man who regularly beat up his wife and children after a few too many drinks. The angry kid walked away and I was left in pieces, feeling stupid, angry and ignorant in my naive approach.

If one adolescent's history so distorted his view of fatherhood, how much more has the painful childhood experience of this nation shaped its belief in divine irrelevance—or worse, rejection and judgment. It is my conviction that the roots of our history have firmly planted within us false, inadequate and prejudicial views of life, meaning and relationships.[1]

As a visitor to Australia, I was not qualified to comment on Smith's views about his own country, but most of us would agree that we are shaped, at least in part, by our national histories, our family histories, and our personal histories. Especially within the past decade, hundreds of books and articles have demonstrated how dysfunctional families, abusive past experiences, and personal traumas have adversely shaped the lives of people who often carry their wounds throughout adulthood. Less prominent are stories of innumerable lives shaped for the good by loving parents, supportive teachers, caring churches, and happy childhood experiences.

What is true of nations, families, and individuals can also be true of organizations, academic institutions, churches, businesses, and professions. Every field of endeavor, including counseling, has been shaped by the past. "Any nation, to some extent, is a reflection of the thinkers who go before it," Smith wrote elsewhere in his book about Australia. "The intellectuals and the thinkers—those who struggle with the great questions of life—may not rule in the political sphere, but in the long run they do so by default."[2]

Even though we have been shaped by the intellectuals, thinkers, and counselors who have gone before us, we are not helpless victims of the past. Just as that past has shaped where we are now, so we can have an impact on the future. We can either chart and steer the ultimate course of Christian counseling or we can allow ourselves to bob about, rudderless, in an ocean of conflicting secular theories, techniques, and trends.

FUTURIST PREDICTIONS

Long before the start of this decade, forward-thinking authors and publishers were rushing to get books into print that would predict what life will be like as we move toward a new century and into the next millennium. If you read these books, you will find that most authors have done their homework, analyzed trends, and presented fascinating glimpses of the future.

Writing about life at the turn of the twenty-first century, for example, a man described as "American's leading forecaster" coauthored an upbeat prediction of what we can anticipate in the year 2000 and beyond. According to these futurists, we can expect that 22 percent of all people will work out of their homes, that universal child care will be free so both spouses can work, that women will earn salaries comparable to those of men, and that job-switching will be the norm. We can further expect that the divorce rate will decline, that artificial blood and "bloodless surgery" will reduce health costs, and that children will be more spoiled than they are now. (Some may wonder if that is possible!) There will be new directions in business, politics, science, technology, and values, these authors suggest. Religion will face major changes, including a return to faith, continued growth in theologically conservative Protestantism, and a greater number of women in positions of church leadership. Surprisingly, the book's four hundred pages never mention mental illness, psychiatry, psychological disorders, or counseling. [3]

Writing about business in the future, Chicago advertising executive Joe Cappo notes that information, technology, and service industries will dominate the economy in the coming years. The population will be older, the middle class will be smaller, interest rates will be lower, and because we have become saturated with possessions, the demand for "experiences" will increase, creating a whole new industry. That industry, Cappo suggests in a statement that will jar some readers, includes "growing interest and involvement in such experiential activities as the *est* movement, group therapy, evangelical religions and yoga."[4]

Writing from a different perspective, Christian researcher George Barna predicts that organizations in the future, including churches, will have to prove their worth or they will be rejected. People will travel more and have less time to volunteer for church-related activities. There will a greater interest in education, an upsurge of involvement in Eastern religions that compete directly with the church, and increasing litigation. "Personally, each of us in leadership positions must be prepared for legal encounters," Barna writes. "Family and psychological counselors may be especially vulnerable during the '90s, as more people seek advice and counsel, but find the outcomes frustrating and unsatisfying."[5]

At the same time, television evangelist (and one-time presidential candidate) Pat Robertson has identified ten rather obvious trends that could impact all of us by the year 2000. His list includes the collapse of communism, the emerging power of Europe and the East, the decline of America as a world leader, scandal in public education, a continuing assault on values and the family, a renewed interest in the supernatural, the impact of space-age technology on the quality of life, the ravaging of our natural resources, and *either* world-wide peace and prosperity or war and collapse.[6]

Slightly more insightful are the power shift ideas presented by futurist Alvin Toffler[7] and the megatrends listed by Naisbitt and Aburdene.[8] The megatrends list has been reported widely in the media although the book, like several of the others, tends to be dull. As the decade ends, according to Naisbitt and Aburdene, we will be seeing a global economic boom, renaissance in the arts (and a parallel declining interest in sports), the emergence of free-market socialism, global lifestyles and cultural nationalism, the privatization of the welfare state, women in significant leadership roles, the age of biology, a religious revival (that appears to be more New Age than Christian), a triumph of the individual, and the rise of the Pacific rim. This, of course, includes the United States, Canada, Australia, and New Zealand; but according to the book authors the Pacific economies will be dominated by Japan, China, and "the Four Tigers—South Korea, Taiwan, Hong Kong and Singapore."

It should come as no surprise that others have picked up the challenge of predicting the future, including psychologists and counselors who are interested in the direction of their professions.[9] Writing about future trends in the practice of psychotherapy, for example, Christian psychologist James D. Guy notes that substantial changes in training and in the delivery of services are likely in the next few years. Guy writes that despite "advances and progress in service delivery, it is now apparent to the general public that psychotherapy is not going to cure society's ills, nor is it going to be helpful to everyone in personal distress. Among some individuals, this has led to a sense of disillusionment and cynicism regarding its utility and effectiveness." There has been a dramatic decrease in third-party payments for professional counseling and this, in turn, has led to increased out-of-pocket expenses for counselees. With increased training facilities, there has been an upsurge in the number of counselors, including Christian counselors. Many of these will have to compete for clients in a time when money for counseling services is short and legal action is more likely whenever there is even a hint of incompetence or malpractice. Consumers no longer regard counselors as mysterious figures but instead come for help with a host of challenging questions and expectations that counselors will be competent and able to help. "Increasing competition and a constantly shifting job market may be a source of considerable anxiety for future practitioners," according to Guy's book.[10]

Some of this may sound academic and far removed from the everyday work of Christian counselors. Nevertheless, these are issues that can shape the course of our work in the future. It may be comfortable to retreat into our offices or church counseling centers and focus solely on our counselees, but potentially significant changes are taking place in the society around us and in the counseling field. Instead of waiting for these changes to come and bring surprise, it is wiser to be aware of the trends in counseling and to help shape their direction.

SUGGESTIONS FOR THE FUTURE

As we have seen, predictions about the future are not always scientific and sometimes they are built more on the predictor's fantasies and interests than on careful analysis. The following suggestions might better be called *hypotheses*, which is a technical word for "good guesses about what might be, based on what we have seen so far." The following Christian counseling "megatrends" (they are not listed in any intended order of importance) may not prove to be accurate predictors of what will concern us in the year 2000, but these are issues that should be discussed if we are to avoid drifting as a group of professional and pastoral caregivers.

The Influence of New Age Thinking

When he began research for a major book on the New Age movement, Russell Chandler, religion writer for the *Los Angeles Times*, interviewed a man who is one of the world's best authorities on New Age thinking. "You can do one of two things," Chandler was told by the consultant. "You can either keep up with the New Age movement, or you can write about it—but not both."[11]

The journalist soon learned how right this was. "New Age is a hybrid mix of spiritual, social, and political forces, and it encompasses sociology, theology, the physical sciences, medicine, anthropology, history, the human potentials movement, sports, and science fiction."[12] It is not an organization to be joined or a creed to follow. "In my opinion," Chandler concluded, New Age thinking is "neither the hellish conspiracy that fundamentalist critics charge, nor the utopian bliss its fondest supporters imagine."

But it may be the fastest growing belief system in this country, a way of thinking that is difficult to define and often too elusive to evaluate carefully. *Time* magazine has called it "a combination of spirituality and superstition, fad and farce, about which the only thing certain is that it is not new." It is a "cloudy sort of religion," according to the magazine, a religion that claims "vague connections with both Christianity and the major faiths of the East . . . plus an occasional dab of pantheism and sorcery. The underlying faith is a lack of faith in the orthodoxies of rationalism, high technology, routine living, spiritual law and order. Somehow, the New Agers believe, there must be some secret and mysterious shortcut or alternative path to happiness and health."[13]

According to most New Age advocates, we live in a universe without a personal God. Each of us is a god in disguise with inner potential, wisdom, and knowledge that can bring out our god-potential. The human race never had a Fall, there is no link between our future happiness and events in the life of Jesus, and salvation is really a matter of self-improvement. We are living at the dawn of a new age, the Age of Aquarius when humanism and brotherhood will come into their own.[14]

This philosophy has spawned a mass of popular books, journals, seminars, and media presentations that feature ghosts, astrology, crystals, channeling, and an "eclectic collection of psychological and spiritual techniques rooted in eastern mysticism." Although some consider it a passing fad and others view it as a harmless diversion, many people, including experts in cultic issues, have noted its potential to be extremely harmful.[15] The movement has attracted attention and followers around the world, and is a serious competitor to both Christianity and the work of Christian counselors.

New Age thinkers are not all ignorant, narrow-minded individuals who have been duped into following some world conspiracy. Many who embrace New Age thinking are highly educated, intelligent people who are frustrated with secularism, empty traditionalism, rigid rationalism, self-centered hedonism, and the spiritual emptiness that pervades Western societies. Often, New Agers are compassionate people who are searching. They have little interest in redemption, forgiveness of sin, and a relationship with God. Instead, they anticipate a "new world order" and seek enlightenment, especially through the ancient religions of the East.

Perhaps it is not surprising that the New Age movement appears to have made its greatest gains through the helping professions, especially psychology.[16] People in the movement make no attempts to preach or coerce people into New Age thinking. Instead, these ways of thinking are introduced gently, often by sincere (but misguided) people who advance their ideas in the context of counseling and compassionate care for hurting people. New Age ideas slip into counseling through journal articles, convention speeches, and professional workshops.

The New Age movement is with us to stay, according to most observers. To be effective in the future, Christian counselors must be aware of and able to counteract popular movements in the culture that are deceptive, ineffective, and in opposition to Christianity.[17] The New Age movement is high on this list of harmful movements.

The Increasing Influence of Cults and Satanism

Almost as difficult as keeping abreast of the New Age movement is keeping aware of cults and their apparently growing influence.[18] Cults are especially attractive to impressionable young people, many of whom are disillusioned with the church; but the cult influence goes further. In a sobering paper presented to an international conference on missionary kids, one speaker described how spiritually committed young Christians, many of whom know the Bible and come from good evangelical homes, nevertheless can be pulled into cults without any awareness of what is happening.[19] Recruitment and indoctrination into cults is subtle and potentially disastrous.

Closely related is the occult-related violence and ritualistic abuse that police departments, media, and counselors have noted during the past few years. While some believe that satanic abuse doesn't exist except as emotionally charged rumor[20] others present convincing evidence that satanic and occult influences are very real, powerful, and the cause of great spiritual and psychological pain or inner turmoil, both for the victims and for their loved ones.[21]

Counselors who know about spiritual warfare cannot ignore these disturbing trends; they are likely to create new counseling challenges in the decade ahead. Christians are beginning to write about counseling and the demonic in ways that are intellectually clear, professionally respectable, and far beyond the sometimes dramatic and over-emotional exorcisms that have characterized segments of the church for centuries.[22] We no longer can counsel completely oblivious of the devil, as if he is nonexistent. The enemy is strong and perhaps getting stronger even though he will face certain defeat in the end.

The Growth of Popular People-Helping Approaches

Sometimes counselors forget the host of nonprofessional helpers who live and have an influence in almost every community. Some, like teachers, clergy, lawyers, doctors, and nurses, are members of professions that have been around longer than ours. Equally important are networks of nonprofessional lay counselors,[23] social-support groups,[24] and neighbors who give help over the back fence or talk over coffee in a restaurant. Church groups, members of bowling leagues, or friends who talk together on the way home from a basketball game may never think of themselves as counselors, but they give help to one another nevertheless—often more than is ever given by therapists or pastoral care specialists who work in offices.

Why is this of concern to counselors who are pondering their futures? First, counselors continue to be mistrusted by many people, including pastors. Some people would never admit that their problems could benefit from counseling, but these same people might have no hesitation talking with a friend in the community. Instead of working against lay counselors and mutual aid groups, we need to be working cooperatively with them. If we eliminate the "we-they" distinctions between helping groups, almost everybody benefits.[25]

Second, when we know about community resources, we can assist those who are trying to decide where they might go for help. Often the counselor's work is greatly aided by small groups in the community, books or other reading materials, tapes, and the influence of a supportive local church.

Third, the counselor has a responsibility to alert people to groups, publications, training materials, and Christian ministries that are fraudulent, promising what they cannot produce, and claiming to be helpful when they really are not. Recent evidence suggests, for example, that some television ministries make claims that are theologically wrong and potentially harmful psychologically.[26] "Don't go to counselors if you have marriage problems," a famous speaker told his television audience. "We don't need counselors. Just bring your marital disagreements to the altar," he advised, and all your problems will fall away and be resolved.

Frequently, counselees realize that such thinking is simplistic and often they know, too, about the latest people-helping trends and fads. Counselors should know about these too. In the future we must be able to help people deal with the trends that claim to help but sometimes do not.

The Problems of Populations at Risk

Some people are more likely to have problems than others. As we have noted, those who grow up in dysfunctional families often have difficulty adjusting to adult life.[27] Children of alcoholics are more prone to become alcoholics. The poor, victims of abuse, school dropouts, teenage parents, the disabled, care-givers who are responsible for chronically ill relatives, victims of rape, the unemployed, survivors of cults, people who have experienced intense trauma—these are what have come to be known as *populations at risk*.

According to Edwin Herr, people who are victims of traumatic backgrounds or "who experience unusual amounts of stress from losing a job or being constantly thwarted in their efforts to become part of the social mainstream are likely to manifest physical symptoms and stress-related disease, mental disorders, chemical dependency, family difficulties and, possibly, abusive behavior. These behaviors . . .

trigger ripple effects that flow through the interpersonal systems of which they are part."[28]

How do we help with these people? With rare exceptions they are not emotionally disturbed and most would not be classified as mentally ill. Nevertheless, many live with intense stress and often they lack the psychological or spiritual resources, knowledge, coping skills, or social support that would help them deal more effectively with the pressures of life. Few would be likely to seek a counselor. If they did, many of our traditional problem-solving therapeutic techniques might not be helpful.

Throughout its history, counseling has been a rehabilitative enterprise. Our goals have centered around interventions that are intended to fix something that has gone wrong within the counselee or in his or her environment. We have tied ourselves to a philosophy of repair and have done little to develop principles of prevention. Many of us have become therapeutic specialists, independent private practitioners in a society where "systems of service delivery—not independent practitioners operating at an *individual* level—will dominate future policies."[29] Because we have built our methods almost exclusively on a one-on-one counseling model and a pay-for-service approach to helping, we may have decreased our ability to help populations at risk and we might even be in danger of contributing to our own obsolescence.[30] Many counselors and counseling students have "too much knowledge about things that do not matter and too little wisdom about things that do."

Counselors in the future will have to be broadly educated, knowledgeable consultants and teachers working with relatively normal people who have made poor decisions, entered unhealthy relationships, or been victims of stress-inducing circumstances. Traditional psychotherapy will always exist, but perhaps most people helpers of the future should be a stress-management experts who can operate in a variety of settings to help others face the challenges of moving through life. According to one creative report, counselors in the years ahead may be most effective if they are facilitators of caring and sharing, facilitators of life transitions, brokers of vital and relevant information, and facilitators of change by which people are helped to acquire needed skills.[31]

In all of this we need to think of new and creative ways to be effective people helpers to populations at risk, including immigrants and native peoples. We must always remember that God's grace and psychological healing are not only for white YAVIS people (young, attractive, verbal, intelligent, successful). As we approach the next century, the counseling fields may have to move beyond a rehabilitation mind-set, focusing instead or in addition, on prevention and on teaching people how to cope. In many ways, this is what the church has been trying to do for centuries.

The Changing Family

Much has been written about the contemporary family, especially the Baby Boomer families. Books and seminars on marriage and family therapy seem to exist in abundance. Surely thousands of sermons have been preached on the subject of families and graduate training programs in counseling almost always include at least one course on family therapy. Even casual newspaper readers are bombarded with statistics about divorce rates, battered women (and men), sex apart from marriage, abused children, the changing roles of women, and nontraditional living arrangements such as multiadult households, homosexual partnerships, and single-parent homes. Family problems differ from one country to another (and from one part of the country to another), but these problems are prevalent everywhere. And regardless of the culture, we know that troubled and dysfunctional families tend to produce troubled and often dysfunctional children.

Christian counselors have a challenge—to do what we can to strengthen family stability and to reduce family dysfunctioning, even though this effort may set us in conflict with numerous antifamily trends within the society.

Within the past decade or two, family counseling has grown significantly in its influence and importance. The methods and theoretical approaches are still being developed and refined, but most assume that problems are better resolved within the context of a family group rather than in one-to-one counseling with an individual family member. Often the focus of counseling is on marital problems or other interpersonal tensions within the home, but family approaches now extend to a variety of related problems including chemical dependency, family abuse, learning problems, adolescent rebellion, eating disorders, and even sexual dysfunction.[32]

Some observers have suggested that family approaches tend to be insensitive to cultural and subcultural differences. Families are shaped by traditions, family rituals, ethnic group membership, personal values of the family members, and religion. Blended families or multiracial families, for example, will be different from Hispanic, wealthy, alcoholic, evangelical, minority, military, inner-city, single-parent, or pastoral families. The unique features of each must be considered if family therapy is to be effective. All of this creates a significant challenge for counselors in the future, especially as multiple stressors continue to affect families and create increasing pressures in the lives of family members.[33]

The Changing Age of Our Population

Almost all of us know that the average age of our population is increasing. Largely because of advances in nutrition and medicine, people are living longer and the elderly are becoming more numerous.

Until recently, only one person in ten could expect to live to the age of sixty-five, but today nearly 80 percent of Americans will live past that age. When the first wave of the Baby Boom generation reaches their mid-sixties (in about twenty years) the numbers of people who are senior citizens will increase radically; and by the year 2020, people over sixty-five are likely to comprise one-fifth of our population. One book has called this "age wave" the most important trend of our time.[34]

The later years can bring a unique set of problems including anxiety, insecurity about the future, frustration, and unrelieved loneliness. Many older people feel in the best of health but they are forced into retirement and feel useless, in the way, or "on the shelf." Often they experience *ageism*, a form of stereotyping and discrimination against the elderly that can be as unfair and as devastating as sexism or racism.

Longitudinal studies confirm that there is little change in overall psychological symptoms as people grow older.[35] Even so, in the later years there are stress-related problems, many of which center around one word: loss. As we get older, we can lose health, the efficiency of our sense organs, mobility, useful employment, self-esteem, independence, memory and other cognitive capacities, physical attractiveness, the ability to control circumstances, purpose for living, relationships with important others, a familiar "old house," and sometimes hope. When a spouse or lifelong friend becomes chronically ill, we lose companionship. When a mate or other close person dies, the loss is irreplaceable.

Although counseling could be helpful in situations like these, many older people resist. Some have the idea that counseling is for people with "nervous breakdowns," or for weak individuals who have to see a "head doctor," because they "can't pull themselves up by their own bootstraps" and go on. Others may be willing to get counseling but they can't afford it, don't know where to find a counselor, or feel too unworthy to take a counselor's time.

Thus far, most of us are ill-equipped to counsel the elderly. Journals such as *Psychology and Aging* describe the changes and stress reactions of older people,[36] but we have a long way to go in developing creative approaches to counseling with older adults. This will be an issue that demands greater attention in the years ahead. There will also be a need for flexibility.

Because they often resist or misunderstand counseling, older people may need to be approached in unique and less threatening ways.[37] This flexibility will still be needed as we move into the next century. Unlike many older people today, members of the Baby Boom generation are more knowledgeable about counseling and less threatened by traditional counseling methods. Because of this, there will have to be further changes in counseling methodology as new generations reach the later years.

For centuries, pastoral counselors have been calling on older parishioners, supporting them in times of grief or loneliness, helping them face loss, giving them purpose for living, and helping them face death. In many ways, therefore, we who are Christians are ahead of our secular colleagues in helping the elderly, although in other ways we are far behind. Christian training programs rarely discuss aging or problems of the elderly and thus far Christian writers have contributed little to the literature on gerontological counseling. In part this may reflect our own *gerontophobia*—fear of getting old. More likely, we have put our attentions and interests on other topics and neglected this important and emerging area of counseling need.

Building Christian Counselor Credibility and Excellence

Throughout its brief history as a scientific discipline, psychology has frequently been at odds with Christianity. Despite genuine efforts at dialogue and integration, psychologists and church members have ignored each other or engaged in conflict, often fueled by vocal critics on both sides.[38] Christian critics, for example, have accused evangelical counselors of being sincere but naive, "psychoheretics," seduced by the counseling profession, advocates of "Christian psychology—the evil within the church," or not appreciative of the sufficiency of Christ. Some of the charges lack substantial backing and many appear to be largely a reflection of the critic's bias or anger. But many of the criticisms are valid and they come from individuals who are genuinely concerned lest Christian counseling undermine the doctrinal purity or the traditional pastoral care ministries of the church.

Although most of our critics are Christians, non-Christian colleagues sometimes criticize us as well, citing our theological commitments and desire to be *Christian* counselors. All of the criticisms and conflicts could be dismissed as academic skirmishes that have no special significance, but the attackers leave many people confused—especially pastors, students, counselees, others in need of help, and bright young minds who might like to enter our field. We need to respond to these criticisms without making the critics into heroes who in turn might use our responses as fuel for the fires of further criticism that are burned into their books and speeches.

Each of us can learn from the critics and sometimes we may need to respond to their arguments.[39] More often a better response is for Christian counselors to model growing spiritual maturity, counseling competence, ethical and personal purity, the highest integrity, mutual accountability, and a consistent commitment to excellence.

In the years ahead, we must give greater attention to attracting the best Christian minds to the task of Christian counseling, improving training and certification standards, building quality control into our work and our profession, raising the standards of research and continuing education, and producing articles and books that are well written, psychologically solid, and biblically accurate. Then, like Daniel of old, we must be men and women of the highest moral integrity and the greatest spiritual depth.

These are high standards, but a consistent emphasis on counselor integrity, accountability, spiritual sensitivity, and excellence is most likely to insure the health and vitality of Christian counseling in the future.

In all of this it is well to remember that we are not working alone and neither are we working primarily for ourselves or for our professions. Christian counselors, despite our theological and theoretical diversity, are all servants of Jesus Christ. We are dedicated to honoring God in what we do, and to being led by the Holy Spirit. We can go forth into our counseling activities reminded of these words from Colossians 3: 23, 24: "Whatever you do, work at it with all your heart, as working for the Lord, not for men, . . . It is the Lord Christ you are serving."

CONCERNS ABOUT THE FUTURE

"Is there a future for me as a Christian counselor?"

This question, in various forms, comes to me several times every year in letters from strangers, mostly students, who are thinking about their future careers. Most want to be people helpers but they also hope for stable incomes and fulfilling vocations. These letter writers are realistic people, looking carefully at career possibilities before going ahead with lengthy programs of education.

In the pages of this book, I have tried to show that Christian counseling does have a bright future. Despite the competition for jobs that might come if too many people get into the field, this *is* an area where creative and committed believers can serve Christ and their fellow human beings in ways that are meaningful, useful, and God-honoring.

But as in life, so it is true in counseling: All is not perfect. In a book published many years ago, I listed a number of issues that "must be considered . . . if we are to be effective counselors who are competent professionals but also true to our commitment to Jesus Christ and to the truths of the Scriptures."[40] A revision of this list is summarized in Table 7-1.

Several years ago I also cited some disturbing trends in Christian counseling—trends that still appear to exist:

- Competition between Christian counselors and attitudes of superiority that sometimes leave little respect or understanding for other believers whose counseling perspectives are different;
- An uncritical acceptance of secular psychology or, among others, a blanket rejection and condemnation of psychology;
- A psychological-theological dualism in which therapeutic counseling and biblical truth are separated into two compartments in our lives, even though we talk about integration in our classrooms and journals;

- An overemphasis on selfism, including acceptance of secular views about self-esteem, self-fulfillment or self-actualization, with a corresponding tendency to ignore concepts like self-denial or self-sacrifice; and
- A lack of careful evaluation of our counseling goals, theories and methods.

As we move through the nineties, counselors and followers of Jesus Christ need to consider three additional, somewhat more philosophical, issues.

Specialization

In a creative speech before the American Psychological Association, psychologist William Bevan expressed concern that his colleagues were becoming too narrow and specialized.

Christian Counseling: Challenges and Concerns for the Future[41]

A Christian approach to counseling must:

1. Clearly delineate its presuppositional foundations;
2. Clarify its values (what we believe and hold to be important, and why);
3. Recognize the influence of the culture and subcultures both of our communities and of the clients with whom we work;
4. Constantly evaluate our methodology;
5. Continually work to improve the ways in which we select, train, and evaluate the effectiveness of Christian counselors;
6. Acknowledge and influence the increasing impact of nonprofessional approaches to people helping;
7. Always be aware of the influence of religious experience;
8. Give serious consideration to the prevention of problems;
9. Put special emphasis on family issues;
10. Be research oriented, building our methods and conclusions on factual data instead of on sweeping generalizations and personal experiences;
11. Be "body" oriented, recognizing that the Christian is a part of the body of Christ, the local church; and
12. Be biblically based, seeking to build our counseling on Scriptural principles.

Table 7-1

> My concern is . . . that the character of psychology is increasingly manifest in the rapid proliferation of narrowly focused and compulsively insular camps, a proliferation that seemingly knows no limits. We persevere in looking at small questions instead of large ones and our view of the forest is forever obscured by the trees. . . .
>
> Over the years I have found a disturbingly large proportion of the papers I have read to be trivial, some even contrived. The intellectual processes behind them too often have lacked clarity and crispness; manuscripts have been marked by a mindless and routine recitation of detail. . . . Preoccupation has frequently been at the level of data. Few writers have been concerned explicitly with fundamental metaphysical issues. . . .
>
> My growing discontent with psychology over the past several decades stems from, among other things, my perception that too many psychologists hug the intellectual shoreline and are content to paddle quietly in their own small ponds. We live in a coherent world, although one of never-ending complexity. The big questions about it will never be answered if scholars simply attend to the comfortable little questions.[42]

In this long quotation Bevan has touched on a problem that is not limited to psychologists. Many individuals become specialists who know a lot about one or two narrow areas but who have lost sight of the broader problems of people in the wide world where we live. Scholarly papers in psychological, theological, and counseling journals are sometimes so specialized that they become picayune and seemingly unaware of the larger and more complex issues that are brought to counselors or to the church. Such narrow specialization can be stifling and harmful.

But vague generalizations can be equally bad. Christian counseling needs both specialists and generalists, each of which has an awareness of and a respect for the other. In the past, I have likened this to people in the oil business. To get oil from deep in the earth we need specialists who can drill the wells with precision and depth. But we also need generalists who can survey large areas of land, see the entire range of possible or existing oil fields, and determine where the wells should be dug. There is nothing wrong with specialists who dig deeply into one area of the counseling field. But those who plumb the depths need to keep aware of their colleagues who work more broadly in the people-helping field. In turn, those who are generalists must not look down on fellow counselors whose perspectives and work are more focused.

Modernity

Within some academic, theological, and professional circles there currently is a vigorous debate over a philosophy known as *modernity*. Modernity is the unquestioned belief in progress. It assumes that anything recent and up-to-date is better and more useful than things that are older and presumably out of date. According to theologian Thomas Oden, modernity is "a mentality, found especially among certain intellectual elites, which assumes that chronologically recent ways of knowing truth are self-evidently superior to all premodern alternatives."[43]

Modernity has four fundamental values.[44] First there is moral relativism, a view that what is right depends on the culture, social location, and situation. Second, autonomous individualism assumes that moral values and authority come from within the individual. The third value, narcissistic hedonism, focuses on personal pleasure as a guide to behavior. Fourth, reductive naturalism reduces truth and knowledge to what we can see, hear, touch, and empirically validate. These four philosophies have cut us off from rich traditions of the past and have left us rootless and floundering.

If you reread the list, you probably will agree that each of these values appears to be well ingrained in modern counseling and psychology. Oden would argue that each is ingrained in modern theology as well and has spread throughout Western society. Each is inconsistent with biblical truth. And each, along with the whole belief in the goodness of progress, is being attacked in many different areas, including architecture, literature, and music.[45]

Most of us, I suspect, have accepted modernity and belief in progress without much question. We assume that recent books will be more informative and better than books that were published even a few years ago. We attend seminars to learn the latest techniques, assuming that these will be advances over methods that have come before. "Postmodern" thinkers argue, in contrast, that tried and long-tested methods or ways of doing things sometimes (not always) are superior to the latest ideas.

Few counselors or psychologists seem willing to admit that relevant truth about modern problems can be found in the Bible. How strange that many of these same counseling professionals show great interest in the writings and gurus of ancient Eastern religions. Is it overly optimistic to hope that some of our modern colleagues, in time, will be open-minded enough to look seriously at traditional Christian writings, including the Old and New Testaments, or the writers of works in classical pastoral care and spirituality?

Christian counselors must be cautious lest we follow our secular colleagues in their modernity thinking and cut ourselves from the rich store of relevant truth about psychological issues that can be found in the Scriptures and writings of the ancient church fathers.[46]

Individualism

Not long ago, a friend introduced me to the Japanese concept of *Kaizen*, a word that means "ongoing improvement involving everyone." This is a way of thinking that has been called "the key to Japan's competitive success."[47]

In contrast to the emphases on originality, creativity, and innovation in the West, *Kaizen* assumes that small improvements, made as a result of ongoing efforts involving everyone, are even more important than the drastic, innovative changes that sometimes result from the imaginative energy of high-visibility leaders. *Kaizen* assumes that everybody should continually be committed to making improvements and doing better. "There will be no progress if you keep doing things exactly the same way all the time," Japanese workers are reminded frequently. And unlike Western management practices of reviewing and rewarding performance on the basis of results, *Kaizen* also rewards people on the basis of effort.

Perhaps we need a little *Kaizen* in Christian counseling. The Scriptures are strong in their emphasis on mutual support and accountability.[48] Spiritual growth is ongoing and involves encouragement, stimulation, and caring within groups of believers.[49] Shouldn't we be more involved in working together as counselors?

Of course there always will be leaders in any field. Sometimes God uses people such as Moses, Nehemiah, Daniel, Paul, and the apostles to make special contributions to the work of the kingdom. Leaders do emerge in Christian counseling and their ideas can be challenging, stimulating, thought provoking, and sometimes fresh or innovative.

But we must never forget the equal importance of people working together, in *Kaizen* fashion, to improve the field slowly through mutual encouragement, discussion, suggestions for improvement, accountability, interaction at conferences, and more formal journal articles.

Once again, Bevan's observations are insightful. In the future, he suggests, we need more of *"the three Cs—communication, collaboration, and colleagueship."*

Neither university departments nor professional societies do much to stimulate such mutual interaction. "None of us can think of a university department of psychology in which there are more than a very small handful of faculty members who engage in genuine intellectual exchange with one another. As for the professional and scientific associations, political agitation within them usually works to inhibit their taking forceful, coherent intellectual positions on anything. Look at the American Psychological Association (APA). It generates new divisions faster than one can find names for them...."[50]

Each of us must make an effort to insure that a similar isolationism and hyperindividuality does not occur in Christian counseling.

Conclusion

In an address to his colleagues, the editor of the *Journal of Clinical Psychiatry* gave his views of psychiatry in the 1990s. The speaker noted the emerging biopsychosocial technology that is changing the face of professional treatment. He talked about the rising numbers of homeless people, domestic violence that has reached "epidemic proportions," the need to give priority to the treatment of chemical dependency, depression at all levels of society, the significance of research (assuming that "treatment springs from research"), the importance of continuing education for professionals, and the need to provide cost-effective psychiatric treatment that is likely to include short-term and group approaches. In discussing our work as counselors, the speaker noted that it is "undoubtedly easier and more fun for a clinician to discuss enhanced gratification with a well-bred, behaved patient than to pursue a schizophrenic living under a bridge or an intravenous drug abuser in a shooting gallery."[51] But all of these people can be part of the domain of Christian counseling. Few fields hold as much challenge and potential for the future as ours.

In his analysis of future trends in the church, researcher George Barna wrote about the need for Christian communicators to be technologically literate.[52] Computers, fax machines, desktop publishing, videos, modems, or data banks cannot be ignored by the church, but neither can they be overlooked by counselors who want to have an impact in the future. It is not difficult for me to respond to those strangers who write to ask if there is a future in the field of counseling. We have detractors and critics, but the needs and opportunities in Christian counseling both continue to be great.

And as we will see in the next chapter, it is possible that the best is yet to be.

CHAPTER EIGHT
FUTURE DIRECTIONS IN CHRISTIAN COUNSELING
The Best Is Yet to Be

My interest in psychology began when I was a freshman on the campus of McMaster University. In those days, incoming students were initiated into campus life through a week-long process of friendly hazing that culminated in a good-natured "battle" between the freshmen and sophomore class members. While the upperclassmen cheered and the participants fired rotting tomatoes at each other, the freshmen were given twenty minutes to slither up a heavily greased pole to retrieve a freshman beanie at the top. If they failed, all incoming students were expected to wear beanies for the first three months on campus.

In the midst of preparations for this first challenge of my academic career, I had an appointment with Professor Patrick. As I recall, he was an austere but friendly man, a scholar whose specialty was French literature and language. Later I discovered that he was a good teacher, highly respected in the academic community. But in our first meeting I learned that he was an expert in dealing with confused incoming freshmen whose main attention was focused on the initiation activities. At the time, I knew nothing about graduation requirements, credits, or scholarship aid, but I knew how to respond when the professor told me that all freshmen were required to take either philosophy or psychology. I didn't know the difference between these two but I did understand the schedule. The psychology class planned to meet on Monday, Wednesday, and Friday. Philosophy would be taught on Tuesday, Thursday, and Saturday mornings. Since I had a Saturday job, I selected psychology. I have been in the field ever since.

In those days there appeared to be few Christians in the fields of psychology or psychiatry. There were no Christian counselor training programs, few licensing laws, no Christian journals, and only a handful of books—most written by a Swiss physician named Paul Tournier. Division 36 of the American Psychological Association—Psychologists Interested in Religious Issues—did not exist and neither did any uniquely Christian organization for professionals in counseling. The pastoral counseling movement was well established and influential, but the theology tended to be liberal and there was little place for nonpastors or for counselors who were theologically conservative.

During the past two or three decades much of this has changed. Counseling has become more acceptable within the church. Counseling courses have become common in colleges and Bible schools, degree programs in Christian counseling have appeared at the master's and doctoral level, several new professional organizations and journals for Christian counselors have come into being, and we have seen a proliferation of radio programs dealing with counseling issues. The publishing industry has seen an exploding interest in self-help books and volumes related to counseling issues. As the field of Christian counseling has grown, there has also been an increase in the numbers of bright, enthusiastic, potential-filled counseling students. Pastoral counseling has made significant strides both in influence and sophistication. And as all of this has been emerging, so too have a handful of vocal, sometimes hostile, critics of Christians in psychology and related fields.

These developments (including the criticisms) have shown that Christian counseling is alive and making an impact. The past few years have been good, but is it possible that the best is yet to be?

In the 1950s, when I was a college freshman, few people had heard of the Ten Boom family from Holland. *The Hiding Place* had not been produced as a major motion picture, and few of us knew about Corrie ten Boom and her family. These brave Christians lived in the Netherlands during the Nazi occupation and hid Jews who were fleeing from capture and almost certain death. Eventually, the Ten Booms were arrested and sent to prison camps where the elderly Papa ten Boom died shortly after his incarceration.

Casper ten Boom had little education, but he was known as the wise man of Haarlem. He had no formal theological training but he was a student of the Scriptures who consistently led Bible studies in several different languages. He had never studied social work or people-helping techniques, but he stimulated his family members to care for young people, to spend hours working with retarded children, to smuggle Jewish babies out of Holland, and to risk their lives to hide Jewish adults who were attempting to escape. Old Mr. ten Boom had no training in counseling, but he was consulted by many people who sometimes traveled for many miles to get his advice and wisdom while they struggled with some problem or decision.

According to one of his neighbors who knew him well, Casper ten Boom had a life motto that guided much of his thinking and behavior. He believed that "the best is yet to be!"

As Christian counseling moves into a new century, its best years could be ahead, especially if its practitioners are guided by important basic values. The following six characteristics are not listed in any special order of importance and neither is this list intended to be complete. If the best is yet to be in Christian counseling, however, much will depend on the traits counselors develop, with the help of God and with the guidance of his Holy Spirit.

INTEGRITY

Integrity is a difficult word to define. It has been described as moral fiber, strength of character, and living beyond reproach. "Integrity is a word for our times!" according to James Dobson. "It may mean different things to different people, but it certainly means keeping our promises . . . doing what we said we would do . . . choosing to be accountable, and taking as our motto, *semper fidelis*—the promise to be *always faithful*.[1]

Most of us, at least in America, are familiar with the much publicized sexual sins of some prominent television evangelists, the reported immorality among some members of Congress, scandals on Wall Street, and the accounts of public officials whose ethical standards are questionable. On television, even prime-time programs show repeated dramas where the heroes have few or no scruples and seem, instead, to be motivated by what Richard Foster has called the lust for money, sex, and power.[2]

Our counselees live in this culture, and so, of course, do we. We too are tempted, sometimes by our fantasies or by our counselees. We too can proclaim one set of values but live by a different set. We can joke about the politicians and television evangelists, but those of us who think we stand firm should be careful that we don't fall (1 Cor. 10:12).

Edgar Guest once wrote a poem that could apply to every counselor:

Myself

> I have to live with myself, and so
> I want to be fit for myself to know,
> I want to be able, as days go by
> Always to look myself straight in the eye;
> I don't want to stand, with the setting sun,
> And hate myself for the things I have done.
>
> I don't want to keep on a closet shelf
> A lot of secrets about myself,
> And fool myself, as I come and go,
> Into thinking that nobody else will know
> The kind of a man I really am;
> I don't want to dress up myself in sham.
>
> I want to go out with my head erect,
> I want to deserve all men's respect;
> But here in the struggle for fame and pelf
> I want to be able to like myself.

> I don't want to look at myself and know
> That I'm bluster and bluff and empty show.
>
> I can never hide myself from me;
> I can see what others may never see;
> I know what others may never know,
> I never can fool myself, and so,
> Whatever happens, I want to be
> Self-respecting and conscience free.

That is integrity. It means personal purity, honest accountability, impeccable Christian standards, and the highest of ethical standards. It must be the mark of Christian counselors—we who seek to guide and help others.

SPIRITUALITY

A graduate student once made a challenging observation. "In our training programs we talk about 'Christian counseling' but almost all of our classes, reading, and therapy seem to focus on 'counseling,' while we hear very little about anything Christian. We emphasize the traits of good counselors, things like empathy, warmth and genuineness, but we give little attention to Christian attributes such as love, joy, peace, patience, kindness, goodness, faithfulness, gentleness or self-control."[3] The student challenged me to develop a seminar course on Counseling and Spirituality. (Subsequently I did.) Such a course, I suggest, should be required for all who enter the field of Christian counseling.

According to Lawrence Richards, "Christian spirituality is living a human life in this world in union with God."[4] Spirituality does not mean withdrawal into esoteric mysticism, monastic separationism, or rigid legalism. The spiritual Christian does his or her work as effectively as possible, lives in his or her community, understands and interacts with the world around, but seeks to be in continuing union and communication with God.

Spirituality does not come automatically and neither does it necessarily lead to continual feelings of ecstasy or mountaintop spiritual exuberance. Spirituality must be nurtured by consistent, disciplined periods of prayer, meditation on the Word of God, study, and corporate worship. Spirituality grows from inward disciplines such as prayer and fasting, outward disciplines like submission or service, and corporate disciplines such as confession and praise.[5]

If the best is yet to be in Christian counseling surely we need practitioners and students who are committed to these spiritual disciplines and are growing in their walks with God. A man or woman may be knowledgeable and skilled in counseling methods but such a person is unlikely to be effective as a *Christian* counselor if he or she neglects personal spirituality.

Perhaps this brings us to the core of Christian counseling. What are we trying to accomplish? What makes our counseling uniquely Christian?

Probably we will never arrive at a clear-cut, categorical, universally accepted definition of who we are and what we do that is distinctive. We have theological, theoretical, personality, and methodological differences that set us apart both from our secular colleagues and from each other. In an earlier book I attempted to give a definition that could allow for these differences and would focus on the counselor's character, traits, and goals. I suggested that the Christian counselor seeks to be "a deeply committed, biblically knowledgeable, Spirit-guided (and Spirit-filled) servant of Jesus Christ who applies his or her God-given abilities, skills, training, knowledge, and insights to the task of helping others move to personal wholeness, interpersonal competence, mental stability, and spiritual maturity."[6] Stated more simply, Christian counselors are committed believers, doing their best to help others, with the help of God. At the core of this is spiritual commitment.

Regardless of our different theologies and religious experiences, surely we cannot claim to be genuine Christian counselors unless we are first of all genuine Christians: followers of Jesus Christ who have acknowledged his lordship, who freely confess their sin and believe that he forgives, who seek to grow in their knowledge of Christ, and who obediently seek divine guidance in their daily lives.

FLEXIBILITY

A few weeks prior to the first International Congress on Christian Counseling someone called to ask if the convention would smooth out individual differences and create a unified approach to Christian counseling. At no time is this likely to happen and neither would it be desirable. Even if we could agree on one "true" theory of personality and one clearly Christian way to counsel, we would be in great danger of becoming rigid, legalistic, insensitive, proud, critical of others and, as a result of all this, largely ineffective. Of course each counselor, each counselee, each problem, and each counseling situation is unique. Despite some early theorists who suggested that counseling should have the same goal for everyone, we now recognize that the goals in counseling are unique.[7] And our approaches to helping have to be unique.

Christian counseling often occurs away from the offices of professionals. Pastors sometimes counsel in hospital rooms and at grave sides. Forensic counselors, including prison chaplains, may meet their counselees in noisy, crowded prison cells. Psychologists who work with victims of disaster are most effective when the counseling takes place close to the trauma location. A recent report described a counselor in New York who works with prominent corporate executives who would never risk appearing at a psychiatrist's office. Instead, the counseling takes place in the back seat of each executive's limousine while the chauffeur drives the car around town. Some might question the ethics or the effectiveness of such variations in therapy, but each is an example of counselor flexibility. Competent counselors know that they have to be flexible in terms of their methods, locations, goals, and times of availability for counseling.

This flexibility will be of increasing importance as counselors face some emerging social trends in the coming years. Let me mention only four of these, some of which have been mentioned in earlier chapters.

Increasing Numbers of People Affected by AIDS. How do we counsel people with AIDS, their families, the people in their churches or communities, and (in some cases) their homosexual lovers? These people may resist coming to our offices and sometimes they are unable to come. In his work with a fundamentalist couple whose son had AIDS, psychologist James Powell had no hesitation in using a variety of methods and working in several different settings to bring a family through an extremely difficult situation.[8] That is Christian counseling flexibility.

The Needs of the Poor and the Homeless. At some time, every counseling student hears that counselors most often focus their efforts on the YAVIS people whom we mentioned in a previous chapter—the *y*oung, *a*ttractive, *v*erbal, *i*ntelligent, and *s*uccessful. These are people most likely to have the time, money, motivation, and verbal skills to benefit from traditional counseling.

In contrast to many of us, Jesus didn't spend much time with *YAVIS* people. More often he moved among the poor, the sick, the lonely, the outcasts, and people in seemingly hopeless situations. He was surrounded by swarms of needy individuals who would not have been helped by our counseling methods or in the places where we do much of our counseling today. Of course the culture was different at that time and so were the people, but we cannot follow Christ and ignore his people-priorities.

Nothing is accomplished by authors who write about social needs and send their readers on guilt trips because they don't work with non-YAVIS people. Certainly no one counselor can or should try to meet all of the social needs that exist at our time of history. But the needy in this world should motivate all Christians to at least some limited action. For counselors this may involve adapting Christian counseling methods so that they can apply to people who are not as verbal or as well educated as many of our clients.

The Aging of the Population. In 1950, people over sixty-five comprised less than 8 percent of the U. S. population. By the early 1990s that figure was around 12 percent. Within the next twenty-five years that number will rise to almost 20 percent. Many of these older people are skeptical of counseling and counselors sometimes resist working with the elderly.

"Geriatric clients are clearly a challenge to most therapists," according to one professional counselor. "They often remind you of your parents, stir up all kinds of countertransference feelings, call you 'dearie,' argue about your fees, and resist having their long stories interrupted when the time is up. Many older people have never discussed feelings with anyone, particularly feelings toward the very person with whom they are talking. They sometimes have cognitive deficits and often have hearing and visual deficiencies. They demand special attention: they want you to fill out their insurance forms, talk to their doctors, call a taxi and wait for it with them. Many times progress means slowing their decline rather than helping them get better."[9]

It has been estimated that older people currently comprise only 2 percent of the case load of private counseling practitioners. This will change as the aging population increases, but if we are to work effectively with such a diverse population it is likely that we will have to be flexible and willing to change some of our approaches to counseling.

The Presence of the Demonic. In one sense, all counseling is in opposition to the influence of Satan and his forces. As Christians, we don't struggle only against flesh and blood. According to the Bible, we struggle against the rulers, authorities, and powers of this dark world and against spiritual forces of evil in the heavenly realms (Eph. 6:12). The devil does create havoc and stimulate sin in this world, and much of our work involves trying to undo what the evil forces have done.

When we focus on the demonic, however, Christian counselors encounter some disturbing attitudes. In the professions that we represent, many of our colleagues are closed-minded and intolerant of anything Christian. Yet they are naively open to a host of Eastern religions and occult practices. In the churches that we represent, many of our fellow worshipers are critical of psychology and related professions but sometimes are naively convinced that all problems are demonic and solvable by exorcisms or other confrontations with the devil.

Most Christian counselors recognize that demonic forces do exist. They hinder our efforts, disrupt the lives of our counselees and often lead us into faulty ways of thinking. But often we go into counseling oblivious to the battle and unaware of the enemy. In some places, naive believers do incredible harm with their frequent and sometimes flamboyant efforts at exorcism, but there are times (not usually and certainly not always) when prayers for deliverance and exorcism are more important and more needed than therapeutic intervention or unconditional positive regard. All of this calls for counselor sensitivity and flexibility.

Beginning counselors tend to look for counseling formulae and never-fail counseling recipes. But these do not exist, largely because each counseling case is unique. We will be of limited effectiveness if we rigidly rely on one approach to counseling amidst the changing social and cultural conditions in which we live. If we are to remain competent, and if the best is yet to be, Christian counselors must be flexible.

GENERATIVITY

In his well-known theory of human development, Erik Erikson describes a time in life when maturing adults turn their attention to *generativity*, the concern for encouraging, establishing, and guiding the next generation. People (and groups of people) who ignore this task tend to stagnate and to experience a "pervading sense of . . . personal impoverishment."[10]

Christian counseling is a young profession and many of our colleagues are in the beginning stages of their careers. For those of us who are in the prime of life (people in our forties and fifties), however, there should be concentrated efforts at encouraging, guiding, teaching, strengthening, mentoring, stimulating, and serving as models for those who are younger.

None of us will be here forever. In the early years of the next century, many of the people who now counsel, present papers, teach, and write books (like this book) will have reached retirement age. A new generation of Christian counselors will have become influential and prominent. These will be the visionaries, leaders, and molders of Christian counseling in the early twenty-first century. They need our prayers, encouragement, and guidance as they pick up the work that we have been doing and try to do it better.

If you look at counseling students or at the younger participants in our professional meetings and denominational conferences, you are likely to spot people with great potential. Some of these future counseling leaders live in North America, but others are scattered around the world. Many are developing approaches to Christian counseling that apply uniquely to their cultures and ethnic groups. We do them (and ourselves) a great disservice if we ignore their efforts or show a "know it all" attitude toward people whose cultures and whose worlds are different from ours. Many of these upcoming colleagues are ahead of us. Even as we encourage and teach them, we can learn from them and become more effective Christian counselors because of our interactions with them.

Sensitivity

Every counselor knows that we must be sensitive to our counselees, but if the best is yet to be, we must also be sensitive to our colleagues, our critics, and the cultures in which we live and work.

Sensitivity to Our Colleagues. Christian counselors are not rescuers, saviors, messiahs, or judges. Neither are we always right, wise, patient, aware of what to do, omniscient, sinless, or available. But we want to help people. We recognize their needs and realize that we have the training and skills to help. Is it surprising that we sometimes fail to say no to the constant requests that come our way? Often we get involved in our people-helping activities and don't get away to rejuvenate, to take care of our own needs, or to gain sufficient rest.

In the midst of our busy activities it is easy to miss the fact that some of our colleagues may also be tired, frustrated, and discouraged. Some may feel like failures. They may struggle financially and feel alone and in danger of sinking in a sea of human need. All of us, at times, can encounter burnout, fragmentation, and impairment.

The term *burnout* probably entered the literature first in 1974 with an article by H. J. Freudenberger.[11] Since that time a number of popular books, seminars, and professional papers have discussed the subject of people (frequently counselors) who reach a state of emotional and physical exhaustion because of the demands that come from working with others.[12] Burnout is an occupational hazard in our profession. It occurs most often in people who work alone without colleague support, have little variation in their schedules (they see one client after another), feel time-pressured, give freely to others without considering their own needs, work with deeply troubled or demanding clients, have stresses in their own homes and careers, and/or sense that their clients may not be getting better.

Fragmentation is a term that is similar to burnout and refers to the problem of feeling overextended, rushing from project to project, pressured by too many commitments and with too little time to finish all that has to be done.

Separately or in combination, burnout and fragmentation can lead to counselor *impairment*. This refers to the personal distress, inner turmoil, feelings of inadequacy, and decline in competency that many counselors face. Our professional colleagues are concerned about helping impaired therapists who are in distress,[13] but do we Christians have a similar concern for our counselor brothers and sisters?

We can begin with ourselves. Burnout, fragmentation, and impairment can be lessened and often prevented when we recognize our own limitations, take time to be with colleagues and with those who are not counselors, and set limits on demanding clients and others who would put us under pressure. Further, we can help ourselves by taking time out for prayer, Bible study, meditation on the Scriptures, reflection, exercise, and diversionary activities, by learning to develop a sense of humor, and never forgetting that we are working, not for other people, but for the Lord (Col. 3:24).

We who are counselors spend many hours helping others, but where does the counselor go for help? Can we find ways to give competent and confidential help to one another? We need to be sensitive to these needs in our colleagues and in ourselves.

Sensitivity to Our Critics. Christians in counseling often encounter criticism both from professional colleagues and from fellow believers. Within recent years several widely read authors have launched broadsides at those of us who work as Christians in the counseling field.

Some of these critics appear to be trouble makers and some may be troubled. A few may be attention-seekers who enjoy the publicity, notoriety, and ego-boost that comes from attacking others, especially those who are prominent, and hoping that those attacked will respond. Some of our critics may be immature. Many appear to be naive and poorly informed. Often their efforts create confusion and harm.

I am torn between answering the critics and ignoring them,[14] but I take the time to be aware of them and to go on doing my work in spite of them. When the critics are other counselors who claim that they are right and I am wrong, I read their books, try to understand their arguments, and learn from their critiques. However vicious or irrational the criticisms, there often are kernels of truth in what they say and we can profit from their observations.

Several years ago I asked Billy Graham's son-in-law (who is a psychologist) how the famous evangelist responded to criticism. The answer was simple and helpful. "Mr. Graham always tries to determine what is right and then he does it!"

The apostle Paul expressed a similar philosophy when he wrote:

> We are taking pains to do what is right, not only in the eyes of the Lord but also in the eyes of men.   (2 Cor. 8:21)

We can learn from other believers without spending our time and energies in fighting them.

In one of his books, Ted Engstrom wrote about a distinguished and generally competent politician who was running for reelection but was being attacked by his opponent in a vicious, mud-slinging, campaign. "Fight back," the politician's advisors suggested, but the man responded instead with a story about his childhood.

The family lived in the country where they had a dog who liked to bark at the moon. Every month, on clear nights when the moon was full, the dog would run up and down barking and snarling at the moon. But the moon never barked back. Instead it just kept on shining—calmly, brightly, beautifully.

When the critics bark at us in their books and lectures, we must not get distracted and let the quality of our work slip while we bark back in endless, fruitless arguments. Instead, we strive to keep on shining, calmly engaged in the work through which we serve God and bring counseling help to others.

Sensitivity to Our Culture. Counseling does not take place in a cultural vacuum. All of us are molded, in part, by family, geographical, economic, ethnic, religious, educational, and gender influences. All of these can have an influence, both in the development of problems and in how people are counseled.

Most of us are aware of these cultural issues and how they influence our counseling, but we have less awareness of the ways by which Christians, including counselors, can influence the culture. Several years ago, a Lutheran businessman named William Diehl had a similar concern. He wondered why his corporate colleagues were so often affected by their culture but had so little impact in return. He wrote:

> Whereas the first-century Christians were part of a movement that ultimately penetrated every nation and class of people in the world, twentieth-century Christians have become virtually invisible in today's world. . . . One looks in vain for evidence that American Protestantism, either mainstream or evangelical, either corporately or through its members, is exerting any lasting influence on this nation's political, social, or economic institutions. Yet the church of the twentieth century proclaims exactly the same message and mission as the church of the first century. What has happened to the Christian faith? . . . Where are God's faithful people? What do they look like?[15]

In an effort to find an answer, William Diehl conducted surveys and interviews, mostly within his own denomination, mostly with businessmen and other lay people. Seven characteristics emerged consistently. These, according to Diehl, are the marks of individuals who have found a way to penetrate their communities and make a difference as Christians.

First, these Christian "difference makers" felt a sense of ministry in their professions and jobs. They sensed that God had allowed them to be where they were, in their vocations, so they could serve him. Do we have a similar sense of calling in our work as Christian counselors? This work can be as significant as any of the more traditional Christian ministries.

Second, Christian difference makers were motivated to grow spiritually. They studied the Bible and were determined to learn how the life and teaching of Jesus could apply to their everyday lives. In discussions with business people, Diehl discovered that they wanted to deal with the "how-tos" of connecting their faith with issues such as the union movement, protectionism, tariffs, competition, government regulation of business, or discrimination against minorities. In counseling, we might consider how the gospel relates to professional ethics, licensing laws for professionals, interdisciplinary issues between mental health professionals, lawsuits against counselors, and training-practice standards. Spiritual growth implies that we seek to apply the truths of Scripture to our everyday lives and work.

Third, the Christian difference makers spent regular times in prayer and meditation on the Scriptures. This was a consistent part of their lives, often scheduled into their daily calendars.

Fourth, almost all of the difference makers in Diehl's study were also involved in a community of believers. For some, this was a church. In addition, most were also involved in small groups or Bible studies. Church growth experts consistently report that strong and growing churches almost always put emphasis on cell groups involving members of the congregation. The same, apparently, is true for individuals who grow spiritually and who are difference makers—for Christ.

Fifth, the difference makers in Diehl's study were generous givers. They resisted the perpetual-accumulation mind-set. Their lives were not motivated by the drive for possessions and affluence. Instead, they were willing to give freely of their time, money, and energy.

Sixth, these Christian difference makers were strongly aware of social issues. They weren't always sure how to help, but they were well-informed about social injustice, poverty, mistreatment of people with different skin color, and similar issues. The Christians in Diehl's research studied social issues, prayed about them, and then took some actions as best they could.

Finally, these people whose faith really made a difference, tended to maintain a relatively simple lifestyle. They were not pushing for power, possessions, and position.

This is not the kind of research that most of us like to hear about. It is easy to dismiss such findings as the chance conclusions of a nonpsychologist who probably didn't know much about research and whose sample was not representative. If we are honest with ourselves, however, most of us are likely to admit that the Diehl research states some principles that are clearly consistent with biblical teaching and applicable to us all.

Christian counselors often use the term *integration* to describe the ways in which psychology and biblical theology can be related. In contrast, William Diehl uses the word to describe how we integrate our Christian principles into our daily lives and work. In his opinion, all of us should be specialists in that kind of integration. If we are to be effective followers of Jesus Christ, surely we must be people whose lifestyles are pleasing to Christ, whose daily work is both psychologically sound and consistent with biblical teachings, and whose professional activities have a penetrating effect (like salt and light) on the cultures in which we live.

QUALITY

When Lyndon Johnson was President of the United States he selected a Republican psychologist to serve in a cabinet level post. Prior to his appointment the cabinet minister, John W. Gardner, had written a book that was required reading in many graduate schools. First published in 1961, Gardner's book is as relevant now as it was then.

Gardner complained about mediocrity in our society, noted that apathy and easiness had become common and suggested that discipline, tenacity, vitality, and drive were no longer valued by most Americans. Few people know the pride and satisfaction that comes in setting standards and keeping them, Gardner wrote, and he issued a call for the pursuit of excellence. Gardner was concerned both about competence and about quality of work. He said:

> We must learn to honor excellence (indeed to *demand* it) in every socially accepted human activity, however humble the

activity, and to scorn shoddiness, however exalted the activity. . . . An excellent plumber is infinitely more admirable than an incompetent philosopher. The society which scorns excellence in plumbing because plumbing is a humble activity and tolerates shoddiness in philosophy because it is an exalted activity will have neither good plumbing nor good philosophy. Neither its pipes nor its theories will hold water.[16]

This emphasis on excellence gets us back to where this book began. As we have seen, quality in counseling is difficult to measure and hard to maintain. The field of counseling is diverse and no one person can be consistently excellent and completely competent in every area of life. Nevertheless, if the best is yet to be, we who are Christian counselors must be knowledgeable in our field, committed to continuing education about counseling issues, astute and growing in our spiritual lives, sensitive to client rights and the ethics of our profession, and committed to the highest possible standards in our work. We could apply the words of Jesus to our work as counselors:

"You are the light of the world. . . . let your light shine before men, that they may see your good deeds and praise your Father in heaven." (Matt. 5:14, 16)

Conclusion

The New Testament book of James is a gold mine of relevant information for counselors. James writes about trials and suffering, perseverance and compassion, maturity and instability. He discusses listening, self-control, anger expression, and behavior change. He mentions the poor, people who stumble, and those who have interpersonal conflict. He warns us about the dangers of envy, selfish ambition, self-indulgent luxury, and insensitivity. He even discusses healing, confession, small groups, and prayer.

In James 1:27, the writer gives the only definition of religion found in the New Testament: "Religion that God our Father accepts as pure and faultless is this: to look after orphans and widows in their distress and to keep oneself from being polluted by the world."

This definition has two parts: to look after widows and orphans (that is, people helping) and to keep oneself from being polluted by the world (that is, personal holiness).

Casper ten Boom knew about this. His life was characterized by integrity, spirituality, flexibility, generativity, sensitivity, and commitment to quality. He was caring, compassionate, and Christlike—and in the end he was ridiculed and martyred because of his beliefs. He knew that he only had one life to live—one chance to make a difference. He chose to live a life characterized by people helping and personal holiness. And when he was taken off to die, apparently he was at peace.

Even then he knew: The best is yet to be.

EPILOGUE
A LETTER TO CHRISTIAN COUNSELORS

A revision of an article by Gary R. Collins which appeared in the Spring, 1990 issue of the Journal of Psychology and Christianity. *It is published here with permission of the Christian Association for Psychological Studies.*

DURING A TIME WHEN the early Christians were under persecution, the apostle John was banished to the lonely and uninviting Isle of Patmos. There he wrote the poetic and symbolic book that concludes our New Testament. Much of Revelation is difficult to understand and Bible scholars continue to debate its meaning. Chapters 2 and 3, however, record several brief letters written with special clarity and apparently intended to challenge and encourage seven churches in Asia Minor.

The seven letters have a common outline. They begin with the words "To the angel of . . . " and preface the main message by listing one or two characteristics of Christ. This is followed by words of *praise* for the good qualities found in the churches, *criticism* for the believers' faults or weaknesses, *instruction* that challenges Christians to change, and *promise* for those who alter their ways and become more like Christ.

In reading these letters, recently, my mind began to wonder how the risen Christ might view churches today. And how might he respond to those of us who are involved in Christian counseling? The hypothetical letter that follows is, of course, speculative and subjective, but even subjective self-examination can be healthy for individuals or professions. Too much introspection can be immobilizing; honest self-evaluation can be thought provoking and challenging, especially when it is followed by a willing effort to make changes for the better.

To the angel of the believing counselors in North America write:
These could be the words of him who is called Wonderful Counselor, Mighty God, Everlasting Father, and Prince of Peace.

I know your works: your journals, training programs, seminars, books, and articles, many of which are insightful, helpful, and good. I know of your sincere desire to make the church and individual Christians more sensitive and caring. I am well aware of your efforts to train others, to "give psychology away," and to devote your time, effort, and skills in diligent attempts both to help those who are hurting and to heal those who are emotionally and spiritually crippled.

I know of your labors in attempting to integrate psychology and theology in ways that will be true to the teachings of Scripture and accurate in terms of the current state of psychological knowledge. I know, too, of your strong desire to keep Christian counseling professionally competent, ethically impeccable, thoroughly practical, and always consistent with biblical teachings. And I know of your frustration, and anger, when your critics speak all manner of evil against you; pontificate in their pulpits by declaring that counseling is unnecessary or irrelevant; teach simplistic, naive, and erroneous views of human nature; and preach that all problems will disappear in those who "only believe" as a response to public messages. I know that it is not easy to be criticized by fellow believers who sincerely think that they are honoring God when they tear down those brothers and sisters who, like many of you, are committed to "make disciples" by teaching and healing, as well as by preaching (Matt. 28:19-20; 10:7, 8).

Nevertheless, I have a few things against you. Some of you have become empire builders who name the name of Christ, but whose energies are devoted primarily to the propagation of your theories, systems, schools, books, videotapes, foundations, "ministries," films, or talk-show appearances. Your efforts are too often directed to the building of your own kingdoms, to fund raising, or to the development of organizations that boost the name of the founder rather than the name of Christ. You have allowed yourselves to become "big name superstar counselors" who are greedy for publicity, pompous, lacking in humility, and rigidly intolerant of brothers and sisters who might disagree with your interpretation of what it means to have a biblical approach to counseling.

Many of you have become dual personalities. You are both "Christian" and "counselor," but you have developed the fine art of keeping these as two distinct and nonoverlapping parts of life. You are faithful in church attendance, firm in your commitment to creeds or to the Scriptures, and inclined to pray in your times of personal devotion. But you never pray with a counselee, never name the name of Christ in a counseling session, and have convinced yourselves that talk of religion or evangelism in counseling is unethical. It appears that some of you don't believe 2 Peter 1:3. You never think about the Holy Spirit's availability to lead in counseling, are unconvinced that a knowledge of Christ can help clients cope more effectively with the problems of living, and are embarrassed about praying or mentioning anything religious in a counseling session. Is it also true that some of you are afraid that a clear Christian witness might lead to loss of business, status, professional credibility, or acceptance by counselees?

Then there are those among you who are compromisers. Like the church at Thyatira, these counselors are known for their deeds, their love, and their faith, but they tolerate immorality, ignore biblical teachings about divorce or marital infidelity, attempt to justify overt homosexuality, and make little effort to condemn adultery. Their minds say that they believe in the destructive power of sin, but their actions, acquiescence, and silence show that they have little awareness of either the destructive nature of evil or the powerful influence of the evil one. These counselors want to be professionally respectable, and this goal is to be admired, but their desire to be respected silences their need to speak the truth as God has revealed it in the Scriptures.

Most dangerous are those of your numbers who are insensitive to the influence of Satan and the power of the demonic. Most of you are appalled by the excesses of well-meaning but naive exorcists who have done incredible harm with their simplistic explanations for human problems and their emotionally charged, overly dramatic, sometimes psychotic-like efforts to drive out demons. Most counselors have seen the abuse of such practices and have rightfully attempted to avoid these nonbiblical and destructive activities. Nevertheless, you have forgotten the warning in Ephesians 6 that all believers are in a battle against supernatural forces of wickedness, forces that are stronger than any system of psychology. You have failed to heed the warning of C. S. Lewis that it is equally dangerous both to ignore the existence of demons or to develop an excessive interest in their influence. You know intellectually that the Holy Spirit who is in us is greater than the devil who is in the world (1 John 4:4), but you have failed to see counseling as one part of a spiritual battle that cannot be won by psychology alone.

I counsel you, therefore, to repent of your merger with humanistic and self-centered theories, to reevaluate your pet approaches to counseling, to be sensitive to spiritual issues, to start every day in prayer, and seek continual divine guidance and wisdom in all that you do—including when you counsel, and especially if you work in a secular setting.

Strive to be humble, knowing that the Lord will lift you up and that there are few things more futile and empty than the building of one's own kingdom, even when that is seen as a "ministry." Work consistently to be a diligent student of the Scriptures, and a competent, knowledgeable practitioner of your counseling art. Ask God to give you boldness to speak the truth in love, to talk freely both of sin and of forgiveness, to show compassion and sensitivity, and to pray regularly for—and at least sometimes with—your counselees. Make it a practice also to pray for your critics and with your colleagues, so that in your counseling as in your life Christ will be honored and preeminent in all things.

To the one who overcomes and is obedient, I do not promise consistent success, counselees who always get better, critics and colleagues who understand, or clients who never commit suicide.

I do not promise family stability, freedom from burnout, or material prosperity.

But I promise abundant life on earth, true inner peace, and the assurance that God will ultimately bring justice. I promise you the certainty that he who knows all of our ways (Prov. 5:21) will eventually welcome us into his presence with the only reinforcement that a counselor will ultimately find satisfying: "Well done, good and faithful servant, come and share your Master's joy."

APPENDIX A
A CODE OF ETHICS FOR CHRISTIAN COUNSELORS

Adapted from the article by Robert R. King, Jr., "Developing a Proposed Code of Ethics for the Christian Association for Psychological Studies," in the Journal of Psychology and Christianity, Fall, 1986. *Published with permission of the Christian Association for Psychological Studies, this Code of Ethics is an earlier version of a revised Code of Ethics yet to be published.*

BIBLICAL FOUNDATION

Note: Each of the biblical blocks of the foundation that follows has one or more references. The references are not exhaustive, nor are they meant to be convenient proof-texting. Rather, the Scriptures cited are meant to be representative of the many biblical references that build the foundation of this Code. The complete foundation is the total message of the Gospel of Jesus Christ. Also, it is recognized that each believer in Christ has the capacity—even the privilege and duty—to explore the depths of God's Word and discover personal guidance for daily living. This Code could not hope to explore all the richness of the Bible as it relates to ethical conduct.

Biblical Building Blocks of the Foundation

Conflicts, difficulties, power struggles, trials and tribulations are normal and to be expected, whether one is a Christian or not (John 16:33; Psalm 37:7; Romans 2:9).

We are to grow and mature through the conflicts, problems, trials and tribulations, and discipline that we experience (James 1:2–4; 1 Thessalonians 5:18).

We are to support and encourage each other (John 15:17; Ephesians 4:32; John 13:35).

We are to admonish and, if necessary, discipline each other, especially those Christians in positions of leadership and trust. However, such discipline is to be constructive rather than judgmental, done in love, and with caution about our own shortcomings (Matthew 18:15, 17; 1 Corinthians 5:11–13; Galatians 6:1).

We are to demonstrate the lordship of Christ in our lives by servant-like leadership, a sense of community, and a life style that reflects the will of God (Matthew 20:25–28; John 12:26; 1 Peter 4:8–11; Colossians 3:12–17).

We are to reach out to others in love and concern (Matthew 25:31–40; Hebrews 13:16; 2 Corinthians 1:3–7).

BASIC CRITERIA AND PRINCIPLES OF THE CODE

1. The Code includes a broad range of morality, yet it is specific enough in certain areas to offer guidance for ethical conduct in a variety of situations. It is intended to be universal without being platitudinous. On the other hand, it aims to be functional without being legalistic.

2. The Code calls for commitment to a distinctively Christian code of ethical behavior in our helping professions. Yet it recognizes that ethical behavior is certainly not the hallmark only of Christians, thus there is no implication of judging persons of different faiths or value systems.

3. The Code is not a credo or doctrinal statement of CAPS. Article II of the CAPS Constitution and By-Laws contains the basis for our association:

> The basis of this organization is belief in: God, the Father, who creates and sustains us; Jesus Christ, the Son, who redeems and rules us, and the Holy Spirit, who guides us personally and professionally, through God's inspired Word, the Bible, our infallible guide of faith and conduct, and through the communion of Christians.

4. The Code is not a position paper on major social issues. While CAPS has genuine interest in social issues, it has traditionally encouraged members

to become involved personally, as led by God, rather than as prescribed by CAPS. Also, CAPS has traditionally encouraged the free exchange of ideas among members, rather than defining truth or a partisan viewpoint for its members.

5. All humans are created in the image of God. We are holistic in our being and thus most descriptions of our parts, such as mind, body, soul, spirit, personality or whatever, are primarily to make it easier to discuss and evaluate our nature. Much of being created in the image of God is still a mystery to us. However, it does mean that we and those persons we serve have basic dignity and worth, along with basic human rights and essential human responsibilities. Also, we are to glorify God in worship, service and stewardship.

6. The family is the basic unit of our culture; it merits honor, encouragement and protection. In addition, "family" to the Christian includes our "neighbor" (Luke 10:29–37). Thus, our "circle of love" embraces God, neighbor and self (Luke 10:27). Not only that, we are to love our enemies (Matthew 5:43). Also, our influence, our activities in the helping professions, are to be "salt and light" in this world (Matthew 5:13,14).

7. Scientific and humanistic activities in the helping professions are good, even excellent, but not good enough. While love without professional standards can become mere sentimentality, scientific observations and professional standards without love and Godly ethics can become mere clinical experiments. Thus, the Christian is called to maximize helping others by integrating the distinctives of Christian commitment—including prayer—with professional education, training and, if appropriate, licensing.

8. The world as we know it is a temporal place of human existence with the ever-present contrasts or polarities such as good and evil, order and disorder, joy and sorrow, generosity and selfishness, love and apathy, abundance and scarcity. Further, we do not necessarily know the reasons for any particular situation, event or relationship.

9. Exploiting or manipulating another person for our own or yet another's pleasure or aggrandizement is unethical and sinful.

10. Pretending to have expertise beyond our abilities or practicing beyond the scope of our licensure is unethical, very likely illegal, and does not value the person who needs help, nor does it glorify God.

11. Attempting to do for others what they are able and responsible to do for themselves, especially those persons who are seeking counsel, tends to create dependency and is thus unethical.

12. Some persons—such as children, for example—are more dependent than others and thus merit a greater degree of protection from persons who would thoughtlessly or selfishly take advantage of or manipulate them.

13. Each of us, whether helper or the person being helped, is a fallible human being who has limits that are universal in human nature yet unique in magnitude and proportion within each individual.

14. The helping professions are both art and science, with much to be learned. Also, each of us who serves, whether as professional or layperson, needs to be competent enough in what we do and of sufficient personal stability and integrity that what we do promotes healing rather than disorder and harm.

Articles of the Code of Ethics

Note: In an effort to avoid awkward and lengthy descriptions of persons we serve, the somewhat neutral word "client" is used. According to the perspective of members, words such as "peer," "parishioner," "communicant," "patient," "helpee," "counselee" or even "prisoner" may be used.

Also, the word "service" or "serving" is used frequently in the Code to describe what we do. Again, according to the perspective of members, words such as "helping ministries," "helping professions," "counseling," "ministering" or "pastoring," for examples, may be substituted. Admittedly, no word is neutral, since language shapes (and reflects) our reality. Thus, the word "service" or its derivatives is meant to reflect Christ's statement that He came to serve, rather than to be served.

1. *Personal Commitment as a Christian*

1.1 I agree with the basis of CAPS, as quoted earlier in this Code, stated in the Constitution and By-Laws.

1.2 I commit my service, whether as professional or layperson, to God as a special calling.

1.3 I pledge to integrate all that I do in service with Christian values, principles and guidelines.

1.4 I commit myself to Christ as Lord as well as Savior. Thus, direction and wisdom from God will be sought, while accepting responsibility for my own actions and statements.

1.5 I view my body as the temple of the Holy Spirit and will treat it lovingly and, respectfully. Balance in my priorities will be prayerfully sought.

2. *Loving Concern for Clients*

2.1 Clients will be accepted regardless of race, religion, gender, income, education, ethnic background, value system, etc., unless such a factor would interfere appreciably with my ability to be of service.

2.2 I value human life, the sanctity of personhood, personal freedom and responsibility, and the privilege of free choice in matters of belief and action.

2.3 I will avoid exploiting or manipulating any client to satisfy my own needs.

2.4 I will abstain from undue invasion of privacy.

2.5 I will take appropriate actions to help, even protect, those persons who are relatively dependent on other persons for their survival and well being.

2.6 Sexual intimacy with any client will be scrupulously avoided.

3. Confidentiality

3.1 I will demonstrate utmost respect for the confidentiality of the client and other persons in the helping relationship.

3.2 The limits of confidentiality, such as those based on civil laws, regulations and judicial precedent, will be explained to the client.

3.3 I will carefully protect the identity of clients and their problems. Thus, I will avoid divulging information about clients, whether privately or publicly, unless I have informed consent of the client, given by express, written permission, and the release of such information would be appropriate to the situation.

3.4 All records of counseling will be handled in a way that protects the clients and the nature of their problems from disclosure.

4. Competency in Services Provided

4.1 I pledge to be well-trained and competent in providing services.

4.2 I will refrain from implying that I have qualifications, experiences and capabilities which are in fact lacking.

4.3 I will comply with applicable state and local laws and regulations regarding the helping professions.

4.4 I will avoid using any legal exemptions from counseling competency afforded in certain states to churches and other nonprofit organizations as a means of providing services that are beyond my training and expertise.

4.5 I will diligently pursue additional education, experience, professional consultation and spiritual growth in order to improve my effectiveness in serving persons in need.

5. My Human Limitations

5.1 I will do my best to be aware of my human limitations and biases, and openly admit that I do not have scientific objectivity or spiritual maturity, insofar as my subjective viewpoint will permit.

5.2 I will avoid fostering any misconception a client could have that I am omnipotent, or that I have all the answers.

5.3 I will refer clients whom I am not capable of counseling, whether by lack of available time or expertise, or even because of subjective, personal reasons. The referral will be done compassionately, clearly and completely, insofar as feasible.

5.4 I will resist efforts of any clients or colleagues to place demands for services on me that exceed my qualifications and/or the time available to minister, or that would impose unduly on my relationships with my own family.

6. Advertising and Promotional Activities

6.1 I will advertise or promote my services by Christian and professional standards, rather than commercial standards.

6.2 Personal aggrandizement will be omitted from advertising and promotional activities.

7. Research

7.1 Any research conducted will be done openly and will not jeopardize the welfare of any persons who are research, i.e., test, subjects. Further, clients will not be used as publicly identifiable test subjects.

8. Unethical Conduct, Confrontation, and Malpractice

8.1 If I have sufficient reason to believe a Christian colleague in CAPS has been practicing or ministering in a way that is probably damaging to the client or the helping ministries, I will confront that person. The principles and procedures specified in Matthew 18:15–17 will be followed in confronting the person who appears to be behaving unethically. In addition, the more stringent actions against pastors specified in I Timothy 5:19–20 will be considered, if relevant.

8.2 In addition to the confrontation procedures based on Scriptural guidance, civil law will be followed if relevant or applicable.

8.3 If the CAPS Board becomes aware that a member has been accused of unethical conduct, the Ethics Committee (either standing or ad hoc) will investigate the situation and recommend ethical discipline, including expulsion from membership, if appropriate.

8.3.1. If a person has been expelled from membership for unethical conduct, the Ethics Committee will maintain loving and concerned liaison with the person and others involved, as appropriate, and will attempt to bring about actions for repentance, forgiveness and restoration into the membership.

8.4 The Ethics Committee will also provide consultation to CAPS as an organization and/or to individual members who may be confronting ethical dilemmas and want some guidance.

8.4.1 Since ethical concerns may be complex and/or have legal implications, the consultation provided will be primarily in helping think through a situation, without assuming responsibility for the case.

8.5 The value of malpractice insurance will be carefully considered, especially if a lawsuit—whether justified or not—would possibly drain financial resources of the ministry organization with which I am associated, or my family.

9. General Prudential Rule

9.1 Recognizing that no code of ethics is complete, I will make day-to-day decisions based on the criteria and principles stated at the beginning of this Code. Even more important, I will do my best to serve and to live in a way that is congruent with the stated basic principles of this Code and with my faith as a Christian.

APPENDIX B
INFORMED CONSENT: A SAMPLE OF THE INFORMATION THAT COULD BE PRESENTED TO NEW AND POTENTIAL COUNSELEES

Description of services: Counseling psychology is a specialized science that seeks to understand and improve human behavior. I, a counseling psychologist (sometimes called a counselor, therapist, or psychotherapist), am a trained and licensed professional who uses my special skills to help persons with their efforts to lead effective and satisfying lives. I am prepared to work with individuals, couples, groups, and entire families. I provide guidance for my clients as they present their problems or concerns and set goals for the counseling process. I then assist them in reaching their goals. I use a variety of counseling methods and strategies in my office and assign appropriate homework activities to aid my clients in learning how to help themselves and run their own lives successfully.

Confidentiality: What you say and do in the sessions with me will be kept in strict confidence. Information concerning you will not be shared with other persons without your permission. Nor will diagnostic terms or codes be used to describe you and your behavior to third parties such as insurance companies without your consent. You need to know, however, that if ever there is reason for me to believe that you are likely to do harm to either yourself or another person, then it is my professional responsibility to notify the appropriate persons or authorities.

Length, frequency, and number of sessions: Individuals usually meet once a week for sessions that run about fifty minutes with adults and thirty minutes with children. Sessions with couples are also scheduled weekly and last about sixty minutes. Groups and families normally meet weekly as well but for ninety minutes. Group counseling sessions for children are weekly fifty-minute sessions. In some cases, it is possible to schedule appointments every two or three weeks. The number of sessions varies with individuals and the nature of their particular problems, but a minimum of ten to twelve sessions should be expected.

Client freedom and responsibility: I respect your values and will not ask you to do anything that would cause you to feel badly about yourself. Nor will I attempt to force you to do anything against your will or good judgment. Although you are encouraged to remain in counseling until you have successfully reached your goal(s), termination or quitting counseling is your right from the very beginning. I don't have any "magic" or power to change your life or solve your problems without your doing some hard work; therefore, it is important that you cooperate with me in carrying out the plans you make for your therapy program. You have the ultimate responsibility for the growth and change you make in counseling and therapy.

Fees: All the services I provide will be billed at the rate of $_____ per session. Clients with insurance coverage, after meeting their annual deductible amount, may choose either to pay the full scheduled fee and be reimbursed later by their insurance company or pay their percentage part and assign payment of the insurance portion directly to me. Clients who are not covered by mental-health insurance will pay the full scheduled fee. Special adjustments can be made for persons who do not have insurance coverage or those who have other difficult financial situations.

Payment of fees: It is expected that you pay either the full scheduled fee or your percentage part when the services are received. You will be given a receipt for each payment for your personal records. If you have insurance and wish to be reimbursed for the total cost of psychological counseling, I will prepare itemized statements to assist you with the reimbursement

Informed Consent

procedure. If you choose to pay only your percentage part and assign payment of the insurance portion directly to me, you are expected to provide me with an official insurance form that is dated and signed by you and/or the authorized party, indicating that payment has been assigned to me.

Canceled appointments: Fees are charged for all scheduled appointments. You will be billed for the full scheduled fee for any appointment that is canceled or broken without twenty-four hours' advance notification. Exceptions will be made in emergency situations such as illness or a death in the family.

Other services: My practice of counseling psychology is one of several options for receiving professional mental-health services in this community. I want you to be fully aware of this now and be assured that I will assist you in seeking another source of help if/when either you or I consider a referral to be in your best interest. Also, it is desirable that you know about the other services before you consent to begin a therapy program with me.

Questions: You are encouraged to discuss openly and freely with me any question or concern you might have about your counseling program at any time you wish.

Consent: I have read, discussed with you the psychologist, and understand what I can expect from a counseling or therapy program offered by you. I give my consent to enter a psychological counseling program with this understanding. I agree to pay $_____$ for each scheduled appointment. I understand that my signing this form does *not* commit me to a binding contract but merely indicates my consent to begin therapy with you.

_____   _____
          Signature   Date

NOTES

Chapter 1. Excellence in Christian Counseling

1. Bob Greene, "Jordan, Before the Cheering Starts," *Chicago Tribune*.
2. John W. Gardner, *Excellence: Can We Be Equal and Excellent Too?* (New York: Harper and Row, 1961), 92.
3. The book that gave impetus to this "excellence revolution" was by Thomas J. Peters and Robert H. Waterman, Jr., *In Search of Excellence: Lessons from America's Best-Run Companies* (New York: Harper and Row, 1982). See also Thomas J. Peters and Nancy V. Austin, *A Passion for Excellence: The Leadership Difference* (New York: Random House, 1985).
4. John D. Krumboltz, "The 1990 Leona Tyler Award Address: Brilliant Insights—Platitudes That Bear Repeating," *The Counseling Psychologist* 19 (1991), 298–315.
5. Personal communication from Clayton Baumann of Chicago North Area Youth for Christ. I am grateful that he has permitted me to publish what originally was written as a personal letter.

6. For a good overview of the growth, see Edwin L. Herr, *Counsel in a Dynamic Society: Opportunities and Challenges* (Alexandria, Va.: American Association for Counseling and Development, 1989).

7. For an overview, see Aaron T. Beck, "Cognitive Therapy: A 30-Year Retrospective," *American Psychologist* 46 (1991), 368–75. An earlier book in this series summarizes cognitive therapy from a Christian perspective. See Mark R. McMinn, *Cognitive Therapy Techniques in Christian Counseling* (Dallas: Word, 1991).

8. Everett L. Worthington, Jr., "Religious Counseling: A Review of Published Empirical Research," *Journal of Counseling and Development* 64 (1986), 421–31.

9. See, for example, Manuel Ramirez, III, *Psychotherapy and Counseling with Minorities: A Cognitive Approach to Individual and Cultural Differences* (Elmsford, N.Y.: Pergamon, 1991).

10. Emory L. Cowen, "In Pursuit of Wellness," *American Psychologist* 46 (1991), 404–408.

11. For a series of articles on counseling and spirituality written from an evangelical perspective, see the Spring 1991 (vol. 19) issue of the *Journal of Psychology and Theology*.

12. For a Christian example, see Gregg R. Albers, *Counseling and AIDS* (Dallas: Word, 1990). For a good secular book, see Mark C. Winiarski, *AIDS-Related Psychotherapy* (Elmsford N.Y.: Pergamon, 1991).

13. For what has been called "a groundbreaking perspective on community mental health," see Patrick Tolan, Christopher Keys, Fern Chertok, and Leonard Jason, eds., *Researching Community Psychology: Issues of Theory and Methods* (Washington, D.C.: American Psychological Association, 1991).

14. S. L. Halleck, *The Politics of Therapy* (New York: Harper and Row, 1971), 36.

15. Jay E. Adams, *Competent to Counsel* (Grand Rapids: Baker, 1970), 18.

16. Martin Bobgan and Deidre Bobgan, *How to Counsel from Scripture* (Chicago: Moody, 1985), 89, 90. A similar viewpoint is expressed in John MacArthur, Jr.'s sharply critical views of psychology in *Our Sufficiency in Christ* (Dallas: Word, 1991).

17. This statement from C. B. Truax and K. M. Mitchell ("Research on Certain Therapist Interpersonal Skills in Relation to Process and Outcome," in *Handbook of Psychotherapy and Behavior Change*, A. E. Bergin and S. L. Garfield, eds., [New York: Wiley, 1971]). It is quoted in Bobgan and Bobgan, *How to Counsel from Scripture,* page 87. The issue of counselor training will be discussed in more depth in chapter 6.

18. Rowland C. Croucher, "Ambition, Excellence and Success," *Grid* (World Vision of Australia, Winter 1987).

19. Allen E. Bergin, "Psychotherapy and Religious Values," *Journal of Consulting and Clinical Psychology* 48 (1980), 95–105. For perspectives that are more evangelical, see the Summer 1991 (vol. 10) issue of the *Journal of Psychology and Christianity*—a special issue devoted to "Religious Values in Psychotherapy."

20. This decade of work was summarized by Bergin when he received an award from the American Psychological Association for "distinguished professional contributions." See Allen E. Bergin, "Values and Religious Issues in Psychotherapy and Mental Health," *American Psychologist* 46 (1991), 394–403.

21. See, for example, chapter 3, "Values and the Helping Relationship," in Gerald Corey, Marianne Schneider Corey, and Patrick Callanan, *Issues and Ethics in the Helping Professions*, 3d ed. (Pacific Grove, Calif.: Brooks/Cole, 1988).

22. Hunter Lewis, *A Question of Values: Six Ways We Make the Personal Choices That Shape Our Lives* (New York: Harper and Row, 1990). The quotation is from page 20.

23. Lewis M. Andrews, *To Thine Own Self Be True: The Rebirth of Values in the New Ethical Therapy* (Garden City, N.Y.: Anchor Press, Doubleday, 1987).

24. The six categories are taken from the book by Hunter Lewis, *A Question of Values*.

25. For a concise, logical evaluation of the ways by which Christians can be manipulated by deceptive arguments, see Mark McMinn and James Foster, *Christians in the Crossfire: Guarding Your Mind Against Manipulation and Self-Deception* (Newberg, Ore.: Barclay, 1990).

26. Ray S. Anderson, *Christians Who Counsel: The Vocation of Wholistic Therapy* (Grand Rapids: Zondervan, 1990), 196.

27. In two revealing charts, Oden looks at some representative writings of Hiltner, Clinebell, Oates, Wise, and Tournier—all of whom were early writers in Christian counseling. Together, they made 111 references to Freud, Jung, or Rogers; there was not a single reference in the text to Luther, Calvin, or the other leaders. See Thomas C. Oden, *Care of Souls in the Classic Tradition* (Philadelphia: Fortress, 1984), 29, 31. See also T. Oden, "What Psychologists Can Learn from the Historical Pastoral Care Tradition," a paper presented at the Rech Conference on Christian Graduate Training in Psychology, Lisle, Illinois, 27 October 1990. The importance of drawing on the wisdom of historical pastoral care leaders is also emphasized in David G. Benner, *Psychotherapy and the Spiritual Quest* (Grand Rapids: Baker, 1988).

28. There are, of course, great differences between countries.

29. N. A. Cummings, "The Future of Clinical Psychology in the United States," *Clinical Psychologist* 37 (1984), 19–20; and James D. Guy, Jr., *The Personal Life of the Psychotherapist* (New York: Wiley, 1987).

30. I described some of these approaches in the first volume in this series. See Gary R. Collins, *Innovative Approaches to Counseling* (Waco, Texas: Word, 1986).

31. Some of the conclusions in this section are drawn from the discussion of professionalism by Ray S. Anderson, *Christians Who Counsel*, 195–213.

32. Ibid., 207.

33. This is a major argument in a book by Jon Johnson, *Christian Excellence: Alternative to Success* (Grand Rapids: Baker, 1985). The paraphrase from Anthony Campolo is taken from Dr. Campolo's foreword to the Johnson book.

34. I am grateful to the Reverend Ted Olsen of Trinity Evangelical Divinity School for suggesting this outline.

Chapter 2. Ethics in Christian Counseling

1. The issue of sharing one's religious faith in counseling has been discussed in an article by two Christian psychiatrists, Alan A. Nelson and William P. Wilson, "The Ethics of Sharing Religious Faith in Psychotherapy," *Journal of Psychology and Theology* 12 (1984), 13–18.

2. To date there has been no definitive published book on the ethics of Christian counseling, although at least one of these is in preparation. For a Christian overview of general ethics see Norman L. Geisler, *Christian Ethics: Options and Issues* (Grand Rapids: Baker, 1989). For discussions of counseling ethics see Gerald Corey, Marianne Schneider Corey, and Patrick Callanan, *Issues and Ethics in the Helping Professions*, 3d ed. (Pacific Grove, Calif: Brooks/Cole, 1988); Mary Ann Carroll, Henry G. Schneider, and George R. Wesley, *Ethics in the Practice of Psychology* (Englewood Cliffs, N.J.: Prentice-Hall, 1985); Patricia Keith-Spiegel and Gerald P. Koocher, *Ethics in Psychology: Professional Standards and Cases* (New York: Random House, 1985); W. H. Van Hoose and J. A. Kottler, *Ethical and Legal Issues Counseling and Psychotherapy*, 2d ed. (San Francisco: Jossey-Bass, 1985); Barbara Herhily and Larry B. Golden, *Ethical Standards Casebook*, 4th ed. (Alexandria, Va.: American Association for Counseling and Development, 1990); Kenneth S. Pope and Melba J. T. Vasquez, *Ethics in Psychotherapy and Counseling: A Practical Guide for Psychologists* (San Francisco: Jossey-Bass, 1991); and Martin Lakin, *Coping with Ethical Dilemmas in Psychotherapy* (Riverside, N.J.: Pergamon, 1991). Psychiatric ethics are discussed in a book by Rem B. Edwards, ed., *Psychiatry and Ethics: Insanity, Rational Autonomy and Mental Health Care* (Buffalo, N.Y.: Prometheus, 1982).

3. Lewis, *A Question of Values*.

4. See, for example, D. Rosenthal, "Changes in Some Moral Values Following Psychotherapy," *Journal of Consulting Psychology* 19 (1955), 431–36;

Alan C. Tjeltveit, "The Ethics of Value Conversion in Psychotherapy: Appropriate and Inappropriate Therapist Influence on Client Values," *Clinical Psychology Review* 6 (1986), 515–37; Everett. L. Worthington, Jr., "Understanding the Values of Religious Clients: A Model and Its Application to Counseling," *Journal of Counseling Psychology* 35 (1988), 166–74; and Allen E. Bergin, "Values and Religious Issues in Psychotherapy and Mental Health," *American Psychologist* 46 (1991), 394–403.

5. Corey, Corey, and Callanan, *Issues and Ethics*, 67.
6. Geisler, *Christian Ethics*, 17.
7. Geisler summarizes these in the first chapter of his book, *Christian Ethics*.
8. Kenneth S. Pope and Theresa Rose Bajt, "When Laws and Values Conflict: A Dilemma for Psychologists," *American Psychologist* 43 (1988), 828–29.
9. M. Wilkins, et al., "Willingness to Apply Understood Ethical Principles," Journal of Clinical Psychology 46 (1990), 539–47. See also Todd S. Smith, et al., "Clinical Ethical Decision Making: An Investigation of the Rationales Used to Justify Doing Less Than One Believes One Should," *Professional Psychology: Research and Practice* 22 (1991), 235–39.
10. Mary Sykes Wylie, "Looking for the Fence Posts," *Family Therapy Networker* 13 (March/April 1989), 22–33. The quotation is taken from page 33.
11. Mark S. Oordt, "Ethics of Practice Among Christian Psychologists: A Pilot Study," *Journal of Psychology and Theology* 18, no. 3 (1990), 255–60. For a contrasting study with psychologists who were not necessarily Christian, see Kenneth S. Pope, Barbara G. Tabachnick, and Patricia Keith-Spiegel, "Ethics of Practice: The Beliefs and Behaviors of Psychologists as Therapists," *American Psychologist* 42, no. 11 (1987), 993–1006.
12. American Psychological Association, "Ethical Principles of Psychologists," *American Psychologist* 36 (1981), 633–38. See also American Psychological Association, "Ethical Principles of Psychologists (amended June 2, 1989)," *American Psychologist* 45 (1990), 390–95. Other organizations with professional codes of ethics include the American Association for Counseling and Development, American Association for Marriage and Family Therapy, National Association of Social Workers, National Federation of Societies for Clinical Social Work, American Psychiatric Association, American School Counselor Association, the Commission on Rehabilitation Counselor Certification, and the American Mental Health Counselors Association. Each of these ethical codes (except for the AMHCA) is included in the appendix of Corey, Corey, and Callanan, *Issues and Ethics*.
13. Notice the title of the article by Wylie, "Looking for the Fence Posts."
14. John Jefferson Davis, *Evangelical Ethics: Issues Facing the Church Today* (Phillipsburg, N.J.: Presbyterian and Reformed, 1985).

15. For further discussion of these issues see Al Deuck, "Ethical Contexts of Healing: Ecclesia and Praxis," *Pastoral Psychology* 35 (1987), 49–62. See also Ray S. Anderson, *Christians Who Counsel*, chapter 10.

16. Don Browning has discussed this in *The Moral Context of Pastoral Care* (Philadelphia: Westminster, 1967).

17. Deuck, "Ethical Contexts of Healing: Ecclesia and Praxis," 56.

18. This reference to Mother Teresa and the paragraph that follows are drawn from an article by Al Dueck, "Ethical Contexts of Healing: Character and Ritual," *Pastoral Psychology* 36 (1987), 69–83.

19. Jerry Bridges, *The Practice of Godliness* (Colorado Springs: NavPress, 1985).

20. Augustus E. Jordan and Naomi M. Meara, "Ethics and the Professional Practice of Psychologists: The Role of Virtues and Principles," *Professional Psychology: Research and Practice* 21 (1990), 107–14.

21. The following are among the writers who deal with these issues from an evangelical perspective: Jack O. Balswick and J. Kenneth Morland, *Social Problems: A Christian Understanding and Response* (Grand Rapids: Baker, 1990); Davis, *Evangelical Ethics*; Richard A. Fowler and H. Wayne House, *Civilization in Crisis: A Christian Response to Homosexuality, Feminism, Euthanasia and Abortion*, 2d ed. (Grand Rapids: Baker, 1988); Robert N. Wennberg, *Terminal Choices: Euthanasia, Suicide, and the Right to Die* (Grand Rapids: Eerdmans, 1989); and Geisler, *Christian Ethics*.

22. Lewis B. Smedes, *Mere Morality: What God Expects from Ordinary People* (Grand Rapids: Eerdmans, 1983), 15.

23. Alan R. Mabe and Stephen A. Rollin, "The Role of a Code of Ethical Standards in Counseling," *Journal of Counseling and Development* 64 (1986), 294–97.

24. For more information about the CAPS code of ethics and its development, see the articles on this subject in the *Journal of Psychology and Christianity* 5 (1986), 78–101.

25. For a more detailed discussion of graded absolutism, see Geisler, *Christian Ethics*, chapter 7.

26. Please see this chapter's note 2.

27. Jay E. Adams, *Competent to Counsel*.

28. These are among the issues discussed by Steve Levicoff in *Christian Counseling and the Law* (Chicago: Moody, 1991).

29. Pope et al., "Ethics of Practice."

30. *Tarasoff v. Regents of the University of California*, 13 Cal. 3d 177, 529 p. 22 553, 118 Cal. Rptr. 129 (1974). This case is discussed in more detail in chapter 3. It illustrates what sometimes are called "duty-to-protect" issues. See, for example, John Bales, "Duty-to-protect Issues Pressing for Guidelines," *APA Monitor* 19 (January 1988), 15.

31. Gregory W. Brock and Jeanette D. Coufal, "Ethics in Practice," *Family Therapy Networker* 13 (1989), 29.

32. AIDS and the duty to warn is discussed in several articles. See, for example, John J. Pietrofesa, Cathy J. Pietrofesa, and John David Pietrofesa, "The Mental Health Counselor and 'Duty to Warn,'" *Journal of Mental Health Counseling* 12 (1990), 129–37; L. A. Gray and A. K. Harding, "Confidentiality Limits with Clients Who Have the AIDS Virus," *Journal of Counseling and Development* 66 (1988), 219–23; and Elliott D. Cohen, "Confidentiality, Counseling, and Clients Who Have AIDS: Ethical Foundations of a Model Rule," *Journal of Counseling and Development* 68 (1990), 282–86.

33. There is debate in the counseling literature about whether such a revelation biases the counselee for or against counseling. Earlier research suggested that the label "Christian counselor" was equated with incompetence in the minds of some people, but more recent research has refuted that conclusion. See Julia A. Pecnik and Douglas L. Epperson, "Analogue Study of Expectations for Christian and Traditional Counseling," *Journal of Counseling and Psychology* 32 (1985), 127–30 and Steven C. Wyatt and Ray W. Johnson, "The Influence of Counselors' Religious Values on Clients' Perceptions of the Counselor," *Journal of Psychology and Theology* 18 (1990), 158–65.

34. The statement is included with permission from the author and publisher, Darrell Smith, *Integrative Therapy: A Comprehensive Approach to the Methods and Principles of Counseling and Psychotherapy* (Grand Rapids: Baker, 1990), Appendix C.

35. This leads to the issue of adolescent informed consent. A recent survey showed that most practitioners seek consent even from very young clients. See David G. Beeman and Norman A. Scott, "Therapists' Attitudes Toward Psychotherapy Informed Consent with Adolescents," *Professional Psychology: Research and Practice* 22 (1991), 230–34.

36. For a discussion of informed consent in Christian counseling see Kathleen N. Lewis and Douglas L. Epperson, "Values, Pretherapy Information, and Informed Consent in Christian Counseling," *Journal of Psychology and Christianity* 19 (1991), 113–31.

37. Carroll et al., *Ethics in the Practice of Psychology*, 27.

38. In his survey, Oordt ("Ethics of Practice") found differences between Christian and non-Christian counselors regarding fees. Christians, for example, were less likely to use a collection agency but more willing to accept goods, rather than money, as payment for counseling.

39. The issue of fees is discussed in more detail in a chapter titled "Why Is Professional Counseling So Expensive?" in Gary R. Collins, *Can You Trust Psychology?* (Downers Grove, Ill.: InterVarsity, 1988).

40. The issue of therapist-patient sex and its impact has been discussed frequently in the professional literature. See, for example, K. S. Pope and J. C. Bouhoutsos, *Sexual Intimacy Between Therapists and Patients* (New York: Praeger, 1986). For a discussion of this issue from Christian perspectives, please see the following three articles, all included in a special issue of the *Journal of Psychology and Christianity* 8 (1989): John F. Schakelford, "Affairs in the Consulting Room: A Review of the Literature on Therapist-Patient Sexual Intimacy," 26–43; Raymond T. Brock and Horace C. Lukens, Jr., "Affair Prevention in the Ministry," 44–55; and Peter L. Steinke, "Clergy Affairs," 56–62. The discussion in this section of the chapter draws from the above articles. For a discussion of sexuality and the ministry see Terry C. Muck, ed., *Sins of the Body: Ministry in a Sexual Society* (Dallas: CTI and Word, 1988).

41. This list is taken from Brock and Luken's, "Affair Prevention in the Ministry." The article applies equally well to Christian counselors who are not ministers.

42. J. L. Bernard and C. S. Jara, "The Failure of Clinical Psychology Graduate Students to Apply Understood Ethical Principles," *Professional Psychology: Research and Practice* 17 (1986), 313–15.

43. American Psychological Association, "Ethical Principles," section 7g.

44. Keith-Spiegel and Koocher, *Ethics in Psychology*, 30–36.

Chapter 3. Liability in Christian Counseling: Welcome to the Grave New World

1. *Nally v. Grace Community Church of the Valley*, 47 Cal.3d 278, 763 P.2d 948, 253 Cal. Rptr. 97, at 99 (1988) cert. denied 109 S. Ct. 1644 (1989). *Malpractice* (which shall be more fully explained later in the text) is a negligent tort, a noncriminal civil wrong that describes a misconduct, incompetence, or failure to deliver a minimum standard of professional care whereby someone suffers some loss or harm that the law will grant redress in the form of money damages.

2. Ibid., hereinafter cited as the *Nally* case or as *Nally III*.

3. Those interested in a fuller treatment of this subject can consult the forthcoming book by G. Ohlschlager and P. Mosgofian, tentatively titled *Legal Guidebook in Christian Counseling*, Word; or S. Levicoff, *Christian Counseling and the Law* (Chicago: Moody, 1991); the excellent secular work by R. Meyer, E. Landis, and J. Hays, *Law for the Psychotherapist*, (New York, Norton 1988).

4. D. B. Hogan, *The Regulation of Psychotherapists, Vol. III: A Review of Malpractice Suits in the United States* (Cambridge, Mass.: Ballinger, 1979).

5. Ibid., table 1, 373.

6. See "Alarm over Malpractice," *Time* (Jan. 28, 1985), 75.

7. Hogan, *The Regulation of Psychotherapists*, table 2, at 373.
8. Ibid., tables 3, 4 and 46, 374, 416.
9. Ibid., at 14.
10. Ibid., tables 5 and 6, 375–76.
11. Ibid., tables 7–10, 377–78.
12. Ibid., tables 11 and 12, 379–80.
13. Ibid., tables 13–20, 381–88.
14. Ibid., tables 21 and 22, at 389–90.
15. S. Fulero, "Insurance Trust Releases Malpractice Statistics." *State Psychological Association Affairs*, v.19 (1—1987), 4–5.
16. See K. Austin, M. Moline, and G. Williams. *Confronting Malpractice: Legal and Ethical Dilemmas in Psychotherapy*. (Newbury Park: Sage Publications, 1990) 16.
17. N. Gartrell, et al. "Psychiatrist-Patient Sexual Contact: Results of a National Survey, I: Prevalence." *American Journal of Psychiatry*, v. 143 (9—1986), 1126–1131.
18. *Tarasoff v. Regents of the University of California*, 13 Cal.3d 117, 118 Cal. Rptr.129, 529 P.2d 334, (1976).
19. M. L. Gross, *The Psychological Society* (New York: Random House, 1978); and J. K Lieberman, *The Litigious Society* (New York: Basic Books, 1983).
20. See C. Colson, *Kingdoms in Conflict* (New York: William Morrow/Zondervan, 1987), and C. Lasch, *The Culture of Narcissism* (New York: Norton, 1979).
21. Y. Aharoni, *The No-Risk Society* (Chatham, N.J.: Chatham House Publishers, 1981) 1.
22. T. L. Needham, "Insurance Protection for Church and Clergy." In H. N. Malony, T. L. Needham, and S. Southard, *Clergy Malpractice* (Philadelphia: The Westminster Press, 1986), 127 [hereinafter cited as *Clergy Malpractice*].
23. T. L. Needham, "Helping When the Risks Are Great," *Clergy Malpractice*, 93.
24. See G. R. Collins, *Can You Trust Psychology?* (Downers Grove, Ill.: InterVarsity, 1988), P. Vitz, *Psychology as Religion: The Cult of Self-Worship* (Grand Rapids : Eerdmans,1977).
25. T. L. Needham, "Malpractice in the ministry." In *Clergy Malpractice*, 13.
26. R. Slovenko, "Malpractice in Psychiatry and Related Fields." *Journal of Psychiatry and Law*, v.9 (2—1981), 5.
27. R. J. Cohen, *Malpractice: A Guide for Mental Health Professionals* (New York: The Free Press, 1979) 21.
28. See, for example, *Our Sufficiency in Christ* (Dallas: Word, 1991) by John MacArthur Jr.; M. and D. Bobgan, *PsychoHeresy* (Santa Barbara, Calif.: Eastgate, 1987); and W. K. Kilpatrick, *Psychological Seduction: The Failure*

of Modern Psychology (Nashville: Nelson, 1983). But compare Collins, *Can You Trust Psychology?*

29. Needham, *Clergy Malpractice*, 18.

30. See J. Dobson, and G. Bauer, *Children at Risk: The Battle for the Hearts and Minds of Our Kids* (Dallas: Word Publishing, 1990) 23.

31. B. Furrow, *Malpractice in Psychotherapy* (Lexington, Mass.: Lexington Books, 1980).

32. D. Kasper, *Liability Workshop 1989: Balancing Prevention and Risk for Clergy, Counselors, Administrators and Educators* (Los Angeles: Caldwell and Toms, Inc., 1989) 2.

33. English common law, including the precedent-following principle of "stare decisis," follows the practice of judge-made law which developed slowly and incrementally over many centuries as a dominant form of English rule. Though much changed and supplemented by all forms of law-making in America, this common law system retains significant influence.

34. Charitable immunity referred to a privilege granted the church, many hospitals and institutions of social welfare that exempted them from numerous legal duties and obligations imposed by governments in recognition of their fundamental value and service to society. This doctrine has been all but abolished in twentieth-century America due to public policy favoring compensation to injured persons and the rise of the insurance industry to protect such institutions from dissolution when sued for injuries caused by their work.

35. "Congress shall make no law respecting an establishment of religion, or prohibiting the free exercise thereof." *U.S. Constitution*, amend. I, clause 1 and 2.

36. See *Black's Law Dictionary*, rev. 4th ed. (1968), p. 1660. "Three elements of every tort action are: existence of legal duty from defendant to plaintiff, breach of duty, and damage as a proximate result."

37. See Hogan, *Regulation*, Vol. 3, supra note 4.

38. W. L. Prosser, *Handbook of the Law of Torts*, 4th ed. (St. Paul, Minn.: West Publishing, 1971) note 43. Prosser's handbooks are considered the "bibles" of American tort law.

39. See Comment, "Tort Liability of the Psychotherapist." *University of San Francisco Law Review*, v.8, (1973), 405; see also D. B. Hogan, (1979b). *The Regulation of Psychotherapists*, vol. 2: *A Handbook of State Licensure Laws* (Cambridge, Mass.: Ballinger, 1979).

40. S. A. Chase, "Clergy Malpractice: The Cause of Action that Never Was." *North Carolina Central Law Journal*, v.18 (1989), 163–85.

41. *Oregon Employment Division v. Smith*, 110 S. Ct. 1595 (1990). [hereinafter cited as *Smith*].

42. See, for example, *O'Neil v. Schuckardt*, 112 Idaho 472, 733 P.2d 693 (Idaho 1986); *Hester v. Barnett*, 723 S.W.2d 544 (Mo. Ct. App. 1987);

Handley v. Richards, 518 So.2d 682 (Alabama 1987); and review, on the controversial issue of intentional emotional distress, L. Brooks, "Intentional Infliction of Emotional Distress by Spiritual Counselors: Can Outrageous Conduct Be 'Free Exercise?'" *Michigan Law Review*, v.84 (1986) 1286.

43. Chase, "Malpractice: The Cause of Action," 173.

44. *Destefano v. Grabrian*, 763 P.2d 275 (Colorado 1988).

45. Ibid., 284. See also *Strock v. Presnell*, 527 N.E.2d 1235, at 1238, (Ohio 1988); where the Supreme Court of Ohio used essentially the same reasoning in rejecting the First Amendment defense of a Lutheran pastor charged with a sexual affair while involved in marital counseling. The court assertively held that this behavior was not religiously motivated but was instead a "bizarre deviation from normal spiritual counseling practices of ministers in the Lutheran church."

46. See Hogan, *Regulation*, vol. 4.

47. *Lake v. Cameron*, 364 F.2d 657 (D.C. Cir. 1966); see also *Lessard v. Schmidt*, 349 F.Supp. 1078 (E.D. Wis. 1972).

48. *Wyatt v. Stickney*, 325 F.Supp. 781 (M.D. Ala. 1971), 344 F.Supp. 373 (M.D. Ala. 1972), aff'd sub nom *Wyatt v. Aderholt*, 503 F.2d 753 (5th Cir. 1974).

49. *O'Connor v. Donaldson*, 422 U.S. 563 (1975).

50. See A. Brooks, "Mental Health Law: The Right to Refuse Treatment," *Administration in Mental Health*, v. 4 (1977), 90–95.

51. See P. Brown, *The Transfer of Care: Psychiatric Institutionalization and Its Aftermath* (Boston: Routledge and Kegan Paul, 1985).

52. S. Halleck, *Law in the Practice of Psychiatry* (New York: Plenum Medical Books, 1980).

53. See J. Fischer,. "State Regulation of Psychologists." *Washington University Law Quarterly*, v.58 (1980), 639; D. A. Hardcastle, "Certification, Licensure and Other Forms of Regulation." In A. Rosenblatt and D. Waldfogel (Gen. Eds.), *Handbook of Clinical Social Work* (San Francisco: Jossey-Bass, 1983).

54. This, of course, includes members of the clergy. "Nothing in this article shall prevent qualified members of other professional groups from doing work of a psychosocial nature consistent with the standards and ethics of their respective professions. . . . These qualified members of other professional groups include, but are not limited to, the following: . . . (e) A priest, rabbi or minister of the gospel of any religious denomination." *California Business and Professions Code*, ch.14, sect. 4996.13.

55. See, for example, Title 16 on Behavioral Science Examiners of the *Cal. Bus. and Profess. Code*.

56. See E. Belser, "BBSE Joint Hearing with the Board of Psychology: Public Input Sought Regarding Dual Relationships," *NASW California News*, v.17(5—1991), at 6.

57. Some of the many ways a license can be denied or revoked in California include misrepresentation of qualifications or competence, aiding and abetting unlicensed practice, any manner of sexual relations or solicitation with a client, failure to maintain confidentiality, failure to disclose fees, false advertising, intentional infliction of emotional distress, negligent supervision of staff and subordinates, failure to report child or elder abuse, and any act of gross negligence. *Cal. Bus. and Profess. Code*, ch. 18, sect. 1881.

58. "Judge Upholds Professional Ethics Codes," *Marriage and Divorce Today*, v.6 (1981) 1.

59. See *Cantwell v. Connecticut*, 310 U.S. 296, 303–304 (1940)

60. *Reynolds v. United States*, 98 U.S. 145 (1879).

61. See *Sherbert v. Verner*, 374 U.S. 398, at 398, 403 (1963); also *Wisconsin v. Yoder*, 406 U.S. 205 (1972). Chase, "Malpractice: The Cause of Action," 166, stated well the application of this historic constitutional standard to Christian counseling: ". . . a clergy counselor who is sued for clergy malpractice can find sanctuary in the free exercise clause if he can convince the court that his conduct was an important part of a sincere religious practice, that a finding of malpractice liability will impose a substantial burden on the exercise of his religious practices, and that such burden is not outweighed by a compelling state interest."

62. E. M.Gaffney, D. Laycock, and M. W. McConnell, "An Answer to Smith: The Religious Freedom Restoration Act." *Christian Legal Society Quarterly*, v.11(4—1990), 17.

63. M. S. Paulsen, and R. K. Smith, "A Luxury . . . We Cannot Afford: Religious Freedom after the Peyote Case," *Christian Legal Society Quarterly*, v.12(2—1990), 18.

64. *Nally III*, 253 Cal. Rptr. at 99.

65. Ibid., 100.

66. Ibid. Compare Justice Kaufman's concurring opinion, p 115, in which he clearly saw that a counseling relationship had begun. This shows the differences by which case facts are understood and used to support the legal reasoning undergirding the judicial rule.

67. Ibid., 115. Although the majority opinion strained to distinguish these statements as referring to trouble living the Christian life, p 100, footnote 2, Nally's suicide and Pastor Rea's deposition testimony, p 115–16, footnote 3, clearly indicate that suicide was at issue.

68. Ibid., 100, footnote 3. This judgment was made in the face of strong clinical evidence of suicidal risk, including open discussion by Nally about suicide and his past struggles with it. Pastor Thomson, who considered himself competent to work with severe depression and suicide, believed that "biblical counseling" and prayer were sufficient for this crisis. Presumably, Pastor Thomson held this position even after Nally's first suicide attempt, p 116.

69. Ibid., 100. The medical side of this tragedy begins to reveal itself here. No psychiatrist or knowledgeable general practitioner would prescribe Elavil (or would do so at very low dosage and with strictest monitoring) to a person at risk for suicide due to its lethality in overdose.

70. Ibid., 101. The record also reveals that Nally told Pastors MacArthur and Rea, while visiting him at the hospital, that he was sorry he didn't succeed in dying and that he would try again. The pastors never informed hospital staff of these statements, presuming, it seems, that they already knew this and had taken precautions.

71. Ibid., 101.

72. Ibid., 102.

73. *Nally v. Grace Community Church of the Valley*, 194 Cal. App. 3d 1147, 240 Cal. Rptr. 215 (Cal. App. 2 Dist. 1987), hereinafter cited as *Nally II*. In California the Court of Appeal is an intermediary between the trial court and the Supreme Court. It is the first appellate review court for disputed trial judgments, but is always subject to the higher authority of the California Supreme Court.

74. Prosser and Keeton, (1984). *The Law of Torts*, 5th ed., section 56, at 374.

75. *Nally II*, 240 Cal. Rptr. at 224–26.

76. See *Meier v. Ross General Hospital*, 69 Cal.2d 420, 71 Cal. Rptr. 903, 455 P.2d 519 (1968); and *Vistica v. Presbyterian Hospital*, 67 Cal.2d 465, 62 Cal. Rptr. 577, 432 P.2d 193 (1967).

77. *Nally* III, 253 Cal. Rptr. at 106

78. Ibid., 108.

79. Ibid., 109. See also S. E. Ericsson, "Clergyman Malpractice: Ramifications of a New Theory," *Valparaiso University Law Review*, v.16, (1981), 163. Ericsson, a Christian attorney and a leading constitutional scholar on church/state relations, was Grace Community Church's defense counsel in the Nally case.

80. Ibid. The court stated that because of "the differing theological views espoused by the myriad of religions in our state and practiced by church members, it would certainly be impractical, and quite possibly unconstitutional, to impose a duty of care on pastoral counselors. Such a duty would necessarily be intertwined with the religious philosophy of the particular denomination or ecclesiastical teachings of the religious entity."

81. Ibid., 110, footnote 8.

82. Ibid., 113.

83. Ibid., 116–17.

84. Ibid., 114–15. The church had fifty pastoral counselors, employed a counseling appointments secretary, served the larger church and community beyond their membership, including advertising its services in the Yellow

Pages, and many counselors taught classes and published books, tapes and various aids on biblical counseling ministry.

85. Ibid., 117–18.
86. Ibid.
87. Ibid., 114–15.
88. Ibid., 102.
89. See N. C. Andreason, *The Broken Brain: The Biological Revolution in Psychiatry* (New York: Harper and Row, 1984).
90. For example, the Code of Ethics of the *American Association of Pastoral Counselors*, which the church successfully fought as an expert witness, requires that "Pastoral counselors accurately represent their professional qualifications . . ." and " . . . are responsible for correcting any misrepresentation of their professional qualifications . . . "(sect. II.A.). Further on, the code states, "Announcements of pastoral counseling services are dignified, accurate and objective, descriptive but devoid of all claims and evaluations" (sect. II.D.).
91. See Christian Association for Psychological Studies: Proposed Code of Ethics (1985). This code, grounded in Scripture and committed to the Lordship of Christ, contains two sections on "Competency in Services Provided" and "My Human Limitations." The church-based counselor would gain much from this standard of practice. See Appendix A.
92. *Nally III*, at 100.
93. Ibid., 100–102.
94. See *Clergy Malpractice*.
95. *Nally III*, at 115–16, footnotes 3–6.
96. *Nally II*, at 233–34.
97. *Nally III*, at 101, 116–17.
98. J. MacArthur, Jr. *Our Sufficiency in Christ*.
99. *Nally III*, at 108–109
100. Letter to the Reverend Clarence Kinzler from James Barringer, Esq. (Nov. 23, 1987). Re: *Clergy Malpractice: the Nally Case*.
101. Compare, for arguments against the "chilling effect" such broad duty would have on pastoral counseling, Comment, "Clergy Malpractice: Bad News for the Good Samaritan or a Blessing in Disguise?" *University of Toledo Law Review*, v.17 (1985), 209.
102. *Nally III*, at 110, footnote 8.
103. See G. Slater, "Nally v. Grace Community Church of the Valley: Absolution for Clergy Malpractice?" *Brigham Young University Law Review*, v.1989, 913.
104. See L. M. Burek, "Clergy Malpractice: Making Clergy Accountable to a Lower Power," *Pepperdine Law Review*, v.14, (1986) 137, pp 156–57. "With the rapid movement of fundamentalist churches into the arena of emotional

counseling comes the increased perception among parishioners of competency on the part of the clergy—a perception often fostered by the members of the clergy themselves . . . [these] clergy have elevated themselves to a new level of competence, skill, or knowledge, thereby making themselves susceptible to the imposition of a duty owed to their counselees."

105. *Nally III*, at 118.

106. H. N. Malony, "The Future of Ministry in a Changing World," in *Clergy Malpractice*, 146.

107. See, for excellent reviews on these subjects, J. F. Shackelford, "Affairs in the Consulting Room: A Review of the Literature on Therapist-Patient Sexual Intimacy." *Journal of Psychology and Christianity*, v.8(4—1989), 26–43; P. L. Steinke, "Clergy Affairs," *Journal of Psychology and Christianity*, v.8(4—1989), 56–62.

108. See *Zipkin v. Freeman*, 436 S.W.2d 753 (Missouri 1968). This leading precedent-setting case was finally won by the plaintiff who eventually received $5,000 in damages. This was for behavior in which the psychiatrist induced his patient to leave her husband and move into an apartment above his practice, file lawsuits against and burglarize her husband's home, give the doctor money for speculative business ventures, engage in nude swimming parties and have frequent sex, including when she escorted him on weekend conferences.

109. See the *Cal. Bus. and Profess. Code*, sections 726, 728 and 4982(k).

110. Ibid., section 1881(f).

111. A compilation of the available research data on the incidence of sexual misconduct reveals this male perpetrator/female victim pattern to represent 80–90 percent of all cases.

112. Meyer, et. al., *Law for the Psychotherapist*, 24–25.

113. See J. Marmor, "Some Psychodynamic Aspects of the Seduction of Patients in Psychotherapy," *The American Journal of Psychoanalysis*, v.36, (1976), 319–21, wherein he wryly noted that most encounters are between male therapists and "women who are physically attractive, almost never with the aged, the infirm or the ugly, thus giving the lie to the oft-heard rationalization on the part of such therapists that they were acting in the best interests of their patients!"

114. See, for an excellent review of this problem in the church, R. C. O'Brien, "Pedophilia: The legal predicament of clergy," *Journal of Contemporary Health Law and Policy*, v.4 (1988), 91.

115. See Gartrell, et al., "Psychiatic-Patient Sexual Contact" (the most extensive survey that showed 6.4 percent of psychiatrists have engaged in sexual misconduct); K. S. Pope, P. Keith-Spiegel, and B. G. Tabachnick, "Sexual Attraction to Cients: The Human Therapist and the (sometimes) Inhuman Training System," *American Psychologist*, v.41 (2–1986), 147–158 (revealed

that 9.4 percent of all psychologists had engaged in some form of erotic contact with clients).

116. See J. S. Vinson, "Use of Complaint Procedures in Cases of Therapist-Patient Sexual Contact," *Professional Psychology: Research and Practice*, v.18(2–1987), 159–64; also N. Gartrell, et al., "Reporting Practices of Psychiatrists Who Knew of Sexual Misconduct of Colleagues," *American Journal of Orthopsychiatry*, v. 57 (1987), 287.

117. See chapter 1, T. LaHaye, *If Ministers Fall, Can They Be Restored?* (Grand Rapids: Zondervan, 1990); through my own clinical and mediation practice with The Redwood Family Institute, serving a Northern California region of approximately 150,000 people with 150 churches, we are aware of 7 men in leadership—pastors, church staff and key lay leaders from conservative, evangelical or charismatic churches—who have recently fallen prey to ruinous sexual misconduct within and outside the church.

118. Special report, "How Common Is Pastoral Indiscretion? Results of a Leadership Survey," *Leadership*, v.9(1–1988), 12–13. (Hereinafter referred to as Leadership survey.)

119. Ibid., 13.

120. J. C. Bouhoutsos, et al., "Sexual Intimacy Between Psychotherapists and Patients," *Professional Psychology: Research and Practice*, v.14(2—1983), 185–96.

121. S. Feldman-Summers, and G. Jones, "Psychological Impacts of Sexual Contact Between Therapists or Other Health Care Practitioners and Their Clients," *Journal of Consulting and Clinical Psychology*, v.52(6–1984), 1054; see also P. Chesler, *Women and Madness* (Garden City, N.Y.: Doubleday, 1972) 136–157.

122. W. H. Masters, and V. E. Johnson, "Principles of the New Sex Therapy," *American Journal of Psychiatry*, v.133 (1976), 548–54.

123. J. Benetin, and M. Wilder, "Sexual Exploitation and Psychotherapy," *Women's Rights Law Reporter*, v.11(2–1989), 121–35; D. LeBoeuf, "Psychiatric Malpractice: Exploitation of Women Patients," *Harvard Women's Law Journal*, v.11 (1988), 83–116.

124. Ibid; see J. Robitscher, *The Powers of Psychiatry* (Boston: Houghton Mifflin, 1980) 417.

125. Available through the California Department of Consumer Affairs, 1020 N Street, Sacramento, CA 95814.

126. A compilation of the data from the various studies noted herein indicates that victims report the incidence of sexual misconduct by therapists only 1 to 5 percent of the time. Considering that sexual misconduct cases are now the most prevalent and successful legal actions for plaintiffs, it is easy to conclude that even a small increase in the barely existent reporting rate will

influence a major increase in sucessful legal actions of all types against sexually abusing therapists.

127. See American Psychiatric Association,"The Principles of Medical Ethics with Annotations Especially Applicable to Psychiatry," *American Journal of Psychiatry*, v.130 (1985), 1057; *Ethical Standards of Psychologists* (Washington, D.C.: National Association of Social Workers, 1980). *NASW Code of Ethics* (Washington, D.C.); American Association for Marriage and Family Therapy, "Ethical Principles for Family Therapists," in *Clergy Malpractice*, 149; American Association of Pastoral Counselors: Ethical Code, in *Clergy Malpractice*, 154; Christian Association for Psychological Studies: Code of Ethics, see Appendix A.

128. NASW Task Force on Ethics, "Ethics Analysis—Conduct and Responsibility to Clients," *NASW News* (May 1980), 12.

129. *Roy v. Hartogs*, 85 Misc.2d 891, 381 N.Y.S.2d 587 (Sup.Ct. 1976).

130. In *Cotton v. Kambly*, 101 Mich.App. 537, 300 N.W.2d 627 (1980), the Michigan court ruled that psychiatrist's sexual actions were "under the guise of psychiatric treatment" and therefore the patient could not consent to sex related to therapy.

131. *Wisconsin Statutes Annotated*, section 895.70; *Minnesota Statutes*, section 148A; and *California Civil Code*, section 43.93.

132. *Wisconsin Statutes Annotated*, section 940.22; *Minnesota Statutes*, section 609.343; *Colorado Revised Statutes*, section 18–3–405.5; *California Business and Professional Code*, section, 729.

133. *Wisconsin Statutes Annotated*, section 940.22(1)(i).

134. See, however, Leadership survey, p. 13. One of the disturbing findings that raise legitimate questions about the church's control of this problem was the number of pastors who thought sexual fantasy about other women (not one's spouse) was okay (39 percent). Gary Collins noted how temptation begins in the mind and asserted that while behavior may be effectively controlled by personal accountability, "we need to be even more careful what we let our minds dwell on, because there can be no outside accountability there. Only the person knows what he's thinking." The failure of accountability and fear of loss of confidentiality was reflected by nearly half the pastors who stated they talk to no one, not even their wives about this problem. Larry Crabb noted that pastors aren't allowed to admit their struggles and temptations, "Most churches require their pastors to live in denial."

135. See R. J. Magnuson, "Law: The Harness and the Guidepost," *Christian Legal Society Quarterly*, v.7(1–1985), 6–11.

136. See T. Frankel, "Fiduciary Law," *California Law Review*, v. 71 (1983), 795–836; also H. Kutchins, "The Fiduciary Relationship: The Legal Basis for Social Workers' Responsibilities to Clients." *Social Work*, v.36(2—1991), 106–13.

137. Destefano, at 284.

138. *Erickson v. Christenson*, 99 Or.App. 104 (Oregon 1989).

139. See Frankel, "Fiduciary Law."

140. A. D Hart, "Being Moral Isn't Always Enough," *Leadership*, v. 9 (2—1988), 24–29.

141. D. Reeck, *Ethics for the Profession: A Christian Perspective* (Minneapolis: Augsburg, 1982).

142. J. R. Beck, and R. K. Mathews, "A Code of Ethics for Christian Counselors," *Journal of Psychology and Christianity*, v. 5(3—1986), 78–84.

Chapter 4. Theory in Christian Counseling

1. Nolan Saltzman and John C. Norcross, eds., *Therapy Wars: Contention and Convergence in Differing Clinical Approaches* (San Francisco: Jossey-Bass, 1990).

2. John D. Krumboltz, "The 1990 Leona Tyler Award Address," 298–315. The quotation is from pages 305–306.

3. Ron Crawford, "Theory into Practice: Choosing an F-Stop," *Journal of Counseling and Development* 67 (1988), 127.

4. Krumboltz, "The 1990 Leona Tyler Award Address," 309.

5. This is the main thrust of an article by William J. Lyddon, "Root Metaphor Theory: A Philosophical Framework for Counseling and Psychotherapy," *Journal of Counseling and Development* 67 (1989), 442–48.

6. Bryant Myers, "Reflections: Doing Research with Eyes to See," *MARC Newsletter* 90 (1990), 3–4.

7. Thomas Kuhn, *The Structure of Scientific Revolutions*, 2d ed (Chicago: University of Chicago Press, 1970). For a brief but useful evangelical critique of Kuhn's work see J. P. Moreland, *Christianity and the Nature of Science: A Philosophical Investigation* (Grand Rapids: Baker, 1989).

8. A. Toffler, *Powershift: Knowledge, Wealth and Violence at the Edge of the 21st Century* (New York: Bantam, 1990).

9. Peter Drucker, *The New Realities* (San Francisco: Harper and Row, 1989).

10. L. Newbigin, *Gospel in a Pluralistic Society* (Grand Rapids: Eerdmans, 1989).

11. A recent survey indicated that the majority of counselors who hold humanistic beliefs agree that "becoming a believer in religion is consistent with humanistic beliefs." Presumably many evangelicals would disagree. See Nelson Goud, "Spiritual and Ethical Beliefs of Humanists in the Counseling Profession," *Journal of Counseling and Development* 68 (1990), 571–74.

12. The following discussion is adapted from an old but highly useful book by Buford Stefflre and Kenneth Matheny, *The Function of Counseling Theory* (Boston: Houghton-Mifflin, 1968).

13. Perry London, *The Modes and Morals of Psychotherapy* (New York: Holt, Rinehart and Winston, 1964).

14. Gerald Corey, Marianne Schneider Corey, and Patrick Callanan, *Issues and Ethics in the Helping Professions*, 105–108. These four models are built on the work of P. Brickman, V. Rabinowitz, J. Karuza, D. Coates, E. Cohn, and L. Kidder, "Models of Helping and Coping," *American Psychologist* 37 (1982), 368–84.

15. Table 4–1 is adapted from P. Brickman et al., "Models of Helping and Coping," *American Psychologist* 37 (1982), 368–84.

16. Stephen Arterburn and Jack Felton, *Toxic Faith: Understanding and Overcoming Religious Addiction* (Nashville: Oliver-Nelson, 1991).

17. Stefflre and Matheny, *Counseling Theory*, 42–44.

18. Ibid., 58.

19. Gary R. Collins, "Wanted: A Christian Theory of Personality," *Journal of the American Scientific Affiliation* 19 (1967), 39–44.

20. As an editor of counseling books, I have learned that these two groups also tend to be poor writers. Clear and helpful writing, like useful counseling theory, is most likely to come from people who learn from both reading and experience.

21. In an earlier book I suggested a proposed new foundation for Christian psychology. See Gary R. Collins, *The Rebuilding of Psychology: An Integration of Psychology and Christianity* (Wheaton: Tyndale, 1977).

22. Darrell Smith, *Integrative Therapy*, 7.

23. A notable exception is a book by Stanton L. Jones and Richard E. Butman, *Modern Psychotherapies: A Comprehensive Christian Appraisal* (Downers Grove, Ill.: InterVarsity, 1991).

24. Mormon psychologist Allen Bergin is more tolerant. He writes that some religious influences seem "like the mental equivalent of nuclear energy.... sometimes manifested in dramatic personal healing or transformation. When this kind of experience is also linked with social forces, its effect can be extraordinary." See Allen E. Bergin, "Values and Religious Issues in Psychotherapy and Mental Health," 394–403. The above quotation is from page 401.

25. Probably most Christian professional counselors would have disagreements and perhaps some discomfort with the work of John and Paula Sanford, who wrote *The Transformation of the Inner Man* (Plainfield, N.J.: Bridge, 1982), or with the views of the late Ruth Carter Stapleton in *The Gift of Inner Healing* (Waco, Texas: Word, 1976). For a more psychologically informed discussion of inner healing, see David A. Seamands, *Healing of Memories* (Wheaton, Ill.: Victor Books, 1985).

26. M. J. Lambert, D. A. Shapiro, and A. E. Bergin, "The Effectiveness of Psychotherapy," in S. L. Garfield and A. E. Bergin, eds., *Handbook of Psychotherapy and Behavior Change* (New York: Wiley, 1986), 157–212. See also

W. B. Stiles, D. A. Shapiro, and R. Elliott, "Are All Psychotherapies Equivalent?" *American Psychologist* 41 (1986), 165–80.

27. The first edition of a new *Journal of Psychotherapy Integration* appeared in 1991. Described as "a conduit for a unified approach to psychotherapy," the journal "encourages attempts to . . . improve the effectiveness of psychotherapy based on integrative approaches to the field."

28. Lisa M. Grencavage and John C. Norcross, "Where Are the Commonalities Among Therapeutic Common Factors?" *Professional Psychology: Research and Practice* 21 (1990), 372–78. In the text I note that these researchers were "patient." Since Grencavage is a graduate student and Norcross is her professor, we can guess which of the two was the more patient in doing the work; and we who are professors can understand and appreciate why!

29. Grencavage and Norcross, "Where Are the Commonalities?" 374.

30. This criticism was directed at me, I think with justification, in an article that discusses commonalities in Christian approaches to therapy. See W. Brad Johnson and Charles R. Ridley, "Sources of Gain in Christian Counseling and Psychotherapy," 1991, in press (*The Counseling Psychologist*).

31. Smith, *Integrative Therapy*, 7, 10.

32. Ibid., 11.

33. For an excellent and well-documented evangelical summary of the secular and Christian foundations of Christian counseling, see Roger F. Hurding, *The Tree of Healing* (Grand Rapids: Zondervan, 1985).

34. D. Smith, "Trends in Counseling and Psychotherapy," *American Psychologist* 37 (1982), 802–809.

35. This is cited in an article that gives an excellent discussion of eclecticism and the dangers of syncretism. See Martha C. McBride and G. Eric Martin, "A Framework for Eclecticism: The Importance of Theory to Mental Health Counseling," *Journal of Mental Health Counseling* 12 (1990), 495–505.

36. C. H. Patterson, *Theories of Counseling and Psychotherapy*, 4th ed. (New York: Harper and Row, 1986), 460.

37. McBride and Martin, "A Framework for Eclecticism," 500.

38. Corey et al., *Issues and Ethics*, 102–104.

Chapter 5. Effectiveness in Christian Counseling

1. Hans J. Eysenck, "The Effects of Psychotherapy: An Evaluation," *Journal of Consulting Psychology* 16 (1952), 319–24.

2. For example, Martin Bobgan and Deidre Bobgan, *PsychoHeresy*, 163–65.

3. Hans J. Eysenck, Letter to the Editor, *American Psychologist* 35 (1980), 114, and Hans J. Eysenck, "The Effectiveness of Psychotherapy: The Specter at the Feast," *The Behavioral and Brain Sciences*, 1983, 290.

4. A. E. Bergin, "The Evaluation of Therapeutic Outcomes," in A. E. Bergin and S. L. Garfield, eds., *Handbook of Psychotherapy and Behavior Change.*

5. Within hours after I had written this paragraph I was shown a copy of the newly issued (May 1991) *Moody* magazine (vol. 91, no. 9). The cover story, written by Jim Morud, is titled "Christians on the Couch," and subtitled "Amid debate, the Christian counseling movement keeps growing." The article quotes California pastor John MacArthur, Jr., whose book, *Our Sufficiency in Christ*, condemns psychology as one of the "three deadly influences" that undermine the spiritual life of Christians and their churches.

6. Martin L. Gross, *The Psychological Society* (New York: Simon and Schuster, 1978), 4. See also Bernie Zilbergeld, *The Shrinking of America: Myths of Psychological Change* (Boston: Little, Brown, 1983).

7. Sol L. Garfield, "Issues and Methods in Psychotherapy Process Research," *Journal of Consulting and Counseling Psychology* 58 (1990), 273–80.

8. M. L. Smith, G. V. Glass, and T. I. Miller, *The Benefits of Psychotherapy* (Baltimore: Johns Hopkins University Press, 1980), 87.

9. M. J. Lambert, D. A. Shapiro, and A. E. Bergin, "The Effectiveness of Psychotherapy" in S. L. Garfield and A. E. Bergin, eds., *Handbook of Psychotherapy and Behavior Change*, 157–211. The quotation is from page 201, italics added.

10. Hans H. Strupp, "Psychotherapy: What Can the Practitioner Learn from the Researcher?" *American Psychologist* 44 (1989), 717–24.

11. J. A. Sandell, *An Empirical Study of Negative Factors in Brief Psychotherapy* (Nashville: Vanderbilt University Press, 1980).

12. Jane M. Raguepaw and Rowland S. Miller, "Psychotherapist Burnout: A Componential Analysis," *Professional Psychology: Research and Practice* 20 (1989), 32–36. See also Gary D. Ackerley, Juliann Burnell, Dale C. Holderane, Lawrence A. Kurdek, "Burnout Among Licensed Psychologists," *Professional Psychology: Research and Practice* 19 (1988), 624–31.

13. Many of the conclusions in this section are adapted from Linda Seligman, *Selecting Effective Treatments* (San Francisco: Jossey-Bass, 1990), 45–50.

14. L. E. Beutler, M. Crago, and T. G. Arizmendi, "Therapist Variables in Psychotherapy Process," in S. L. Garfield and A. E. Bergin, eds., *Handbook of Psychotherapy and Behavior Change*, 257–310.

15. J. S. Berman and N. C. Norton, "Does Professional Training Make a Therapist More Effective?" *Psychological Bulletin* 98 (1985), 401–407.

16. M. L. Smith, G. V. Glass, and T. I. Miller, *The Benefits of Psychotherapy*. See also Beutler et al., "Therapist Variables," and M. Greenspan and N. M. Kulish, "Factors in Premature Termination in Long-term Psychotherapy," *Psychotherapy: Theory, Research, and Practice* 22 (1985), 75–82.

17. Berman and Norton, "Does Professional Training Make a Therapist More Effective?" See also J. A. Durlak, "Comparative Effectiveness of Para-Professional and Professional Helpers," *Psychological Bulletin* 86 (1979), 80–92.

18. R. B. Sloane, F. R. Staples, A. H. Cristol, N. J. Yorkston, and K. Whipple, *Psychotherapy Versus Behavior Therapy* (Cambridge, Mass.: Harvard University Press, 1975).

19. Everett L. Worthington, Jr., "Religious Counseling: A Review of Published Empirical Research," *Journal of Counseling and Development* 64 (1986), 421–31.

20. C. A. Everett and A. Seaton-Johnson, "An Analysis of Pastoral Counseling Supervisors: Their Identities, Roles and Resources," *Journal of Pastoral Care* 37 (1983), 50–59.

21. H. A. Virkler, "The Facilitativeness of Parish Ministers: A Descriptive Study," *Journal of Psychology and Theology* 8 (1980), 140–46.

22. Kevin R. Kelly, Alex Smith Hall, and Kenneth L. Miller, "Relation of Counselor Intention and Anxiety to Brief Counseling Outcome," *Journal of Counseling Psychology* 36 (1989), 158–62; and Adam O. Horvath, Ronald W. Marx, and April M. Kamann, "Thinking About Thinking in Therapy: An Examination of Clients' Understanding of Their Therapists' Intentions," *Journal of Consulting and Clinical Psychology* 58 (1990), 614–21.

23. Seligman, *Selecting Effective Treatments*, 49.

24. Beutler et al., "Therapist Variables," and M. J. Lambert, *The Effects of Psychotherapy* (New York: Human Sciences Press, 1982).

25. Seligman, *Selecting Effective Treatments*, 50.

26. Smith, Glass, and Miller, *The Benefits of Psychotherapy*.

27. Seligman, *Selecting Effective Treatments*, 53. See also M. J. Horowitz et al., "Brief Psychotherapy of Bereavement Reactions," *Archives of General Psychiatry* 41 (1984), 438–48.

28. David C. Mohr et al., "Identification of Patients at Risk for Nonresponse and Negative Outcome in Psychotherapy," *Journal of Consulting and Clinical Psychology* 58 (1990), 622–28.

29. G. S. Howard, D. W. Nance, and P. Myers, *Adaptive Counseling and Therapy: A Systematic Approach to Selecting Effective Treatments* (San Francisco: Jossey-Bass, 1987).

30. Beutler et al., "Therapist Variables," 282.

31. This list is taken from research by E. L. Worthington, Jr., and G. G. Scott, "Goal Selection for Counseling with Potentially Religious Clients by Professional and Student Counselors in Explicitly Christian or Secular Settings," *Journal of Psychology and Theology* 11 (1983), 318–29. See also R. R. King, Jr., "Evangelical Christians and Professional Counseling: A Conflict of Values?" *Journal of Psychology and Theology* 6 (1978), 226–81.

32. Some of these conclusions are summarized by Michael J. Lambert, Dean E. Barley, and Ellie L. Wright, "Research in Psychotherapy Effectiveness," in David G. Benner, ed., *Psychotherapy in Christian Perspective* (Grand Rapids: Baker, 1987), 61–74.

33. Horowitz et al., "Brief Psychotherapy," 439.

34. Adam K. Lehman and Peter Salovey, "Psychotherapist Orientation and Expectations for Liked and Disliked Patients," *Professional Psychology: Research and Practice* 21 (1990), 385–91.

35. Harvey R. Freeman, "Influence of Client and Counselor Characteristics on Satisfaction with Counseling Services," *Journal of Mental Health Counseling* 11 (1989), 375–83.

36. One study that demonstrated a clear link between therapeutic alliance and effectiveness was published by D. E. Hartley and H. H. Strupp, "The Therapeutic Alliance: Its Relationship to Outcome in Brief Psychotherapy," in J. Masling, ed., *Empirical Studies in Analytic Theories* (Hillsdale, N.J.: Erlbaum, 1983).

37. For a sample of this research see P. Forrest Talley, Hans H. Strupp, and Leslie C. Morey, "Matchmaking in Psychotherapy: Patient-Therapist Dimensions and Their Impact on Outcome," *Journal of Consulting and Clinical Psychology* 58 (1990), 182–88. See also M. R. McMinn, "Religious Values and Client-Therapist Matching in Psychotherapy," *Journal of Psychology and Theology* 12 (1984), 24–33.

38. Lisa M. Grencavage and John C. Norcross, "Where Are the Commonalities Among the Therapeutic Common Factors?" 372–78.

39. D. E. Orlinsky and K. I. Howard, "Process and Outcome in Psychotherapy," in S. L. Garfield and A. E. Bergin, eds., *Handbook of Psychotherapy and Behavior Change*, 311–81.

40. S. Perry, A. Frances, and J. Clarkin, *A DSM-III Casebook of Differential Therapeutics* (New York: Brunner/Mazel, 1985).

41. R. L. Propst, "The Psychology of Religion and the Clinical Practitioner," *Journal of Psychology and Christianity* 5 (1986), 74–77; Worthington, "Religious Counseling," and Everett L. Worthington, Jr. et al., "Christian Therapists' and Clients' Perceptions of Religious Psychotherapy in Private and Agency Settings," *Journal of Psychology and Theology* 16 (1988), 282–93. For a survey report of the extent to which religious practices are used by Christian counselors, see Robert A. Ball and Rodney K. Goodyear, "Self-Reported Professional Practices of Christian Psychotherapists," *Journal of Psychology and Christianity* 10 (1991), 144–53.

42. T. Karasu, "The Specificity Versus Nonspecificity Dilemma: Toward Identifying Therapeutic Change Agents," *American Journal of Psychiatry* 143 (1986), 687–95.

43. This and the following paragraph are adapted from Seligman, *Selecting Effective Treatments*, 14.

44. W. Brad Johnson and Charles R. Ridley, "Sources of Gain in Christian Counseling and Psychotherapy" (1991), in press.

45. Jay Adams, *Competent to Counsel*, 20.

46. Johnson and Ridley, "Sources of Gain."

47. Clara E. Hill, "Exploratory In-Session Process Research in Individual Psychotherapy: A Review," *Journal of Consulting and Clinical Psychology* 58 (1990), 288–94. The quotation is from page 292.

48. This view is expressed succinctly by George S. Howard, "The Scientist-Practitioner in Counseling Psychology: Toward a Deeper Integration of Theory, Research and Practice," *The Counseling Psychologist* 14 (1986), 61–105.

49. Worthington, "Religious Counseling," 429.

Chapter 6. Growth and Training in Christian Counseling

1. Siang-Yang Tan and Stanton L. Jones, "Christian Graduate Training in Professional Psychology: The Rech Conference," *Journal of Psychology and Christianity* 10 (1991), 72–75. Training, of course, is of concern to educators in a number of mental health related disciplines. See, for example, Margaret L. Fong and Peter A. D. Sherrard, "Mental Health Counselor Training: Directions for the 1990s" *Journal of Mental Health Counseling* 13 (1991), 167–71, and Susan Moses, "New Image Affirmed for Graduate Training," APA Monitor, March 1990, 30.

2. See, for example, C. Stephen Evans, *Wisdom and Humanness in Psychology: Prospects for a Christian Approach* (Grand Rapids: Baker, 1989). From my perspective, "new breed" writers include, but are not limited to the following: Stanton Jones, Siang-Yang Tan, Mary Stewart Van Leeuwen, Ray Anderson (author of *Christians Who Counsel*), Alan C. Tjeltveit, Rebecca Propst, Charles R. Ridley, Darrell Smith (author of *Integrative Therapy*), and perhaps Samuel Southard (author of *Theology and Therapy: The Wisdom of God in a Context of Friendship*). These writers are of different ages and many, like Evans and Anderson, are not professional psychologists.

3. C. Stephen Evans, "Developing Wisdom in Christian Counseling," unpublished paper presented at the Rech Conference on Christian Graduate Training in Psychology, Lisle, Illinois, 26 October 1990. The quotation is from page 14.

4. Evans, "Developing Wisdom," 16.

5. Gary W. Moon et al., "Training in the Use of Christian Disciplines as Counseling Techniques Within Religiously Oriented Graduate Training Programs," *Journal of Psychology and Christianity* 10 (1991), 154–65.

6. R. L. Propst, "A Comparison of the Cognitive Restructuring Psychotherapy Paradigm and Several Spiritual Approaches to Mental Health," *Journal of Psychology and Theology* 8 (1980), 107–14. The quotation is from page 107. Some more recent evidence on the self-reported practices of Christian counselors suggests that "religious interventions" (most often prayer) are used, at least periodically. See Robert A. Ball and Rodney K. Goodyear, "Self-Reported Professional Practices of Christian Psychotherapists."

7. Jeremiah W. Canning, ed., *Values in an Age of Confrontation* (Columbus, Ohio: Charles E. Merrill, 1970), 148–49.

8. David B. Hershenson and William Strein, "Toward a Mentally Healthy Curriculum for Mental Health Counselor Education," *Journal of Mental Health Counseling* 13 (1991), 247–52.

9. Eileen Gambrill, *Critical Thinking in Clinical Practice* (San Francisco: Jossey-Bass, 1990). The quotation is from page 55. Agoraphobia is fear of being in open spaces.

10. It should be noted that this debate is not limited to counselor education. When I taught undergraduates, the faculty debated what needed to be included in the curriculum. When I taught in theological seminaries, there was debate over what a seminarian needs to know if he or she is to be prepared for ministry. These debates are ongoing, often bogged down in "turf defending," but frequently productive in boosting the quality and relevance of education.

11. This is emphasized by Gerald Corey, Marianne Schneider Corey, and Patrick Callanan, *Issues and Ethics in the Helping Professions*, 142.

12. J. Hollis and R. Wantz, *Counselor Preparation 1986–1989: Programs, Personnel and Trends* (Muncie, Ind.: Accelerated Development, Inc., 1986).

13. Some of these lay counselor training approaches are described in chapter 7 of the book by Siang-Yang Tan, *Lay Counseling: Equipping Christians for a Helping Ministry* (Grand Rapids: Zondervan, 1991).

14. See, for example, J. Hansen, T. Robins, and J. Grimes, "Review of Research on Practicum Supervision," *Counselor Education and Supervision* 22 (1982), 15–24.

15. See, for example, Dale Larson, ed., *Teaching Psychological Skills: Models for Giving Psychology Away* (Monterey, Calif.: Brooks/Cole, 1984). For further information about the role of theories in training, see R. Goodyear and F. Bradley, "Theories of Counselor Supervision: Points of Convergence and Divergence," *The Counseling Psychologist* 11 (1983), 59–67, and L. Bradley, *Counselor Supervision* (Muncie, Ind.: Accelerated Development, Inc., 1989).

16. This is a major conclusion of research by Timothy E. Clinton, "Assessment of Behavioral and Personality Characteristics of Masters Level

Counselor Education Students Across Training and Supervision," unpublished doctoral dissertation, William and Mary College, 1990. See also L. Borders, "A Pragmatic Agenda for Developmental Supervision and Research," *Counselor Education and Supervision* 29 (1989), 16–24, and C. Stoltenberg and E. Delworth, *Supervisory Counselors and Therapists: A Development Approach* (San Francisco: Jossey-Bass, 1987).

17. Jack Martin et al., "Conceptualizations of Novice and Experienced Counselors," *Journal of Counseling Psychology* 36 (1989), 395–400.

18. Gambrill discusses experience in *Critical Thinking*, 61–62.

19. For example, see Gambrill, *Critical Thinking*, page 67; H. Grayson, "Ethical Issues in the Training of Psychotherapists," in M. Rosenbaum, ed., *Ethics and Values in Psychotherapy: A Guidebook* (New York: Free Press, 1982); and Sherry Cormier, "Systematic Training of Graduate-Level Counselors: A Reaction," *The Counseling Psychologist* 18 (1990), 446–54. For an excellent discussion on Christian mentoring (but with no attempt to relate this to counseling), see Ted W. Engstrom with Norman B. Rohrer, *The Fine Art of Mentoring: Passing On to Others What God Has Given to You* (Brentwood, Tenn.: Wolgemuth and Hyatt, 1989).

20. The best and most complete treatment to date dealing with the training of Christian lay counseling, is Tan's *Lay Counseling*.

21. E. Holloway and P. Wolleat, "Style Differences of Beginning Supervisors: An Interactional Analysis," *Journal of Counseling and Psychology* 28 (1981), 373–76, and Allen K. Hess, "Advances in Psychotherapy Supervision: Introduction," *Professional Psychology: Research and Practice* 18 (1987), 187–88.

22. Research is being done on a variety of supervision issues, however. For one review, see Michael J. Lambert and Robert C. Arnold, "Research and the Supervisory Process," *Professional Psychology: Research and Practice* 18 (1987), 217–24.

23. The number of training courses has increased within the past decade. For example, compare A. K. Hess and K. A. Hess, "Psychotherapy Supervision: A Survey of Internship Training Practices," *Professional Psychology: Research and Practice* 14 (1983), 504–13, and L. D. Borders and G. R. Leddick, "A Nationwide Survey of Supervision Training," *Counselor Education and Supervision* 27 (1988), 271–83. See also John S. Baranchok and Mark A. Kunkel, "Clinical Supervision Training in Counseling Psychology," *The Counseling Psychologist* 18 (1990), 685–87.

24. For example, L. D. Borders, "Credentialing Supervisors: A Commitment to Professionalism," *Illinois Association for Counseling and Development Quarterly* 112 (1989), 33–42.

25. Michael S. Carifio and Allen K. Hess, "Who Is the Ideal Supervisor?" *Professional Psychology: Research and Practice* 18 (1987), 244–50.

26. H. Allan Dye and L. DiAnne Borders, "Counseling Supervisors: Standards for Preparation and Practice," *Journal of Counseling and Development* 69 (1990), 27–29. See also Carifio and Hess, "Who Is the Ideal Supervisor?"

27. D. Brannon, "Adult Learning Principles and Methods for Enhancing the Training Role of Supervisors," *The Clinical Supervisor* 3 (1985), 27–41.

28. Everett L. Worthington, Jr., "Issues in Supervision of Lay Christian Counseling," *Journal of Psychology and Christianity* 6 (1987), 70–77. For a verbatim example of a one-to-one supervision session, see Tan, *Lay Counseling*, 149–55.

29. For a brief treatment of ethical and legal issues in clinical supervision, see Corey et al., *Issues and Ethics*, 154–60; William R. Harrar, Leon VandeCreek, and Samuel Knapp. "Ethical and Legal Aspects of Clinical Supervision," *Professional Psychology: Research and Practice* 21 (1990), 37–41; and Elizabeth L. Holloway et al., "Relation of Power and Involvement to Theoretical Orientation in Supervision: An Analysis of Discourse," *Journal of Counseling Psychology* 36 (1989), 88–102.

30. George Domino, "Clergy's Knowledge of Psychopathology," *Journal of Psychology and Theology* 18 (1990), 32–39. See also George Domino, "Clergy's Attitudes Toward Suicide and Recognition of Suicide Lethality," *Death Studies* 9 (1985), 187–99.

31. D. E. Linebaugh and P. DeVivo, "The Growing Emphasis on Training Pastor-Counselors in Protestant Seminaries," *Journal of Psychology and Theology* 9 (1981), 266–68. It should be noted that this study is over ten years old and changes may have occurred in the years following the cited research.

32. In a recent published symposium, three Christian professional counselors attempted to assess the impact of integration and theology courses on their practice. Apparently with tongue in cheek, one respondent observed, "Everything I needed to know about integration I already learned in Sunday School." See Clark D. Campbell, John F. Shackelford, and Randy P. Marsh, "Integrative Inquiry," *Journal of Psychology and Theology* 18 (1990), 381–86.

33. For a brief overview of these programs see James P. Sampson and John D. Krumboltz, "Computer-Assisted Instruction: A Missing Link in Counseling," *Journal of Counseling and Development* 69 (1991), 395–97.

34. S. L. Greenburg, G. J. Lewis, and J. Johnson, "Peer Consultation Groups for Private Practitioners," *Professional Psychology: Research and Practice* 16 (1985), 437–47.

35. Of course, people drop out of peer groups for a number of reasons, so we should not assume that the one who leaves is threatened or afraid to face his or her colleagues.

36. Steve Levicoff, *Christian Counseling and the Law* (Chicago: Moody, 1991), 52–55.

37. Information about both organizations is available by writing to 5999 Stevenson Avenue, Alexandria, Va. 22304.

38. S. J. Gill, "Professional Disclosure and Consumer Protection in Counseling," *Personnel and Guidance Journal* 60 (1982), 443–46. Disclosure is discussed in greater detail in Corey et al., *Issues and Ethics*, 148–51.

Chapter 7. Trends in Christian Counseling

1. J. Smith, *Advance Australia Where?* (Homebush West, NSW: Anzea), 7–8.

2. Ibid., 25.

3. M. Cetron and O. Davis, *American Renaissance: Our Life at the Turn of the 21st Century* (New York: St. Martin's Press, 1989).

4. Joe Cappo, *FutureScope: Success Strategies for the 1990s and Beyond* (Chicago: Longman Financial Services, 1989). Perhaps it should be noted that the *est* movement has fallen on hard times since the publication of Cappo's book, and some are predicting that *est* is already passe.

5. George Barna, *The Frog in the Kettle: What Christians Need to Know About Life in the Year 2000* (Ventura, Calif.: Regal Books, 1990), 180.

6. Pat Robertson, *The New Millennium: 10 Trends That Will Impact You and Your Family by the Year 2000* (Dallas: Word, 1990).

7. Alvin Toffler, Powershift: *Knowledge, Wealth, and Violence at the Edge of the 21st Century*.

8. J. Naisbitt and P. Aburdene, *Megatrends 2000: Ten New Directions for the 1990s* (New York: Morrow, 1990).

9. S. S. Rude, M. Weissberg, and G. M. Gazda, "Looking to the Future: Themes from the Third National Conference on Counseling Psychology," *The Counseling Psychologist* 16 (1988), 423–30; E. L. Herr, *Counseling in a Dynamic Society: Opportunities and Challenges* (Alexandria, Va.: American Association for Counseling and Development, 1989); Gerald L. Stone and James Archer, Jr., "College and University Counseling Centers in the 1990s: Challenges and Limits," *The Counseling Psychologist* 18 (1990), 539–607; Stanley B. Baker and Ann T. Greeley, "Looking at the Past and into the Future," *The Counseling Psychologist* 18 (1990), 691–93.

10. James D. Guy, *The Personal Life of the Psychotherapist*. Chapter 8 is titled, "Future Trends in the Practice of Psychotherapy." For a more critical analysis of changes in the field, see Bernie Zilbergeld, *The Shrinking of America: Myths of Psychological Change* (Boston: Little, Brown, 1983).

11. Russell Chandler, *Understanding the New Age* (Dallas: Word, 1988), 17.

12. Ibid.

13. "New Age Harmonies," *Time*, 7 December 1987, 62, 64.

14. This summary is adapted from an article by Gordon Miller, "The New Age Movement," *Grid* (World Vision of Australia, Autumn 1990), 4–5.

15. A. A. Dole, M. D. Langone, and S. Dobrow-Eichel, "The New Age Movement: Fad or Menace?" *Cultic Studies Journal* 7 (1990), 69–71.

16. This is discussed by Robert J. L. Burrows, "The Coming of the New Age," in Karen Hoyt and J. Isamu Yamamoto, eds., *The New Age Rage* (Old Tappan, N.J.: Fleming H. Revell, 1987).

17. Several excellent and well-documented books have been written to summarize New Age thinking for Christian readers. Among the best: Chandler, *Understanding the New Age*; Douglas R. Groothuis, *Unmasking the New Age* (Downers Grove, Ill.: InterVarsity, 1986); Elliot Miller, *A Crash Course on the New Age Movement* (Grand Rapids: Baker, 1989); Walter Martin, *The New Age Cult* (Minneapolis: Bethany House, 1989); and Ron Rhodes, *The Counterfeit Christ of the New Age Movement* (Grand Rapids: Baker, 1990). If you only have time to read one book, I would recommend Miller's.

18. One of the best ways for Christian counselors to know about cults is by subscribing to the *Cult Studies Journal* (available semi-annually for fifteen dollars sent to American Family Foundation, Box 336, Weston, Mass. 02193). This is not a Christian organization, but there are Christians on the board of the journal and the publication is often sympathetic to evangelical thinking. The AFF also publishes other cult-related materials, including books such as a volume by Joan Carol Ross and Michael D. Langone, *Cults: What Parents Should Know* (Weston, Mass.: AFF, 1988).

19. Margaret W. Long, "The Cult Appeal: Susceptibilities of the Missionary Kid," *The Cultic Studies Journal* 4 (1987), 38–60. See also W. Appel, *Cults in America: Programmed for Paradise* (New York: Holt, Rinehart and Winston, 1983); Harold L. Bussell, *Unholy Devotion: Why Cults Lure Christians* (Grand Rapids: Zondervan, 1983), and M. Galanter, *Cults, Faith Healing, and Coercion* (New York: Oxford, 1989).

20. *The Skeptical Inquirer* is a humanistic journal that debunks almost everything that might be considered supernatural, but mature Christians can get good insights into the thinking of contemporary skeptics by reading selected articles, many of which are well written and carefully documented. The Summer 1989 issue was entirely devoted to examining (and generally debunking) the New Age Movement. The Spring and Summer 1990 issues carried articles critical of reports that cite the reality of Satan. See, for example, Robert D. Hicks, "Police Pursuit of Satanic Crime: Part II—The Satanic Conspiracy and Urban Legends," *Skeptical Inquirer* 14 (summer 1990), 378–98.

21. M. D. Langone and L. O. Blood, *Satanism and Occult-Related Violence: What You Should Know* (Weston, Mass.: American Family Foundation, 1990), and Carl A. Raschke, *Painted Black: From Drug Killings to Heavy Metal—The Alarming True Story of How Satanism Is Terrorizing Our Communities* (San Francisco: Harper and Row, 1990). For a more popular

treatment, see Jerry Johnston, *The Edge of Evil: The Rise of Satanism in North America* (Dallas: Word, 1989).

22. See, for example, Rodger K. Bufford, *Counseling and the Demonic* (Dallas: Word, 1988), and the chapter by Lois Motz, "A Case of Ritualistic Abuse," in Gary R. Collins, ed., *Case Studies in Christian Counseling* (Dallas: Word, 1991).

23. Siang-Yang Tan, *Lay Counseling*.

24. B. H. Gottlieb, ed., *Social Networks and Social Support* (Beverly Hills, Calif: Sage, 1981).

25. Stanley F. Schneider, "Psychology at a Crossroads," *American Psychologist* 45 (1990), 521–29.

26 M. Horton, ed., *The Agony of Deceit: What Some TV Preachers Are Really Teaching* (Chicago: Moody, 1990).

27. There are numerous books on this subject. The following, for example, are all written by Christian authors: Sandra D. Wilson, *Counseling Adult Children of Alcoholics* (Dallas: Word, 1989); Sandra D. Wilson, *Released from Shame: Recovery for Adult Children of Dysfunctional Families* (Downers Grove, Ill.: InterVarsity, 1990); Charles Sell, *Unfinished Business: Helping Adult Children Resolve Their Past* (Portland, Ore.: Multnomah, 1989); Jim Conway, *Adult Children of Legal or Emotional Divorce: Healing Your Long-term Hurt* (Downers Grove, Ill.: InterVarsity, 1990); and Dave Carder, Earl Henslin, Henry Cloud, John Townsend, and Alice Brawand, *Secrets of Your Family Tree: Healing for Adult Children of Dysfunctional Families* (Chicago: Moody, 1991).

28. Edwin L. Herr, *Counseling in a Dynamic Society: Opportunities and Challenges* (Alexandria, Va.: American Personnel and Guidance Association, 1989), 189.

29. C. A. Kiesler and T. L. Morton, "Psychology and Public Policy in the 'Health Care Revolution,'" *American Psychologist* 43 (1988), 993–1003.

30. This idea is developed by Scheider in "Psychology at the Crossroads."

31. G. R. Walz and L. Benjamin, *A Futuristic Perspective for Counselors* (Ann Arbor, Mich.: The University of Michigan, ERIC Counseling and Personnel Services Clearinghouse, 1979).

32. For a brief overview of family therapies, especially as they relate to the future, see chapter 3 "The Changing American Family," in Herr's book, *Counseling in a Dynamic Society*. A discussion of family therapy from a Christian perspective is presented by Frederick A. DiBlasio, "Integrative Strategies for Family Therapy with Evangelical Christians," *Journal of Psychology and Theology* 16 (1988), 127–34.

33. To keep abreast of this emerging field, you may want to subscribe to *The Family Therapy Networker*, 8528 Bradford Road, Silver Springs, Md. 20901. The publication is strictly secular, however, and sometimes prints

articles that are in sharp contrast to Christian values. Professionals may also wish to consider joining the American Association for Marriage and Family Therapy, 1100 Seventeenth Street, Washington, D.C. 20036.

34. Ken Dychtwald and Joe Flowers, *Age Wave: The Challenges and Opportunities of an Aging America* (Los Angeles: Jeremy P. Tarcher, 1989).

35. C. M. Aldwin, A. Spiro, III, M. R. Levenson, and R. Bosse, "Longitudinal Findings from the Normative Aging Study: 1. Does Mental Health Change with Age?" *Psychology and Aging* 4 (1989), 295–306.

36. N. Krause, J. Laing, and V. Keith, "Personality, Social Support, and Pathological Distress in Later Life," *Psychology and Aging* 5 (1990), 315–26.

37. For examples of creative approaches to counseling the elderly, see the entire July 1990 issue of *Journal of Mental Health Counseling*, which deals with "Techniques for Counseling Older People." See also Carol P. Hausman, "Treating the Elderly Client," *Family Therapy Networker* 15 (1991), 21–24.

38. For a discussion of Christian criticisms, see James D. Foster and Mark F. Ledbetter, "Christian Anti-Psychology and the Scientific Method," *Journal of Psychology and Theology* 15 (1987), 10–18.

39. I attempted to do this in Gary R. Collins, *Can You Trust Psychology?*

40. Gary R. Collins, ed., *Helping People Grow* (Santa Ana, Calif.: Vision House, 1980), 338. This book is no longer in print and copies are no longer available.

41. Ibid, 338–50.

42. William Bevan, "A Tour Inside the Onion," *American Psychologist* 46 (1991), 475–83. The quotation is from pages 475, 476, and 481.

43. Thomas C. Oden, *Agenda for Theology: After Modernity . . . What?* (Grand Rapids: Zondervan, 1990), 46.

44. From an interview with Thomas Oden by Christopher A. Hall, "Back to the Fathers," *Christianity Today* 34 (24 September 1990), 28–31.

45. Strangely, modernity is still entrenched on university campuses and there appears to be little resistance to modernity within contemporary psychology. The article by Bevan, "A Tour Inside the Onion," is an exception. See also L. Kolakowski, "Modernity on Endless Trial," *Encounter* 66 (1987), 8–12; and R. Nisbit, *The Present Age, Progress and Anarchy in Modern America* (New York: Harper and Row, 1988).

46. Some of these issues are developed further by Oden, *After Modernity . . . What?* and by David G. Benner, *Psychotherapy and the Spiritual Quest* (Grand Rapids: Baker, 1988).

47. Masaaki Imai, *Kaizen (Kay´zen): The Key to Japan's Competitive Success* (New York: McGraw-Hill, 1986).

48. See, for example, 1 Corinthians 12, Romans 12, and Ephesians 4. In these passages, the church is seen as a body where all of the members work together, using their God-given gifts to build the church and advance the

Kingdom of Christ. These passages give little support to the idea of theological super-stars.

49. The clearest examples are in Acts 2:42–47 and 4:32–37, but the concept of mutuality is seen throughout the New Testament.

50. Bevan, "A Tour Inside the Onion," 480.

51. Alan J. Gelenberg, "Psychiatry in the l990s," *Journal of Clinical Psychiatry* 52 (1991), 205–7.

52. Barna, *The Frog in the Kettle*, 62.

Chapter 8. Future Directions in Christian Counseling: The Best Is Yet to Be

1. James C. Dobson, foreword to *Integrity* by Ted W. Engstrom with Robert C. Larson (Dallas: Word, 1987), ix (italics in the original).

2. Richard J. Foster, *Money, Sex and Power: The Challenge of the Disciplined Life* (San Francisco: Harper and Row, 1985).

3. In an earlier chapter I noted that research now exists to back up the student's observations. Spiritual disciplines are rarely included as part of Christian counseling education programs. See Gary W. Moon, Judy W. Bailey, John C. Kwasny, and Dale Willis, "Training in the Use of Christian Disciplines as Counseling Techniques Within Religiously Oriented Graduate Training Programs," *Journal of Psychology and Christianity* 13 (1991), 154–65.

4. Lawrence 0. Richards, *A Practical Theology of Spirituality* (Grand Rapids: Zondervan, 1987), 50.

5. Richard J. Foster, *Celebration of Discipline: The Path to Spiritual Growth*, rev. ed. (San Francisco: Harper and Row, 1988). See also Dallas Willard, *The Spirit of the Disciplines: Understanding How God Changes Lives* (San Francisco: Harper and Row, 1988).

6. Gary R. Collins, ed., *Case Studies in Christian Counseling* (Dallas: Word, 1991), 4.

7. John D. Krumboltz, "The 1990 Leona Tyler Award Address," 298–315.

8. James L. Powell, "Counseling a Fundamentalist Family Whose Son Has AIDS," in Gary R. Collins, ed., *Case Studies in Christian Counseling* (Dallas: Word, 1991)

9. Carol P. Hausman, "Treating the Elderly Client," *The Family Therapy Networker* 15, no. 1 (1991), 24.

10. Erik H. Erikson, *Childhood and Society*, 2d ed. (New York: Norton, 1963), 267.

11. H. J. Freudenberger, "Staff Burn-out," *Journal of Social Issues* 30 (1974), 159–65.

12. G. D. Ackerley, J. Burnell, D. C. Holder, and L. A. Kurdek, "Burnout Among Licensed Professionals"; and C. R. Berry, *When Helping You Is Hurting Me* (San Francisco: Harper and Row, 1988).

13. R. R. Kilburg, P. E. Nathan, and R. W. Thoreson, eds., *Professionals In Distress: Issues, Syndromes, and Solutions Psychology* (Washington, D.C.: American Psychological Association, 1986); J. D. Guy, P. L. Poelstra, and M. J. Stark, "Personal Distress and Therapeutic Effectiveness: National Survey of Psychologists Practicing Psychotherapy," *Professional Psychology and Practice* 20 (1989), 48–50. For an excellent Christian discussion of this issue see Louis M. McBurney, *Counseling Christian Workers* (Waco, Texas: Word, 1986).

14. I have attempted to answer some of their arguments in Gary R. Collins, *Can You Trust Psychology?*

15. W. E. Diehl, *In Search of Faithfulness: Lessons from the Christian Community* (Philadelphia: Fortress, 1987), ix.

16. John W. Gardner, *Excellence: Can We Be Equal and Excellent Too?* 86.

INDEX

Aburdene, P., 136
Accomodation assumption, 108, 110
Accountability, 25, 38, 61, 126, 146, 151, 159
Action therapies, 82
Active agent assumption, 109–10
Adams, Jay, 8, 32, 106, 109, 110, 123
Advertising, 183–84
Age, similarity between counselor and counselee, 99. (*See also* Senior citizens)
AIDS, 7, 34, 161
American Association of Marriage and Family Therapists, 55
American Bar Association, 49
American Psychological Association (APA), 23, 39, 148, 152, 156; Insurance Trust Study, 43, 45

Anderson, Ray S., 13, 15
APA Monitor, 127
Apollos, 87
Aristotle, 22
Arterburn, Stephen, 84
Augustine, Saint, 13
Australian Congress on Christian Counseling, 133
Authority, as basis for values, 11

Baby Boomers, 143, 144, 145
Backus, William, 108
Bakker, Jim, 47
Barna, George, 136, 152
Beck, J.R., 73–74
Behaviorism, 6, 107
Bergin, Allen E., 10
Bevan, William, 148–49, 152
Biopsychosocial technology, 152
Bobgan, Martin, and Bobgan, Deidre, 8

Body of Christ (*See* Christian community)
Bridges, Jerry, 26
Burnout, 99, 125, 126, 127, 165

Caleb, 79, 80
Calvin, John 13
Campolo, Anthony, 16
Cappo, Joe, 135
Catholicism (*See* Roman Catholicism)
Certification, 130
Chandler, Russell, 138
Charitable immunity, 50–51, 52–53. (See also *Nally v. Grace Community Church of the Valley*)
Character, 25–26
Christian Association for Psychological Studies (CAPS), 28;
Code of ethics, 179–84; Ethics Committee, 184
Christian community, 4, 16, 24–25, 48–49, 115, 148, 168
Church growth, 9–10, 168
Clinebell, Howard, 109
Clinical Pastoral Education, 100
Code of ethics, 22–23, 28, 32, 55, 67, 73–74, 168, 174, 179–84. (*See also* Christian Association for Psychological Studies)
Cognitive approach, 107
Commonalities of theories and methods, 87–88
Community Mental Health Centers Act of 1963, 53
Community psychology, 7
Community resources, 140–41

Compensation (*See* Fees)
Compensatory model of counseling, 82–83
Competence, 32–33, 123, 129, 146, 174, 183
Competition between counselors, 147
Confidentiality, 33–34, 123, 183, 186
Consent (*See* Informed consent)
Corey, Gerald, 82, 90–91
Counselee profile, 102, 104
Court of law, 42, 50, 53, 58–59. (*See also* United States Supreme Court)
Crabb, Lawrence, 108
Criticism, 6, 8, 37, 48, 112, 145–46, 166, 174–75, 176
Cross-cultural and multicultural counseling, 6–7. (*See also* Culture)
Croucher, Rowland, 9, 10
Cults, 139–40
Culture: Australian, 133–34; different approaches to counseling, 164; influence on counselee's expectations, 82, 99; in Jesus's time, 162. (*See also* Sensitivity to culture)

Daniel, 146, 151
Davidson, Al, 47
Demonic (*See* Satan)
Dependency, 181
Destefano v. Grabrian, 53
Deterioration effect, 98
Diehl, William, 167–69
Directive approach, 107–8
Distortion of reality, 77, 78

Dobson, James, 157
Drakeford, John, 109
Drucker, Peter, 80
Dysfunctional families, 133, 141, 143

Eclecticism, 89–90
Education, continuing, 116, 124–28, 152, 183. (*See also* Training for counselors)
Elavil, 57, 61
Emotion, as basis for values, 12
Engstrom, Ted, 166
Enlightenment model of counseling, 82–84
Erikson, Erik, 163
Ethical codes (*See* Code of ethics)
Ethical therapy, 11
Ethics, defined, 21–22
Evangelism, 4–5, 90
Evans, C. Stephen, 114–15
Expectations, 103
Experience, as basis for values, 12
Eysenck, Hans, 93–94, 106, 111

Failure to warn, 33, 45–46
Family counseling, 143–44, 181. (*See also* Dysfunctional families)
Federal Civil Rights Act of 1964, 53
Fees, 4, 14, 20–21, 35, 37, 123, 186–87
Felton, Jack, 84
Fiduciary trust, 71–73, 74
First Amendment
Flexibility, 161, 163, 171
Foster, Richard, 158

Fourteenth Amendment, 53
Fragmentation, 165
Frankel, T., 72
Freud, Sigmund, 13, 76, 78
Freudenberger, H. J., 165
Furrow, B., 49
Future: predictions concerning counseling, 136–37; predictions for the twenty-first century, 135–36

Gambrill, Eileen, 119
Gantry, Elmer, 47
Gardner, John W., 2, 169–70
Geisler, Norman, 21–22, 31
Generativity, 163–64, 171
Goals: of Christian counseling, 160; of counseling, 17, 97–98, 142, 161
Grace Community Church (See *Nally v. Grace Community Church of the Valley*)
Graded absolutism, 31
Graham, Billy, 166
Greene, Bob, 2
Gregory the Great, 13
Gross, Martin, 95
Guest, Edgar, 158–59
Guy, James, D., 137

Hart, Archibald D., 73
Halleck, Seymour L., 7, 54
Health psychology, 6–7
Hedonism, 22, 150
Herr, Edwin, 141
Hill, Clara E., 111
Hogan, Daniel, 43
Hogan study, 43–45
Homeless, 161–62

Hope assumption, 109, 110
Humanism, 7, 80–81, 107, 176, 181. (*See also* New Age)

Impairment, 165
Individualism, 150, 151–52
Informed Consent, 34–35, 183, 185–87
Inner healing, 87, 109
Insight therapies, 82
Insurance, 186–87
Integrity, 157–59
International Congress on Christian Counseling, 160
Intuition, as basis for values, 12

John, the apostle, 173
Johnson, Lyndon, 169
Johnson, V. E. (*See* Masters and Johnson)
Johnson, W. Brad, 108, 110
Jordan, Michael, 1–2
Joshua, 79, 80
Journal of Clinical Psychiatry, 152
Jung, Carl Gustav, 13, 76

Kaizen, 151
Kaper, Dennis, 50
Kaufman, California Supreme Court Justice J., 59–60, 63–64
Krumboltz, John D., 3, 76–77, 78
Kuhn, Thomas, 80

Law, 48–50, 70, 73, 183,184; of God, 71, 74
Lawsuits (*See* Liability)
Lawyers, 49
Leadership, 1988 poll, 66

Levicoff, Steve, 129
Lewis, C. S., 176
Lewis, Hunter, 10
Liability, 33–34, 42–43, 49, 51, 63, 68, 70, 72–73; criminal, 69–70
License revocation, 68
Licensing, 13, 51, 54–55, 56, 64, 119, 129–30, 168, 181. (*See also* Certification)
Logic, as basis for values, 11
Luther, Martin, 13

MacArthur, John, Jr., 57, 59, 62
MacNutt, Francis, 109
Malony, H. Newton, 18, 110
Malpractice, 43–46, 49, 51–52, 64, 69, 72, 184. (*See also* Tort law)
Manipulation, 35, 104, 181, 182
Masters and Johnson, 67
Matheny, Kenneth, 85
Matthews, R. K., 73–74
McMinn, Mark R., 108
Media psychology, 7
Medical model of counseling, 82–83
Mediocrity, 16, 17
Meier, Paul, 108
Mental patients, 53–54
Mentor, 120–21, 164
Minirth, Frank, 108
Modernity, 150–51
Moral model of counseling, 82–83
Mormon Church, 55
Moses, 79, 80, 151
Mowrer, O. Hobart, 109
Mutual-aid, 14

Naisbitt, J., 136
Nally v. Grace Community Church of the Valley, 41–42, 47, 56–64
National Association of Social Workers, 55, 57–68
Native American Church, 56
Nazarene, Church of the, 63
Nehemiah, 151
New Age, 135–36, 138–39 (*See also* Humanism)
Newbigin, Leslie, 80
Non-Christian community, 4

O'Connor v. Donaldson, 54
Oden, Thomas C., 13, 150
Oregon Employment Division v. Smith, 55–56, 61, 64, 69, 73, 74

Paradigms, 79–81
Patrick, A. W., 156
Paul, the apostle, 17, 18, 61, 72, 151
Peter, the apostle, 31
Polarity, 4
Political action, 7. (*See also* Social justice)
Populations at risk, 141–43
Powell, James, 161
Pragmatism, 22
Prayer (*See* Inner healing; Religious counseling techniques)
Prevention, 142–43
Professionals, 14–16
"Professional Therapy *Never* Includes Sex", 67
"Professional virtues, 26–27
Propst, Rebecca L. 110
Psychoanalysis, 6, 78, 107

Psychoneurotics, 94
Psychotherapy integration movement, 87

Rea, Duane, 57, 62
Reductive naturalism, 150
Reeck, D., 73
Relationship of counselor to counselee, 105–6, 111
Relativism, 22, 150
Religious beliefs of the counselee, 104
Religious counseling techniques, 6, 107, 109, 115, 175, 176, 181
Research, 84–85, 95–96, 97, 102, 104, 106, 110–11, 124, 148, 152, 168–69, 184
Richards, Lawrence, 159
Ridley, Charles R., 108, 110
Robertson, Pat, 136
Rogers, Carl, 6, 13, 76
Role play, 122, 123, 141, 146
Roman Catholicism, 57, 58
Roy v. Hartogs, 68–69

Sanford, John, and Sanford, Paula, 109
Satan, 86, 140, 163, 176
Satanism (*See* Cults)
Science, as basis for values, 12
Scripture, as authority, 11, 24
Seamands, David A., 109
Selection criteria: for continuing education, 127–28; for accepting students into graduate counseling programs, 114–15
Self-disclosure, 130–31
Seligman, Linda, 101
Senior citizens, 7, 99, 144–45, 162

Sensitivity, 171, 174, 176; to colleagues, 164; to critics, 166; to culture, 1647–69
Sessions, length and frequency, 186
Sexual misconduct, 37–38, 44, 45, 64–70, 183
Sin, 20, 81, 107, 158, 175
Smedes, Lewis, 27
Smith, Darrell, 35, 86, 88–89
Smith, John, 133–34
Smith, 1990 Supreme Court case (*See* Oregon Employment Division v. Smith)
Social justice, 168–69
Solomon, 109
Specialization, 148-50
Spirituality, 159–60
Spontaneous remission, 98
Stapleton, Ruth Carter, 109
Stefflre, Buford, 85
Strupp, Hans H., 97
Supervised counseling, 122–24; ethical and legal issues, 123
Supervision models, 123
Swaggart, Jimmy, 47
Syncretism, 89-90

Tarasoff, Tatiana, 33, 46
Technology, 152–53
Ten Boom, Casper, 157, 171
Ten Boom, Corrie, 31, 157
Ten Commandments, 27
Teresa, Mother, 25
Tertullian, 13
Thomson, Pastor Richard, 57, 58, 62
Toffler, Alvin, 80, 136
Tort law, 49, 51, 52, 68–69

Tournier, Paul, 17, 109, 156
Toxic faith, 84
Training for counselors, 8, 9, 84, 100, 113, 115–21, 156, 174, 181. (*See* Education, continuing; Supervised counseling)
Travel, overseas, 114, 126
Truth assumption, 109, 110

Unethical behavior, 38–40
United States Supreme Court, 42, 50, 52, 54, 55–56

Values, 10–13, 21, 148, 158, 186; Christian, 10, 46, 108, 116
Vande Kemp, Hendricka, 109
Vayhinger, John, 109

Wellness (*See* Health psychology)
Wisdom, 114–15, 176
Worthington, Everett L., Jr., 111, 123

YAVIS (young, attractive, verbal, intelligent, and successful), 142, 161–62

Gary R. Collins

Gary R. Collins is a licensed psychologist with a Ph.D. in clinical psychology from Purdue University. He has published numerous scientific and popular articles, serves as consulting editor to two professional journals, and is a contributing editor to *Christian Herald*. His books include *Christian Counseling, Can You Trust Psychology?, Case Studies in Christian Counseling,* and *The Magnificent Mind*. He is the general editor of the Resources for Christian Counseling series, published by Word, Inc., and writes the monthly *Christian Counseling Newsletter* distributed by Word.

For twenty years Dr. Collins served on the faculty of Trinity Evangelical Divinity School. He is now executive director of the American Association of Christian Counselors and is involved in writing, speaking, and leading workshops, frequently overseas. He and his wife Julie live in northern Illinois; they have two college-age daughters, Marilynn and Jan.